Haynes-Apperson and America's
First Practical Automobile

ALSO BY W.C. MADDEN
AND FROM MCFARLAND

*Baseball's First-Year Player Draft,
Team by Team Through 1999* (2001)

*The All-American Girls Professional
Baseball League Record Book: Comprehensive
Hitting, Fielding and Pitching Statistics* (2000)

*The Women of the All-American
Girls Professional Baseball League:
A Biographical Dictionary* (1997)

BY W.C. MADDEN AND PATRICK J. STEWART
AND FROM MCFARLAND

*The Western League:
A Baseball History,
1885 through 1999* (2002)

Haynes-Apperson and America's First Practical Automobile

A History

W.C. MADDEN

foreword by David Griffey

McFarland & Company, Inc., Publishers
Jefferson, North Carolina, and London

The present work is a reprint of the illustrated case bound edition of Haynes-Apperson and America's First Practical Automobile: A History, *first published in 2003 by McFarland.*

Library of Congress Cataloguing-in-Publication Data

Madden, W.C.
Haynes-Apperson and America's first practical automobile : a history / W.C. Madden ; foreword by David Griffey.
p.   cm.
Includes bibliographical references and index.

ISBN-13: 978-0-7864-2675-1
softcover : 50# alkaline paper ∞

1. Haynes automobile — History. 2. Haynes-Apperson Automobile Company — History. 3. Haynes Automobile Company — History. 4. Apperson Brothers Automobile Company — History. I. Title.
TL215.H38M33   2006   629.222'2 — dc21   2002152268

British Library cataloguing data are available

©2003 W.C. Madden. All rights reserved

No part of this book may be reproduced or transmitted in any form or by any means, electronic or mechanical, including photocopying or recording, or by any information storage and retrieval system, without permission in writing from the publisher.

Cover photograph: Elwood Haynes and his invention *(Haynes Museum)*

Manufactured in the United States of America

*McFarland & Company, Inc., Publishers
Box 611, Jefferson, North Carolina 28640
www.mcfarlandpub.com*

Acknowledgments

Several people were very helpful in making this book possible. The most credit goes to curator Kay Frazer of the Haynes Museum. She allowed me access to all of the Haynes papers and photos at the museum. She also read much of the book to clear up any inconsistencies or possible clarity problems.

The Stan Mohr Local History Library of the Howard County Historical Society provided several photos for the book. Bonnie J. Van Kley and her staff helped provide some valuable information, too.

The Auburn Cord Duesenberg Museum in Auburn, Indiana, provided several photos of Apperson vehicles as well as a lot of information in its research home. Jon Bill and Norb Adams lent me a hand in digging up information for the book as well.

The W.H. Smith Memorial Library at the Indiana Historical Society contained some valuable information that was collected by W.S. Huffman. Huffman collected a vast amount of Indiana automotive information and donated his collection to the Society upon his death.

Several owners of Haynes and Apperson vehicles also did what they could to provide me information and photos. David Griffey provided a rare photo for the book as well as a lot of information that was not available at the Haynes Museum. Dale Etherington drove me around Kokomo to show me where the plants had been located. Not being from Kokomo, I would have never found some of the facilities without his help.

And finally, thanks to my wife for giving a final read of the book and supporting my writing efforts.

Contents

Acknowledgments v
Foreword by David Griffey xx
Introduction 1

1 — America's First Practical Automobile 5
2 — The Haynes-Apperson Company 14
3 — The Apperson Brothers Automobile Company 39
4 — The Haynes Automobile Company 79
5 — Aftershocks 131
6 — Honoring Haynes and Apperson 140
7 — Elwood Haynes 152
8 — Elmer Apperson 172
9 — Edgar Apperson 175

Appendices
I— Haynes-Apperson Models 185
II— Apperson Models 186
III— Haynes Models 193
IV— Roster of Employees 196
V— Biographical Sketches 201
VI— Haynes-Apperson Specificiations 203

VII— Apperson Specifications		207
VIII— Haynes Specifications		211
Bibliography		221
Index		223

Foreword

by David Griffey, President, City of Firsts Automotive Heritage Museum, Inc., Kokomo, Indiana 1991–2000

No single person could have had more influence on the growth of Kokomo, Indiana, than Elwood Haynes. He began planning to build a horseless carriage even before he moved to Kokomo, and soon after his arrival, he contracted with the Apperson brothers to build it. That contract would begin to shape the city's destiny. Haynes would also enlist a local citizen, Jonathan D. Maxwell, to assist with the project. Maxwell would later build the famous automobiles that would bear his name and the company that would become the Chrysler Corporation.

One has to realize the obstacles in building an automobile for the first time. Everything had to be learned by trial and error. Not one company anywhere offered parts of any kind, and no one could imagine just how many components would have to be designed and built for the early automobiles. Many local people joined in the challenge, and by the mid–1920s, over sixty manufacturers of parts would be located in Kokomo.

Special metals with extra strength were required, and that is where Haynes' metallurgical experience was an advantage. He developed several new metal alloys, the best known of which was stellite, a stainless steel, for which he received a patent. The Haynes Stellite Factory was an integral part of the city during those early years. While its ownership has changed over time, the Haynes plant still produces special metals in Kokomo.

By 1923, things began to look very bleak for many of the nation's builders of expensive cars, including the Haynes and Apperson automobile companies. Two years later both were closed, leaving behind many large empty buildings, complete with infrastructure. The automobile manufacturing days were over for

Kokomo, but nearly 76,000 cars had been produced here. Several of the component manufacturers continued in business, many shipping worldwide.

Kokomo's automobile success can be traced directly to Elwood Haynes and the Apperson brothers. Those local pioneers met the challenge.

Introduction

While Elwood Haynes and the Apperson brothers are not as well known as Henry Ford, Ransom Olds and other famous automotive manufacturers, their contributions to the automobile industry are as significant as—if not more than—those automakers'. What kept their names from being prominent in history books was likely their products' lesser commercial success and longevity in the marketplace.

There's an adage: Necessity is the mother of invention. Elwood Haynes came up with inventions that he thought were necessary for the progress of man. Haynes was an educator, inventor, scientist, metallurgist and industrialist. The educator was first a teacher, then a principal. Later in life, he was a member of the Indiana Board of Education and was conferred with an Honorary Doctor of Law Degree from Indiana University. Haynes discovered the inventiveness within himself when he worked for a natural gas company and created the small vapor thermostat to measure natural gas. Then came his work with the automobile. He experimented with different metals that allowed him to come up with a better product. As metallurgist he provided the earliest and most practical superalloys, such as stellite. He made significant advancements in stainless steel as well. He also invented the rotary gas valve engine.

Haynes also claimed that he was the inventor of the first American car, but that title has long been disputed. Haynes had never heard of the Duryeas until he faced them in the Thanksgiving 1895 automobile race in America. He refused to believe that he was not the maker of America's first gasoline-powered automobile. In fact, for the next 30 years that Haynes built cars, his company's advertisements always carried the slogan: "The Haynes is America's first car." He even went as far as putting hood ornaments on his cars boasting, "America's First Car."

An examination of the claim reveals some interesting facts. While George Selden was granted a patent for a "motorcar" in 1877, he did not actually build an automobile until he was engaged in litigation with Henry Ford, who fought the validity of the Selden Patent.

Marshall McClure claimed that he drove a horseless carriage in the summer of 1891 in Spring Lake, Michigan. "The first trip gave me quite a thrill. I think I went about 20 miles an hour—faster than horses anyway." He had borrowed a gasoline engine from a man named Zintz for his experiments. The engine weighed 3,600 pounds. It took him two months to put the buggy together with the engine.

L. Scott Bailey, the respected former editor of *Automobile Quarterly*, declared in a 1960 article that the Lambert built by John W. Lambert in 1891 at Ohio City, Ohio, was the first practical, working automobile built in the United States. While the Lambert effort was not documented prior to its first use, it is better documented by other means than most early automobiles.

Gottfried Schloemer and Frank Toepfer built a car in Milwaukee in 1892 using a Sintz engine like the one Haynes ended up using in his first vehicle. The car was supposedly tested, but they never made another. Also, a Pennsylvania man named Henry Nadig had reputedly built an automobile in Allentown.

The Collector's History of the Automobile mentioned Duryea's car as "America's first gasoline-engined automobile," and the Duryea brothers are recognized by many accounts as the first to use a gasoline-powered engine on a horseless carriage. They modified a horse-drawn buggy by installing a horizontal single-cylinder engine with the crankshaft placed vertically and with the flywheel located on the underside. The vehicle, which weighed about 700 pounds, was first road tested on September 20, 1893. It didn't run very well—about as fast as a horse trotting—and the brothers made some changes before trying it again on November 10. The *Springfield Morning Union* recorded the event, which involved the car running up and down two streets before it stopped. "It ran no faster than an old man could walk, but it did run," Charles Duryea later said of the vehicle. However, another source says that the Duryeas weren't successful until January 1894. This date is still six months before Haynes had his first car ready.

Another report said the car that the Duryea brothers built was really a horseless carriage: a crude vehicle with oak-spoke wheels turned by bicycle chains and guided by a tiller. "When they drove their car out onto the streets of Springfield, no one gasped and said, 'They've done it. They've turned a carriage into an automobile.' It was not a revelation," said Roger White, transportation historian at the Smithsonian. Charles left Massachusetts and returned to his bicycle business in Peoria before the project was completed. "When Charles left, the car was not running," Professor Scharchburg said. "It would not run with the engine he described and the transmission would not work. A year after Charles left, Frank finished the car and made it run. Frank developed an entirely new engine, new transmission, a carburetor and ignition." So exactly when all this transpired is about as clear as a London fog.

After the Duryea Motor Wagon Company split up, the Duryeas even argued between themselves over which one of them was the first to invent the automobile. Historians describe Charles as a visionary with more than 50 patents, a shameless self-promoter whose ideas were brought to life by his younger brother Frank, a master mechanical engineer with 20 patents of his own.

What later hurt the Duryeas' claim to being the first in America was Charles' claim that they built the automobile in 1892, a year earlier than the actual date. The situation was further muddied by claims from other automakers, such as Henry Ford, that their cars predated Haynes' creation.

Haynes doggedly claimed he was the first to build an American automobile, because he said the Duryeas' creation was just a motorized buggy. However, his original creation resembled a buggy as well, except it was a lot more complicated than the Duryea creation. Haynes is credited with making the first clutch-driven automobile with an electric ignition.

What isn't disputable is who manufactured the first automobile for sale. The Duryea brothers formed the Duryea Motor Wagon Company in 1895, a full year before the Haynes-Apperson Automobile Company sold their first car. However, the Duryeas ended up selling only 13 cars and went out of business in 1898, the year the Haynes-Apperson Automobile Company was incorporated, so the title of the oldest automobile company was passed on to Haynes and Apperson. When the trio split up a couple of years later, the Haynes Automobile Company and the Apperson Brothers Automobile Company fought over the "oldest company" title for awhile.

The first Duryea and Haynes automobiles are now exhibited in the Smithsonian Institution. The Smithsonian recognizes the 1893 Duryea as the "first marketable automobile in America." However, the Pioneer leads the automobile display, not because it was the first vehicle, but because it showed more innovation than the Duryea brothers' creation.

In 1920, the National Vigilance Committee of the Associated Advertising Clubs of the World credited Haynes for building the first car. Reaction to the decision came from A.G. Seiberling: "While the Haynes Automobile Company has never participated in the discussion over who made America's first car, further than to state that Elwood Haynes invented, designed and built it, and to rest its case with his story, we admit a glow of satisfaction as we take occasion to express to the advertisement of the world our felicitations to their National Vigilance committee upon the thoroughness of its research and its conscientious insistence upon the verities in public statement."

A current brochure about Kokomo proudly proclaims the city as the "Home of America's First Car," although that fact is still disputed by others.

The discussion on who made the first automobile will likely go on ad infinitum. However, automotive historian Richard Scharchburg best sums up the matter by saying that everyone had a hand in inventing the automobile, because the device was so complicated that it required years of evolution in order to reach a point where it could be manufactured. Unfortunately, the average American thinks that Henry Ford built the first American car. In fact, he didn't produce his first automobile until June 4, 1896. In his haste to get his car completed, Ford failed to take into account the size of the door in his workshop. After he finished his first automobile, he had to demolish the frame with a pickax to get the car out of his small workshop. Ford should be remembered for perfecting mass production and for creating a car, the Model T, that the average American could afford to buy.

Haynes also incorrectly claimed he made the first 1,000-mile trip, which came when he traveled to New York City. Unfortunately, the trip is less than 1,000 miles, as the distance is measured at 729 miles today.

The Haynes Automotive Company compared its founder to Alexander Graham Bell and Thomas A. Edison in *The Haynes Pioneer*, a company publication. Writer Wilbur D. Nesbit undoubtedly got carried away, because he credited Elwood with inventing the motor car. Apparently, he didn't know about Gottlieb Daimler, Karl Benz, Armand Peugeot and the Duryea brothers, who all built well-documented automobiles before Haynes. Nesbit called the feat a commonplace miracle. Indiana historian Ralph D. Gray wrote that Haynes deserves to be better known as a true pioneer in the American automobile industry. In Indiana circles, he is remembered as a pioneer, but on the national level his contributions have eroded with time and he is no longer recognized as one of the great founders of the automobile.

Another fact that somehow got distorted later on was who was responsible for what. Elwood Haynes designed the Pioneer and the Appersons built it; however, in later newspaper and magazine articles, Edgar Apperson was somehow credited with the design of the vehicle as well as its construction. Undoubtedly, Edgar told reporters that's what he did, as he was known to stretch the truth a bit at times. In another newspaper article, the writer documented that the Haynes-Apperson Company was changed to Apperson Brothers Automotive Company. That wasn't exactly the case: the reporter should have explained that the Haynes-Apperson Company was later split into two companies.

The Haynes-Apperson Company boasted in advertising that it had entered 17 contests and won them all, but news reports to the contrary were found. In one of the Buffalo endurance contests, Haynes-Apperson cars finished second and third—not first.

1

America's First Practical Automobile

After driving his horse home after a hard day's work, Elwood Haynes thought to himself that it would be a fine thing if he didn't have to depend on the tired four-legged beast for transportation. The year was 1889. The young Hoosier was in charge of constructing a gas line from Portland to Pennville, Indiana, a distance of about 10 miles, and he had to cover that distance every day by horse. The horse lacked endurance and this became more apparent as the nag was driven day after day. What's more, the roads in Indiana were heavy with sand, so even a good animal soon became tired.

This led Haynes to start thinking about an alternative mode of transportation. His first thoughts on a self-propelled road vehicle involved a steam engine. (He wasn't aware of the steam passenger cars which had been invented long before he ever thought of the idea. In fact, the first steam cars appeared about the time he was a child.) He quickly abandoned the notion of a steam vehicle because a fire would have to be constantly burning to keep the machine running. He feared a collision or fiery accident would make the vehicle very unsafe. Moreover, getting water for the vehicle would be troublesome over a long journey.

Then Haynes considered electricity, but batteries at that time were heavy and crude—the lightest weighed over 1,000 pounds! Also, batteries in those days had the capacity of only ten horse-hours. Electric cars were yet to be invented. He thought about the gasoline engine, too, but they were also very heavy at the time and rather crude in construction. He pondered his ideas for awhile longer.

The following year, Haynes became a field superintendent for a Chicago company to oversee the drilling of new wells. His work on the wells continued, taking him throughout the country. Of course, he continued to use a horse to get to where he was going. He thought a great deal about an alternative to the horse and began making some rough drawings for the construction of a mechanically propelled vehicle for use on the highway.

In December 1892, Haynes moved to Kokomo and was named supervisor of the Kokomo branch of the Indiana Natural Gas & Oil Company. The family moved into a home belonging to the gas company on North Washington Street. Days later, his wife Bertha gave birth to a daughter, Bernice, their first child to survive infancy. In his new position, Elwood had more free time for other endeavors, such as a road vehicle he planned on developing. Then in the summer of 1893, he attended the Chicago World's Fair and came across the gasoline-powered Sintz engines. They were lighter and more to his liking. He decided then and there that the engine would be right for his invention, so he ordered one.

The $225 one-horsepower marine upright, 2-cycle gasoline engine arrived along with Harry Kraft, a troubleshooter from Sintz. Haynes mounted the 180-pound engine, meant for water applications, on sawhorses in his kitchen, because he lacked anywhere else to experiment at the time. After cranking the engine several times, it finally started. The engine vibrated so intensely, running at only 500 revolutions per minute, that it pulled itself from its attachments. Fortunately, one of the battery wires was wound around the motor shaft and thus disconnected the current. The experiment tore up the kitchen floor and disturbed the neighbors so much that the fire department was called upon to see what all the commotion was about. After that, Elwood decided to further test the engine somewhere else.

He went to the local Riverside Machine Shop with his blueprints to ask for help in putting together his dream of a horseless carriage. "Boys," he said to Elmer and Edgar Apperson, "I've bought a one-cylinder gasoline marine engine. Think you can put it in a buggy so it'll run the thing?"

Elmer was speechless, so Edgar spoke up. "Sure, we can make it run," he said. "All we got to do is get the power carried from the engine to the ground."

"That's right. And I have all the drawings here to do just that," Elwood said.

The Appersons agreed to work on the vehicle after hours to avoid conflict with any of their usual work, making saw gummers and sedges for saw mills. That appealed to Haynes, because most of the work would be done at night and wouldn't raise a lot of curiosity. The Appersons told Haynes that they wouldn't be responsible for the outcome. Haynes agreed to pay them 40 cents an hour. The Appersons thought that the project was absurd at first, but as work progressed they became more serious about it.

Everything was made from scratch. In order to protect against the vibration, Haynes designed a frame of hollow steel tubing and used bicycle tires for its wheels. A buggy was set on top of the frame. With the engine in the rear, chains ran from the rear axle to a jackshaft forward of the motor. Edgar devised clutches and gears for each chain, all operated by a single lever outside the driver's seat, which was on the right. The lever was pulled back for low gear, out and farther back for second, out again and back for high. The contraption would have three forward speeds, but no reverse. Fingers pushed the gears into place. A wet battery used for telegraph lines was also employed in the vehicle for electrical power.

Some of the problems that Haynes came across were worked out by the most primitive means. To determine the amount of traction required to overcome road resistance, he had a man on a bicycle towed behind a buckboard drawn by a horse. He attached a spring scale to one end of the towline and the bicycle to the other. The man on the buckboard then took readings of the pull registered on the spring scale. He kept a record of the readings, averaged them, and arrived at the result. The man and the bicycle weighed two hundred pounds and the test showed that it took three and one-half pounds of traction to move this weight, which meant something like seventeen and one-half pounds to a thousand pounds of weight in the motor car. Haynes estimated the torque by means of a brake on the fly wheel of the engine. From these figures he determined the gear ratio on a level road. Two speeds were planned: the low speed was strong enough to move the machine up a four percent incline. The weight of the machine would be over 800 pounds. To cool the engine, a water tank was put beneath the seat.

Another mechanic who helped put together that first car was J. D. Maxwell, who had worked at the Star Machine Works in Kokomo before coming to the company in 1889. Another person who helped with that first car was Warren B. Wrightman.

First Test Drive

After some nine months of tedious work and expenditures of some $750, the motorcar was about as ready as a baby in the womb after the same amount of time. The date was July 4, 1894, and a big celebration was planned for the farming community of 7,500. The Appersons let the public know about the test ride. When the vehicle—named the "Pioneer"—was rolled out that afternoon, a crowd immediately gathered out of curiosity. "The moment it [the car] appeared, a crowd gathered as if by magic forming a circle of not over twenty feet in circumference," the inventor explained. "I deemed it unwise to start the machine under these conditions as none of us had ever seen a machine of that sort, much less operated one. It was therefore attached to the rear of a horse carriage and hauled about three miles into the country, where a start was made on Pumpkinvine Pike." The only witnesses to the event where Elwood's wife and an old farmer. The motor started right away. Haynes took the driver's seat, while Elmer Apperson and Warren Wrightman rode. "I wonder if the little devil can make the hill?" Elmer questioned Haynes. "I think it can," said the confident inventor. The new contraption coughed like a longtime smoker and moved along the road at about seven miles an hour, the speed of a human jogging. After about 15 minutes of chugging along, Haynes stopped the vehicle and the men turned it around manually, since there was no reverse gear. Haynes decided to drive the vehicle all the way back to the machine shop. On the way back, he was convinced that there was a future for his horseless carriage. As the machine entered the town, it was greeted by a bevy of girls on bikes. They gazed wide-eyed in amazement at the vehicle which moved as fast as them, and scattered in all directions like a flock of frightened geese. The Pioneer sputtered and quit as it came to a stop in front of the Riverside shop.

The ride was not mentioned in the local newspapers the next day. That didn't occur for another eleven days when the *Kokomo Daily Tribune* wrote about the Pioneer and called it a "queer-looking vehicle." The paper called it a "cross between a buggy and a bicycle, being mounted on four bicycle wheels, but running without the aid of a horse."

Elwood Haynes sits in his invention. (Courtesy of the Haynes Museum.)

After the initial test run of the automobile, Haynes began either driving his wife around at night when the streets were more quiet, or taking jaunts out in the country. The automobile moved about as fast as a horsedrawn wagon, so sometimes wagon drivers would pull over and let him go by because they feared the new contraption. On one trip out to the country he met up with an old gentleman seated on a load of crated tomatoes in his horse drawn carriage. The man became so intrigued with the horseless carriage that he dropped one of his lines and the other team pulled to one side, resulting in the carriage going down a slight embankment and the load overturning. The tomatoes became tomato sauce. Elwood felt so sorry for the farmer that he settled up with the man for the damaged tomatoes.

While the test run of the Pioneer was a success, Haynes was not very satisfied with the results. He was unhappy with the steering, the engine and a few other things from his first design. It was back to the drawing board. The steering was controlled with a vertical rod that had a horizontal handle attached to it. The mechanism was similar to a bicycle crank and pedal — move forward and backward to steer, not from side to side. The driver moved the stick forward to turn the vehicle to the right and back to turn left. It was awkward and dangerous. A muffler was added to quiet the engine as well. Haynes also felt that the engine was too weak, so he wrote the Sintz company for a more powerful one. He wanted Sintz to lend him an engine, but the company would not accept his proposition. Sintz was about 40 days behind in engine orders at the time and was getting orders from other car makers as well. However, the company was trying to discourage the inventors.

"They have always had more gearing than the power of the engine would draw without the vehicle," the company explained to Haynes in a reply. Haynes settled for trading in the old engine for a new two-horsepower model, which cost him $100 after the trade. Yet the second engine proved to be too difficult, so Haynes and Elmer Apperson decided to build their own engine for a second automobile model. To lighten the engine, Haynes introduced aluminum into the crankcase—

A historical marker now marks the place where Elwood Haynes made his historic ride in a horseless carriage.

the alloy for the crankcase was 93 percent aluminum and 7 percent copper.

America's First Auto Race

By this time, the Europeans were much more advanced in auto making and were already racing cars. In July 1894, fifteen vehicles raced from Paris to Ronen, a distance of 75 miles, and gasoline-powered automobiles made the best showing. The first auto race in America didn't come until 1895. The *Chicago Times-Herald* decided to sponsor the first automobile race in America. The race was designed for the new style of road wagons: the ones run by steam, electricity, gasoline or in any other way without the use of horses. The Horseless Carriage Contest was first scheduled for July 4, but the lack of entries forced the newspaper to delay it until November 2. Haynes and the Apperson brothers wanted to enter their second car in the race, but it was not yet ready. Only the Duryea brothers and a German Benz showed up for the race on November 2, although 80 entries had been received. Entries had to have at least three wheels and two passengers per vehicle. Any fuel was acceptable other than "muscle power." Not wanting to be the laughing stock of other newspapers in Chicago, the paper got the Duryea brothers and Oscar Mueller to run an exhibition race. The real race was rescheduled for Thanksgiving Day, and it came to be called the Race of the Century.

At the start of the exhibition race, Frank and Charles Duryea quickly pulled ahead of Mueller's Benz car. Less than halfway into the race their noisy car frightened a team of horses. The horses, pulling a wagon, bolted into the road and smack into the Duryeas' path. Frank, who was driving, ran the car into a ditch to avoid hitting the wagon. The badly bent car was pulled back to the railroad station by the same team of horses and was shipped back to Springfield, Massachusetts, for some fast repairs before the big race. The Mueller Benz car obviously won the exhibition race.

The delay allowed Haynes and the Appersons to get the second car, called the Trap, ready. In the meantime, they sent the Pioneer for the race in case the second car wasn't ready in time. Rather than driving to Chicago over roads meant more for horses than autos, Haynes shipped the Pioneer by the more reliable train service to Englewood, a suburb of Chicago. Upon arriving, Haynes drove the Pioneer on Michigan Avenue to get to his hotel, but a police officer on bicycle pulled him over. "You can't drive that thing on Michigan Avenue," the officer told Haynes.

"I'm here for the first automobile race, officer," Haynes replied. "Why can't I drive it on this road?"

"Arders, sir," the public official said.

Haynes could do nothing but obey the orders. He turned off Michigan Avenue to take a different route to his hotel. Other entries for the race ran into the same problem, so the *Times-Herald* had to get permission from City Hall for vehicles to use the roads in Chicago. The four-passenger, two-cylinder Trap, which cost Haynes about $2,000 to build, finally arrived in Chicago by train on November 19. Following the arrival of the second Haynes creation, an early snowstorm dumped four to six inches of snow on the city.

By the evening before the race, eleven automobiles had committed to the race. The next morning, below-freezing temperatures and snow-covered streets greeted Haynes. On the way to the starting line, the inventor swerved to avoid a collision with a streetcar and slammed

A Chicago police officer stops Elwood Haynes and Elmer Apperson from driving on Michigan Avenue. This was a re-creation of the actual event which took place in 1895. (Courtesy of the Haynes Museum.)

into a curb. Ironically, the mishap occurred at the corner of Indiana Avenue and Thirteenth Street. Bad luck? The bicycle-type wheel was broken and no spare was available for the car. For Haynes and the Appersons, the race was over before it ever began. The Haynes-Apperson entry wasn't the only vehicle not to make it to the starting line that fatal morning. The race was delayed for an hour until six "motocycles," as the automobiles were called by the newspaper, finally made their way to the starting line. A shivering crowd of spectators lined the streets as the flag dropped and the race officially began. The crowd cheered as six cars inched across the starting line, slowly rolling their way toward history.

Two electric cars that entered the race quickly ran out of power due to the cold temperatures. Because of the snow, the race had been shortened to fifty-five miles. Contestants started at Jackson Park in Chicago and had to drive to Evanston and back again. The race came down to a match-up between the Duryea brothers and three German-built Benz cars. One Benz was driven by Mueller. Another entry was an imported Benz from the R.H. Macy store of New York City. Macy had hoped to sell them in Chicago. The other was a Benz entered by the De LaVergne Refrigeration Company of New York City.

Just outside Chicago, the Macy Benz ran into a horse and was out of the race. On the way back from Evanston, Duryea

ANTIQUE AUTOMOBILES
1893 Duryea

The gasoline-powered automobile was invented in Europe in the 1860s. However, it did not take long for American ingenuity to improve upon the initial designs. U.S. manufacturers drew from a broad spectrum of technologies, including the bicycle and buggy industries. By the turn of the century, they were emerging as leaders in the creation of dependable, economical "horseless carriages."

The pioneers of American gasoline-powered cars were two brothers, Charles and J. Frank Duryea. At the 1886 Ohio state fair, Charles spotted a stationary gasoline engine that was sufficiently compact to power a carriage. Over the next few years, he worked on the design for such a vehicle. Its single-cylinder, four-horsepower engine was mounted in the rear, beneath the body, and featured friction drive.

The 1893 prototype Duryea was built in Springfield, Massachusetts. It was tested for the first time on town streets September 22, 1893. Although it broke down during the outing, the brothers were delighted. "It ran no faster than an old man could walk," Charles noted, "but it did run." An improved two-cylinder, three-gear Duryea, largely J. Frank's work, was entered in America's first motorcar race on Thanksgiving Day 1895. Of the more than 600 cars that set out on the 55-mile trek from Chicago to Evanston, Illinois, only two finished. The Duryea crossed the finish line just ahead of a Mercedes Benz.

By then, the two Duryea brothers had gone their separate ways in the automobile industry. Charles organized the Duryea Motor Wagon Company, the first American manufacturer of gasoline-powered cars, in 1895. Later, he founded the Duryea Power Company of Reading, Pennsylvania, which produced three-cylinder, three-wheel cars. J. Frank became a partner in a firm that created the Stevens-Duryea, one of the best known of the early motorcars. Its production continued into the 1920s.

The 32¢ U.S. stamp picturing the 1893 Duryea was designed by Ken Dallison of Ontario, Canada. Among his previous designs are the five stamps in the 1988 classic car series.

The 1893 Duryea was included as one of the stamps honoring antique automobiles that were issued on Nov. 3, 1995.

passed both the Mueller Benz and the De LaVergne Benz. The automobile continued to pick up speed, despite the cold and snow, and crossed the finish line with no other car in sight. What was left of the frozen crowd cheered wildly. An hour and a half later, the Mueller Benz car crossed the finish line, the only other car to finish the race. The actual time of the race took seven hours and fifty-three minutes.

The Duryea brothers earned the top prize of $2,000. The Sturges Electric Motor Wagon was awarded $500 after running out of power 13 miles into the race. The Haynes-Apperson entry received $150 for its meritorious design. The Chicago race also prompted the formation of the Automobile League, and Haynes became one of its charter members. Many historians believe the race provided the impetus for the development of the automobile industry in the United States. It certainly did for the Duryea brothers, who began the Duryea Motor Wagon Company in February the following year. The Haynes-Apperson Automobile Company soon followed, as did others.

Not long after the Chicago race, the Pioneer was put to rest in a rude shed in the rear of Elwood Haynes' home. It had served him well and had traveled more than a thousand miles. His first automobile gathered dust until the Smithsonian Institution decided in 1910 that it wanted the vehicle to be preserved forever, and the vehicle has been on display there ever since.

2

The Haynes-Apperson Company

While Elwood Haynes and the Appersons began making cars in 1894, they didn't decide to form the Haynes-Apperson Company until after the failed automobile race in Chicago in November 1895. Their venture was jointly financed and began slowly and cautiously in early 1896. Their roles didn't change much, but their responsibilities increased quite a bit. Haynes, who continued to work for the gas company, took care of the company's promotional literature and advertising. He worked closely with the Appersons in designing the vehicles and solving engineering problems.

Haynes had heard about another motorcar that was made before his by John W. Lambert in Ohio. Haynes visited the Ohio inventor to tell him that he was planning to market his own automobile and to call it "America's first car." He obtained Lambert's promise not to dispute Haynes' claim.

Duryea Motor Wagon Company

Meanwhile, the Duryeas formed the Duryea Motor Wagon Company of Springfield, Massachusetts, in early 1896 and got a jump on the Haynes-Apperson Company by putting out a dozen vehicles by the end of the year. It was considered "the first attempt at quantity production of passenger automobiles by an American industrial firm." However, the company broke up after that as the Duryea brothers went their own ways. Several other automotive makers got their start in 1896 as well: Charles King introduced the first four-cylinder auto; Henry Ford introduced his first auto, the "Quadricycle"; Ransom Olds also introduced his first auto in 1896; and Alexander Winton of Cleveland introduced his first auto in *The Horseless Age*.

Haynes and the Appersons also used

The Horseless Age to introduce their "new carriage," which should be "considerably in advance of their previous models." The new model would continue to feature an engine made of aluminum except for the cylinders of steel tubing, as had been the case with their second car. Haynes was concerned with the durability and reliability of the motor more than he was concerned with speed. The notice stated that it would be on display at the Ohio State Fair in Columbus in September. All three Haynes-Apperson mechanical marvels appeared at the fair during the second week of September. Automobiles were so rare back then that many people hadn't seen one, so they received the same status as the fat lady and other freak show characters. The company was paid $400 for the appearance with the John Robinson Circus.

First Order

Shortly after the fair and other exhibits in Ohio, the first order for the new Haynes-Apperson automobile came from P.C. Lewis, a pump manufacturer in Catskill, New York. Another early purchase came from Dr. Sweany of Chicago. Doctors wanted the convenience of a horseless carriage because back in those days they traveled a lot to see patients at their homes. Plus, they could afford to purchase the new contraptions.

The 1896 Haynes-Apperson model was further featured in the November issue of *The Horseless Age*. The article, obviously written by Haynes, contained the company's philosophy of motor construction and reviewed their experience with motor cars. Haynes discussed the advantages of cast aluminum over cast iron in gasoline engines, such as its lightness, strength and ease of casting. Haynes also advocated very strong crankshafts, so that "all the shocks and jars communicated from the momentum of the carriage as well as the force of the sudden explosions of the gaseous mixture in the cylinder" could be withstood. The article also described the features of the open, six-passenger vehicle. Fitted with 2½-inch pneumatic tires, the automobile "should run at least 20 miles per hour on a good level roadway. It is fitted with an 8-horsepower motor which makes 500 revolutions per minute and weighs 340 pounds, including balance wheel." The carriage had four speeds of 4, 8, 12 and 18 miles per hour, and weighed about 1,500 pounds. The one-cylinder model would run 56 miles on a gallon of gasoline, which was six cents a gallon and sold at the general store. Up until this time, gasoline, a byproduct in oil production, wasn't being used much. Now there was a market for the product.

1896-7 Models
One-cylinder
Trap, 4 passenger, 1,500 lbs, $1,000

1897

In 1897, orders for Haynes-Apperson automobiles, which sold for $1,250, came from as far as New York, Massachusetts and Montana. If somebody wanted a car, they either stopped by the shop or sent in a request by mail. One day, Lord Russell from England stopped by the Riverside Machine Shop and ordered an automobile, which may have been the first export automobile in the United States. By August, the Riverside Machine Shop was keeping busy with orders and the plant was staying open as late as 10:30 p.m. every evening. Plans to enlarge the plant were under way, including a woodworking facility to replace

THE HAYNES-APPERSON
Motor Carriage.

Four-Passenger Trap, either Dos-a-Dos or Both Seats fronting forward.

PRICE, $1,000.00.

The above illustration shows our Four-Passenger Trap which was on exhibition at the *Times-Herald* contest at Chicago on November 28th. Although this carriage did not take part in the race on account of an accident to one of the wheels prior to the race, we received the only special prize awarded by the judges for best driving engines. The prize was awarded for best plan of balance in engines and minimum vibration of engine and carriage, extreme lightness, and general design. This carriage was supplied with our regular five-horse power balanced gasoline engine and will travel on ordinary roads from 2 to 17 miles per hour.

Our engines, which are of our own make and which we shall put on all styles of our carriages, are perfectly balanced, very light, and durable.

We shall have a full line of carriages of various styles ready for the market at an early date.

HAYNES & APPERSON, Kokomo, Indiana, U. S. A.

This is one of the first advertisements used by the Haynes-Apperson Company. (Courtesy of Howard County Historical Society, Kokomo, Indiana.)

the need to outsource wood products to a shop in Peru. The Kokomo Rubber Company provided the pneumatic tires for the vehicles.

Incorporation

The success achieved in 1897 — a dozen automobiles were sold — and future orders led Haynes and the Appersons to incorporate the business and use the new capital to finance the planned expansion. The owners made a well-publicized trip to Portland to stir up interest in the company. They traveled seventy-four miles in less than seven hours, and only six hours were needed for the return. A number of Portlanders agreed to purchase stock in the expanded enterprise. Seven Portland investors besides Haynes and Elmer Apperson, purchased stock in the company, but the plant would remain in Kokomo. Two of those investors were Haynes' brothers, Walter and Calvin. So the incorporated company began with $50,000 in capital and a dozen workers. The officers of the company were: Elwood Haynes, president; Elmer Apperson, secretary; and G.W. Charles, treasurer.

Immediately after the corporation papers were filed on May 24, 1898, the decision was made to produce fifty cars as soon as possible for sale. Up until then, the company had only produced vehicles after they were ordered. Some company board directors were against such a bold move, but the majority ruled in favor of it and production began. The 1898 models featured "steel spur gearing," which allowed the driver to vary the speed in each gear. "These speeds are variable from maximum to minimum within the range of

An 1897 Haynes-Apperson visited Kokomo in 1965. Only three were built. This one was owned by Jack Frost of Detroit. (Courtesy of Howard County Historical Society, Kokomo, Indiana.)

Two buildings housed the works of the Haynes-Apperson Company. (Courtesy of the Haynes Museum.)

each, thereby making a gradual variation from the slowest to the greatest speed without friction or loss of power."

The new facility would be able to manufacture an automobile a week, three times faster than the Riverside Machine Shop. The company line included two-, four- and six-passenger vehicles, all powered by a rear-mounted, horizontally opposed two-cylinder engine. However, the four- and six-passenger vehicles were actually trailers to be towed by the two-passenger automobile. One of the carriages-with-trailer was driven all the way to Chicago on July 15. Two passengers rode in the carriage, while one passenger rode in the trailer with all of their luggage. The first leg of the trip was to Lafayette, and it took the car three and a half hours to go the 50 miles—an average of 15 miles per hour. Gas by then had risen to 30 cents a gallon.

Although the company really wasn't the first to build an automobile in America—Duryea's invention came in 1893—the Haynes-Apperson slogan became "America's First Car." The company used the slogan in advertising and marketing materials. It also would later appear on the hood ornaments for the car.

1899

The directors who decided on building fifty cars made a wise decision, because orders began coming in at a quick pace. In fact, by February 1899, the Haynes-Apperson workers were toiling 15-hour days with a backlog of orders that stretched into May. Orders were coming in from everywhere; a government mail agent in Puerto

Practical and Reliable Motor Carriages

Gasoline System.

Two, four, and six passenger pleasure carriages, doctors' carriages, business and delivery wagons. No trouble, no vibration. Strong power. Will go any distance over any road at any speed. Easily managed, durable and convenient. Our 1899 design will be ready after January 1st. If you want a motor carriage for spring delivery, get your order in now. Send 10c. for our beautifully illustrated and descriptive catalog.

THE HAYNES-APPERSON CO., Kokomo, Ind., U.S.A.

Top: The Assembly Room of the Haynes-Apperson Company featured stalls where the automobiles were put together. This was before the assembly line came into being. (Courtesy of the Haynes Museum.) *Bottom:* One of the first advertisements used by Haynes-Apperson. It appeared on Dec. 31, 1898, in *Scientific American*.

The Haynes-Apperson Company claimed their vehicles were practical and reliable in this 1899 ad. (Courtesy of Howard County Historical Society, Kokomo, Indiana.)

Rico requested a three-seated "motocycle," and a Chicago firm wanted a delivery wagon, "almost as pretty as a woman and much more tractable."

The orders prompted the company to plan yet another plant expansion in order to keep up with demand. In April, the company announced that people wanting an 1899 model should get their orders in immediately, because their "output for this year is about sold." C.B. Knox, the gelatin manufacturer, ordered a delivery wagon for advertising purposes in New York. Another order for a carriage as a replacement for a stagecoach came from Arizona. The orders mainly came from the rich — doctors, lawyers, company presidents and the like — because the average American couldn't afford the expense. The automobile was considered a luxury item until years later when assembly-line production brought the price down to an affordable range. Vehicles also tended to break down frequently and repairs were costly. By the end of 1899, the Haynes-Apperson Company had produced and sold thirty vehicles, but the Winton Motor Carriage Company, began by Alexander Winton in March 1897, outdid them by selling a hundred cars on the year. The first Winton sold for $1,000 and twenty-two were sold in 1898. Ironically, one of the buyers was James Ward Packard, who would go on to produce cars by the same name. A total of 3,700 automobiles were produced in the United States in 1899.

The most notable delivery came in July 1899, when Haynes and Edgar Apperson drove all the way to Brooklyn, New York. The company said that the trip marked the first a 1,000-mile journey by an automobile in the United States, but the

Workers of the Haynes-Apperson Automobile Plant gathered together for this photo in the early days of the plant (Courtesy of Howard County Historical Society, Kokomo, Indiana.)

journey was less than thousand miles. While the delivery got coverage in many newspapers, it remained obscure in general automobile history. For some reason, other journeys got more ink than the Haynes-Apperson endurance feat. The first trans–American trip didn't come until 1903 and it didn't involve a Haynes-Apperson vehicle. In 1901, the company made the same trip to New York and back in 73 hours to claim a speed record. The company also received some good publicity when a Haynes-Apperson won a gold medal at the Louisiana Purchase Exposition at Buffalo, New York.

Besides free publicity which the newspapers provided, the company also believed in national advertising to sell their automobiles. The company put advertisements in *Scribner's*, *Cosmopolitan*, *Scientific American* and other magazines. The company's strategy was to use small advertisements in many different publications in order to ready buyers. Since many potential customers still relied on a horse for travel, one ad claimed that driving a Haynes-Apperson was "More Pleasant than Driving a Horse." Another advertisement suggested the vehicle as a Christmas present. The ads emphasized that the company was the oldest in the United States and had better workmanship and correct design. In the advertisements before 1900, the company listed no agents, but after the turn of the century, San Francisco was added as an agent of the company.

1900

Elwood wrote in *The Horseless Age* several articles on the superiority of the gasoline engine over other types of engines,

The Haynes-Apperson Company ran this small ad for its 1899 vehicles. (Courtesy of Howard County Historical Society, Kokomo, Indiana.)

Left: The first Runabouts were called "horseless buggies" for obvious reasons. (Courtesy of the Haynes Museum.)

particularly steam and electricity. His January 1900, article, "The Hydrocarbon Engine as a Source of Energy," spelled out the technical reasons for the superiority of the gas engine. He made direct comparisons with electric and steam automobiles, and pointed out that the "gasoline carriage has always defeated all competitors in long distance runs." Electric cars were popular in the cities where short trips could be made, while the steam cars were used in the country, like the gasoline-powered automobile. Haynes backed those articles with advertisements that stressed the advantages of gasoline-powered vehicles. The company also used testimonials from owners to help sell its automobiles. One owner had made a run of 8,400 miles in three years and was quite impressed with the vehicle, as he had never had any service on it. The company's philosophy about its audience can best be described by a sentence in a company brochure: "Most persons want a carriage which will, to some extent at least, form in general style to the horse-drawn carriage, and so long as it does not interfere with the efficiency and practicability of the carriage, we are entirely willing to gratify their taste."

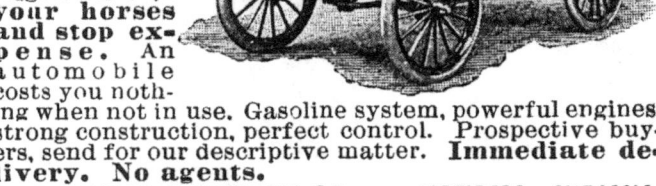

Top: In the early days the largest competitor for Haynes-Apperson was not another auto company, but the horse. (Courtesy of Howard County Historical Society, Kokomo, Indiana.) *Bottom:* The Haynes-Apperson Company advertised all three of its models in 1902.

1898–1900 Models
Two-cylinder, ⅞ hp
Carriage, 2 passenger, $1,250
Carriage, 4 passenger, $1,500
Carriage, 6–8 passenger, $1,800

By the turn of the century, at least one hundred different brands of automobiles were being marketed in the United States. However, only six companies, including Haynes-Apperson, built more than a hundred cars in a year. The other five were the Olds Motor Works in Lansing, Michigan; Winton Company in Cleveland, Ohio; Thomas B. Jeffrey Company in Kenosha, Wisconsin; and Pope Manufacturing in Hartford, Connecticut. The Haynes-Apperson Company separated themselves from those companies by billing itself as the "Oldest Gasoline Automobile Manufacturer in America." The company employed more

Top and bottom: A 1900 Haynes-Apperson on display at the Automotive Heritage Museum in Kokomo.

The Haynes-Apperson Company went after the resort market with its largest carriage. (Courtesy of Howard County Historical Society, Kokomo, Indiana.)

than twenty workers. Sales were up to nearly half a million dollars as production exceeded 190 vehicles. The company continued to make improvements to their product, adopting carburetors for their engines to solve the lack of power at low speeds and the difficulty of changing speeds easily. Haynes and Apperson applied for a patent for the carburetor in January, 1901. Approval came in 1904.

1901

By 1901, the Haynes-Apperson models included one-, two- or three-seat carriages, but the vehicles could accommodate up to eight passengers. The largest model was marketed to stage lines, hotels and resorts. Some marketing was done using advertisements. The automobiles were equipped with twelve-horsepower engines and three-speed forward and reverse transmissions, which made them "especially adapted to country roads and long trips."

1901 Models

Two-cylinder, ⅞ hp
Business Wagon, 2 passenger, $1,000
Pleasure Carriage, 2 passenger, $1,250
Doctor's Carriage, $1,250
Carriage, 4 passenger, $1,500
Carriage, 6 passenger, $1,600
Carriage with trailer, 10–15 passenger, $1,800
Delivery Wagon, $1,800

The disputes over the road use between horse drivers and automobiles were clarified further in 1901, when the Indiana

The Haynes-Apperson Company used women to advertise its carriage in 1901. (Courtesy of Howard County Historical Society, Kokomo, Indiana.)

Supreme Court overturned a decision by the Grant County Circuit Court, which had upheld a decision that prohibited steam-propelled vehicles from traveling on city streets and alleys in Kokomo. The Supreme Court ruled: "Highways and streets are not for the exclusive use of vehicles propelled by animal power, nor are travelers confined to the use of such power and ordinary carriages upon highways." The court also stated that "new means of locomotion cannot be excluded merely because their use may tend to the inconvenience or even to injure those who continue to use the highways and streets by former methods." Haynes carried the ruling in his pocket to show police or others that he had the right to travel on all the roads.

In 1901, the company offered a guarantee of six months on the motor and other items on their vehicles. Buyers had to put one-fourth down in cash when they ordered the car with the balance due when the vehicle was completed. The two-passenger runabout cost $1,000, which was about a dollar a pound since it weighed about a thousand pounds. Featuring a five horsepower, two-cylinder motor, the runabout could motor approximately 125 miles on a tank of gas and manage a top speed of 30 miles per hour. Another two-passenger vehicle was the pleasure carriage, with a speed of about 20 mph and a cost of $1,250. The four-passenger pleasure automobile ran $1,400. A top was an extra $50 and could be installed or removed in a couple of minutes.

More than a thousand dollars for a car was a lot to pay in those days, so some companies sought to provide the American public with a less expensive model. One of those car makers was Ransom Olds, who came out with a comparatively reasonable Oldsmobile Runabout for $650. He also sent his assistant, Roy Chapin, on a nine-day, 800-mile trip from Detroit to New York City in the fall of 1901 to publicize his automobile. Newspaper accounts of the journey helped boost interest in the Runabout and launched a car more affordable to the American public.

Top: This 1901 ad featured the two-passenger carriage. (Courtesy of Howard County Historical Society, Kokomo, Indiana.) *Bottom:* This 1901 advertisement was simple and to the point.

Racing

To further publicize the Haynes-Apperson Automobile Company, Edgar Apperson also began driving in automobile endurance races in 1901. He drove a two-seated, eight-horsepower surrey in the Long Island test run in April, and covered the one hundred miles without a mishap on five gallons of gasoline to earn a blue ribbon. The entry didn't finish first, but the race was more for endurance than speed. A photo of the vehicle with its four mud-splattered occupants appeared in *Horseless Age*.

A Haynes-Apperson car did win the New York City-to-Buffalo Pan-American Exposition run later that year. The 100-vehicle race included three Haynes-Appersons, including one driven by the Apperson brothers, who had driven from Kokomo to enter the race.

Edgar drove in another endurance race in August. He covered the Detroit race of ten miles in seventeen minutes, forty-three and one-fifth seconds, a speed of about thirty-four miles per hour. Two months later on October 5, the Chicago millionaire broker J. C. King broke the Chicago-Milwaukee record, driving an eight-horsepower Haynes-Apperson. King took four hours and two minutes to cover the eighty-five miles.

Although all the publicity and advertising led to record sales in 1901, Haynes and the Appersons decided to part company. Edgar left the company after the Detroit race with his brother, formally resigning on November 15, 1901. The split was a friendly one and they remained on good terms after the departure. About the only thing they squabbled about later was their claims on building the first automobile, which some speculated was the

The Haynes-Apperson Company occupied these three buildings. (Courtesy of the Haynes Museum.)

Elwood Haynes drives a Haynes-Apperson in an endurance contest. (Courtesy of the Haynes Museum.)

reason for the split in the first place. While they never came out publicly and explained their differences, the companies did go in different directions with the styles of their automobiles, which may be another reason for the departure. Their personalities were different as well: Haynes was the scholarly type; the Appersons were mechanics.

The departure of the Appersons led Haynes to resign as manager of the Indiana Natural Gas & Oil Company so he could concentrate more on the automobile business. Although the Appersons were now gone, the name of the company remained the same for the next few years because Elmer Apperson retained a stock interest in the company. Sales remained the same as well. The company sold about 250 vehicles a year, but exact sales figures are not available.

A 1902 Haynes-Apperson on display at the Automotive Heritage Museum in Kokomo.

1902

In 1902, the company raised the price of the runabout from the year before, but made no changes in the model. The top was an additional $50. The two-passenger runabout model also went up in price to $1,500. A four-passenger surrey model, offered for $1,800 with $100 extra for a top, featured a 12-horsepower horizontally-opposed piston engine that the company described as follows: "Each cylinder of our machine is a complete engine in itself capable of bringing the car home under all ordinary conditions." The reliability of the engine was supported by a telegram from Chicago that read: "Nine degrees below zero. Slade and Robinson both still running Haynes-Apperson machines."

Advertising in 1902 emphasized that the Haynes-Apperson Automobile was the most practical automobile in the world and won the Long Island Endurance Contest two years in a row. One advertisement stated that the company had finished first in every contest they entered, but results of a Buffalo endurance contest reported that two Haynes-Apperson cars finished second and third out of a field of 89 who started the race. The ads listed the prices of the cars, unlike some companies, as the Haynes-Apperson automobiles were moderately priced in comparison with other companies. For example, a two-seat hydro-carbon Friedman auto was priced at $750, while a Winton touring car was $2,000 and a Buffalo tonneau cost $1,500.

The two-passenger Haynes-Apperson

AD 2-17 This small ad emphasized the runabout in 1902. (Courtesy of Howard County Historical Society, Kokomo, Indiana.)

Elwood Haynes drives a Haynes-Apperson surrey in the Boston to New York Reliability Contest in 1902. (Courtesy of the Haynes Museum.)

A 1901 Haynes-Apperson Model A could hold four passengers, as seen in this example on display at the Auburn Cord Duesenberg Museum.

runabout was featured in *Scientific American* magazine in 1902. The magazine wrote that the automobile did "embody the latest improvements incorporated in their machines. These include direct gearing, water circulation by means of a radiator and pump, a new design of steel wheel rims of greater strength than used in earlier machines, and improvements in the carburetor, clutch and a new pump feed lubricator. The motor is a double-cylinder engine with cylinders arranged horizontally on opposite sides of the shaft — an arrangement that gets rid of troublesome vibration. The sparking device is of the make and break positive contact type, which the company claims is not affected by wet weather and muddy roads."

The company began using the alphabet to designate its models in 1902. The surrey was the Model A, the phaeton became the Model B and the runabout was dubbed the Model C. In 1903, the models were changed to G, H and I, respectively.

1902 Models

Model A, Surrey, 9 hp, 4 passenger, $1,800
Model B, Phaeton, 9 hp, 2 passenger, 2,100 lbs, $1,500
Model C, Runabout, 6 hp, 2 passenger, 1,250 lbs, $1,200

Although Edgar Apperson was now gone, the company kept racing its cars for the additional publicity. A Haynes-Apperson finished in the top spot in the Long Island Endurance Contest, a 100-mile nonstop affair, on April 25, 1902. Then the company took first place in a five-mile speed run at the Fort Erie Track in Buffalo, New

The New York City-Buffalo Endurance Run was highlighted in this 1902 ad. (Courtesy of Howard County Historical Society, Kokomo, Indiana.)

In 1902 the Haynes-Apperson Company began designating its models by letter. This was the Model A Surrey.

York, on September 27, 1902. That was followed up by a win in a 10-mile speed contest at Grosse Pointe Track near Detroit, Michigan, on October 10. Two Haynes-Apperson cars were among the field of 78 in the New York-to-Boston Reliability Test.

In December 1902, Haynes wrote a series of advertisements featuring the technical improvements in the new Haynes-Appersons for the 1903 models. He emphasized the patented carburetors, which were operated by a button in the floor of the car. The hub pivots produced "exceptionally steering qualities." Steering was still by lever, but a steering wheel was available as an option until a few years later when it became standard equipment. The steering wheel could be tilted out of the way to allow the driver or passenger easy access to the front seat. The tilted steering wheel was the first of its kind though it was still located on the left side, an unusual feature on American cars at the time considering that the vehicles were driven on the right side of the road.

Tiller steering was employed in the early Haynes-Apperson automobiles.

1903

Demand for the Haynes-Apperson automobile was high in 1903. Advertising boasted that the automobiles "have practically been sold before they were built." In fact, the Haynes agent in Brooklyn had to return 23 percent of his deposits as the company couldn't produce enough cars to meet the demand. The company also went after women owners, producing an advertisement with a lady driver that said the powerful automobile was simple enough for a lady to run easily, and reliable enough for her to take far from home and count on getting back without trouble.

The company marketed the 1903 models as "The Only One That Always Won." What they meant was that their cars had won every endurance contest held in America and held more records than any other car made in America. The 12-horsepower Phaeton sold for $1,500, while the Surrey cost $1,800 and the Runabout was $1,200. The prices were the middle of the road in the automotive industry. Features included the double opposed-cylinder motor, four-speed transmission and an adjustable steering wheel. At the time, the company had branch offices in Brooklyn,

The Balanced Motor

Employed in all **Haynes-Apperson cars** is of the famous double cylinder type which has proved its superiority over all other forms. This motor was designed for automobiles by **The Haynes-Apperson Company,** and is used exclusively in every type of carriage they manufacture. Many manufacturers have tried to imitate this construction, but have produced nothing equal to the **original.**

Patents Cover the Three-Speed Transmission, the Most Distinctive Feature of the Haynes-Apperson Car

This transmission produces the various speed changes in easy stages, without the jerky motion characteristic of the French gear, and is more flexible under all road conditions than any other automobile speed changing device in existence. It has been consistently developed through ten years of hard service, and has been more thoroughly tested under all conditions than any other transmission made.

Should this be of interest, we shall be glad to tell you more about it. Send for our literature

THE HAYNES=APPERSON CO., Kokomo, Ind.
(*The Oldest Builders of Motor Cars in America*)

National Automobile Mfg. Co., San Francisco, agents for Pacific Coast, branch store, 381 to 385 Wabash Ave.

Please mention the SCIENTIFIC AMERICAN when you communicate with us.

2 — The Haynes-Apperson Company

Chicago and San Francisco. Meanwhile, Ford had come out with its first Model A and was selling it for $850 in 1903. However, Ford was not the leader in the industry. That honor belonged to Oldsmobile, which topped the charts with its curved dash Runabout, a two-seater that sold for less than a thousand dollars. Cadillac also began producing cars in 1903, and its two-passenger Model A sold for $750.

1903 Models

Model G, Surrey, 9 hp, 4 passenger, 2,100 lbs, $1,800
Model H, Phaeton, 12 hp, 2 passenger, 1,900 lbs, $1,500
Model I, Runabout, 6 hp, 2 passenger, 1,300 lbs, $1,200

The company's interest in racing declined after Edgar Apperson left. However, in July 1903, Nelson McClain drove a Haynes-Apperson to victory in Marion, Indiana. He averaged just under 40 miles an hour against a field of six. A Haynes-Apperson was run in a contest from New York City to Boston and back without any repairs or adjustments of any kind. The last race in which the company drove came in 1904 for the Vanderbilt Cup.

1904

Only two models were produced in 1904, the last full year for the Haynes-Apperson Automobile Company. The Model

The rear entrance of the tonneau was all the rage in 1904, so manufacturers began putting the engine in front after that. This is the Model F.

Opposite: This 1903 advertisement stressed the motor as the best feature.

Apperson was dropped from the name of the 1904 models. (Courtesy of Howard County Historical Society, Kokomo, Indiana.)

F was a four-passenger Tonneau featuring two solar gas headlights, two Dietz Regal oil lights, tail light and horn for $2,550 with a top and front glass. Model J was the Light Touring Car, which had the same outward appearance as their Runabout from the previous year. The standard features included the magneto generator, make-and-break spark ignition, throttle control, the "double cylinder opposed balanced motor" and an aluminum alloy engine block. The motor was moved to the front of the car under a conventional bonnet, although it was still a horizontally-opposed twin. Prices ranged from $1,450 for a two-seater light touring car to $2,450 for a five-seater tonneau and a permanent top and front glass could be added to the tonneau also for an extra $100. Curtains could be rolled down from the top for weather protection. The tonneau came equipped with two Solar No. 1 gas headlights, two Dietz Regal oil lights, tail light and horn. The company advertised the cars as "The Handsomest Car on the American Market — Built for American Roads." All of the Haynes-Apperson cars were more expensive than the Cadillac at the time, which sold a touring car for $900. Also less than a thousand dollars were the curved-dash Oldsmobile and the Buick Model B.

Advertisements in 1904 emphasized that the cars were made more complete than any other factory in the world and that the company had won all contests it had entered, which may not have been correct. Automobiles could be ordered in Chicago, Brooklyn, Buffalo and San Francisco.

This 1904 advertisement ran in such publications as *Scientific American*.

After June 1904, Apperson was dropped from the name of the cars and they became known as Haynes, but the company remained Haynes-Apperson Automobile Company. The company was awarded a Grand Prize at the St. Louis World's Fair. Meanwhile, Olds was the first to make the move to mass production during the year with his Curved Dash model, which sold for $650. Olds sold more than 5,000 Runabouts that year, compared to 250 Haynes cars.

1904 Models

<u>Two-cylinder, 12 hp, 76" wb</u>
Model J, Light Touring Car, 2 passenger, $1,400

<u>Four-cylinder, 93" wb</u>
Model F, Tonneau, 5 passenger, $2,450

1905

The Haynes-Apperson Automobile Company finally came to an end in September 1905, when the official name of the company was changed to the Haynes Automobile Company.

Haynes-Apperson Company Production, 1896–1905

Year	Production
1896	5
1897	12
1898	55
1899	110
1900	192
1901	240
1902	250
1903	250
1904	250

Figures are approximate.

3

The Apperson Brothers Automobile Company

In the fall of 1901, Edgar Apperson was racing Haynes-Apperson vehicles to victory all over the United States, but he wasn't getting paid much from the company. His pay, a mere $20 a week, wasn't much for an automobile designer and race car driver, and this was likely the main reason he quit the company. He probably had other reasons as well, but he kept those to himself and never expressed them to anyone. His departure was the dawning of a new day and a new company. His brother Elmer told him, "Open the old machine shop. Make drawings for a new and better car. I'll be along soon." By the end of the year, Elmer joined his brother. Elmer suggested equal shares, but Ed refused on the ground that Elmer was furnishing all the money. So the compromise became two-thirds share for Elmer and a third for Edgar, until a later reorganization when they became equal partners. The Appersons did need financial help though and turned to Thomas C. McReynolds, Sr., a boyhood friend. Before they made the move officially, they received a number of orders on a trip to New York City. This undoubtedly made their decision a bit easier.

1902

They moved back into their old Riverside Machine Shop in 1902 to begin manufacturing their own automobiles. When he left the company, Edgar envisioned a faster and bigger car, weighing between 1,200 and 1,300 pounds, with a wheelbase of 72 inches. The Model A had a surrey body with French influence, evident in the front-end design and flared fenders. The surrey was powered by a 16-horsepower, horizontally-opposed, two-cylinder engine. Edgar was also the first to use a German magneto. The surrey employed a three-speed sliding gear transmission. A dry battery was used for starting

Top: The Apperson brothers raced their first car in the Boston to New York Reliability Contest in 1902 against Elwood Haynes. (Courtesy of the Haynes Museum.) *Bottom:* The first effort by the Apperson Brothers was this two-cylinder model in 1902. (Courtesy of the Haynes Museum.)

and supplied power to a red tail lamp and two dashboard lamps. The clutch and transmission were put in a gear case. The car was also equipped with the first emergency brake — to keep the car from rolling backward on a hill — and a spare tire. The first car was shipped in July at a cost of $3,500, but others sold for as low as $2,500.

1902 Models

Model A, 2-cyl., 16 hp, 102" wb
Touring, 4 passenger, $2,500

1903

After selling about a dozen Model As for about $2,500 each in 1902, production increased to a couple of cars per week in 1903. The Appersons used a Nesta 75-amp battery for starting. A two-cylinder engine could push the vehicle up to 30 miles per hour. A three-speed transmission was used. The company designed its own radiator and began using it in cars.

Two sizes of four-cylinder engines were added in March 1903. They could develop 40 or 45 horsepower, and drivers could expect about 10 miles per gallon. A four-speed transmission was also offered.

1903 Models

Model A, 2 cyl., 25 hp. 102" wb
Touring, 6 passenger, $3,500

Model B, 2 cyl., 24 hp, 102" wb
Touring, 4 passenger, $3,500

Note: Four-cylinder engines were added in March.

As with the Haynes-Apperson Automobile Company, the Apperson brothers continued to race their cars in order to publicize their vehicles. One of the first by the new company came in 1903, when Elmer Apperson drove an Apperson car to victory in a three-mile race in Marion, Indiana. Two years later he drove a four-cylinder engine model to victory in the Savannah Road Race. The company also won the Chicago to New York City race in 1904, a race that took 72 hours. However, the most important race in 1904 was the Motor Age Cup Road Race. It was won by Jack Frye, the Los Angeles Apperson distributor. His outstanding performance won the car the name of "Frye's Rabbit" in motor magazines. The nickname evolved into the Jack Rabbit, which the company liked so much, it later adopted the name to its whole line of cars. Frye raced again the following year at the Harlem Mile Track in Chicago, but he was beat by a Thomas.

1904

The year 1904 marked the introduction of the Apperson side-door touring car, the first in the country. For many years new automobiles that were sold were not fully equipped. This was likely done to keep down the initial cost of the cars. People then would have to buy the luxuries separately if they wanted them. Most cars were built without tops, windshields and other options. Even so, the Apperson models sold for $3,500 and $5,000, putting the cars on the high end in the automobile market. Compare the Apperson to the most expensive Ford — the Model K — which sold for $2,800. Appersons compared more in price to the first Packards, which sold from around $4,000. The seven-passenger touring car was similar in design to European models. The hood and front looked a lot like the Mercedes.

1904 Models

Model A, 4 cyl., 40 hp, 114" wb
Touring, 6–7 passenger, $5,000

Model B, 4 cyl., 24 hp, 102" wb
Touring, 5 passenger, $3,500

1905

The Appersons made three four-cylinder cars in 1905 and all were alike except for size. The company called them "high class fours, the lightest and strongest in the world for their horsepower." Prices ranged from a low of $3,500 for a touring model to $7,500 for a limousine. For an extra $125, the customer could get a top and standing glass. The cars featured a hand clutch, Michelin tires, and French coils and batteries. The company also featured some parts from Europe and boasted to customers that they were the best parts made in the world.

1905 Models

Model A, 4 cyl., 40 hp, 108" wb
Touring, 7 passenger, $4,150

Model B, 4 cyl., 24 hp, 102" wb
Touring, 5 passenger, $3,500

Special, 4 cyl., 50 hp, 114" wb
Touring, 7 passenger, $5,150
Limousine, 7 passenger, $6,500

1906

Apperson decided to build its own four-cylinder motor in 1906. The T-head with two camshafts employed a double ignition system. A Krebs carburetor was used with the engine. Two different chassis were used in the 1906 line: the larger chassis used a 50–55 horsepower motor, while the smaller chassis used a less powerful engine rated at 40–45 horsepower.

One of the first Jackrabbits built was

The 1904 Apperson sported a hard top. (Courtesy of Howard County Historical Society, Kokomo, Indiana.)

3 — Apperson Brothers Automobile Company

1905 Model B Touring Car. (Courtesy of the Haynes Museum.)

entered in the 1906 Vanderbilt Cup Race. During practice for the race, George Robertson wrapped the $10,500 Apperson Jackrabbit around a Long Island telegraph pole. Robertson escaped injury, while his mechanic sustained broken wrists.

1906 Models

Model A, 4 cyl., 50/55 hp, 116" wb
Special Touring, 7 passenger, $5,500

Model B, 4 cyl., 40/45 hp, 112" wb
Touring, 7 passenger, $4,500

This was the first home of the Apperson Brothers Automobile Company. (Courtesy of Howard County Historical Society, Kokomo, Indiana.)

This ad appeared in the April 1906 issue of *Motor Age*. (Courtesy of the Wallace Spencer Huffman Collection, Indiana Historical Society.)

Model C, 4 cyl., 30/35 hp, 104" wb
Special Touring, 7 passenger, $5,500

1907

In 1907 the Apperson brothers hired A.G. Seiberling, a superintendent from the Haynes Automobile Company, to increase production. Seiberling bought $10,000 worth of the $150,000 inventory of the company. Up until that time, the company had been producing just two to three cars a week. The company in 1907 only carried an inventory worth about $150,000. The company also continued to import some of the best European parts for its cars. In addition, it bought steel from Krupp Gun Works in Essen, Germany. The bodies of the cars were designed in Paris, hence one model was called the Laundaulet.

The Jackrabbits were touted as the nearest thing to a racing car available from a dealer. Indeed, they were among the

1907 Apperson touring car. (Courtesy of the Wallace Spencer Huffman Collection, Indiana Historical Society.)

swiftest cars of the day and helped boost sales of the firm's more prosaic standard models. The two-passenger Jackrabbit runabout featured a round gas tank on the rear deck and guaranteed speeds up to 75 miles per hour. The company also offered a special racing Jackrabbit, called the "Big Dick." It could reach speeds as high as 90 miles per hour and cost a skyhigh $15,000, one of the most expensive models on the market. The company ended up selling just 15 of the special racers. A couple of models were also used for racing by the company.

The Apperson inventory also included in 1907 a limousine with a 50-horsepower engine which listed for $6,700. A duplicate Vanderbilt racer was also offered at the cost of $5,000. The company offered a 60-day warrantee on its cars, with payment of 20 percent required when a car was ordered and the balance due on delivery. The company decided to close its branches around the country and rely on dealers to market its cars.

The Apperson Brothers Automobile Company sponsored a basketball team during its heyday. (Courtesy of Howard County Historical Society, Kokomo, Indiana.)

The Hartford Suspension Company used an Apperson to promote its springs. This ad appeared in *Scribner's* Magazine in 1907. (Courtesy of the Wallace Spencer Huffman Collection, Indiana Historical Society.)

1907 Models

Model A, 4 cyl., 50/55 hp, 115" wb
Touring, 7 passenger, $4,000
Chassis, 5 passenger, $3,500
Chassis, 7 passenger, $4,250
Chassis, 7 passenger, with full extension top, $4,700
"Kimball" Limousine, $6,200
Runabout, $4,500
Jackrabbit Cup Racer, (60 hp., 100" wb), $5,000

Model B, 4 cyl., 40/45 hp, 114" wb
Touring, 5 passenger, 3,800 lbs, $3,800
Touring, 7 passenger, 4,200 lbs, $4,200
"Kimball" Limousine, $5,600
Runabout, light chassis, $3,800

Racing, 4 cyl., 96 hp, 110" wb
Jackrabbit "Big Dick" racer, 2 passenger, $15,000

1908

In 1908 the company hired Herbert Lytle as a driver of its Jackrabbit racer. He drove the car to victory over the 180-mile inaugural road race in Savannah, Georgia, at the new Vanderbilt Cup course on March 21. He also drove in the Briarcliff race and finished in the money. Another Jackrabbit showed it was quick as a hare on July 4, 1908. The car was so fast against two other cars that it made the Elks-sponsored race at the Indiana Fairgounds seem dull. The successes that season were overshadowed by the tragic death of Frank Croker at Daytona Beach. He was driving an Apperson. The early Apperson vehicles had problems with gears, as they broke with frequency. Edgar solved the problem by purchasing alloy steel from Krupp in Germany, the first used in an American car. Gears were now cut using a hacksaw.

The company offered a shaft drive and a six-cylinder engine in 1908. Edgar Apperson designed the new six cylinder that was put in the Model S, a seven-passenger touring model, which cost $5,000. Four-cylinder engines were still used in the Model M, K and Jackrabbit. The Jackrabbit, however, had a more powerful engine that produced 60 horsepower and a shorter wheelbase of 105 inches.

1908 Models

Model K, 4 cyl., 50/55 hp, 114" wb
Touring, 7 Passenger, $4,200
Runabout, $4,000
Jackrabbit (60 hp, 105" wb), $5,000

Model M, 4 cyl., 35 hp, 106½" wb
Roadster, 4 passenger, $2,750

Model S, 6 cyl., 55 hp, 114" wb
Touring, 7 passenger, $5,000
Runabout, 3 passenger, $5,000

Vehicles are lined up outside the Apperson Brothers Automobile Test Shed. (Courtesy of the Haynes Museum.)

1909

The six-cylinder engine models didn't sell well, so they were dropped for the 1909 model year. The company offered four models that year, the I, O, M and Jackrabbit, all with four-cylinder engines. The O Model Roadster and Runabout were the cheapest models at $2,250, and a top could be added for another $50. The Jackrabbit Runabout was the most expensive at $5,000. The company also decided both to change to Diamond Tires and to also extend the warrantee from 60 days to 90 days.

Racing Troubles

In July 1909, California Apperson distributor Harris Hanshue drove a Jackrabbit to victory in the Ferris Trophy road race at Santa Monica. He averaged 64.4 mph to thrill the crowd of 50,000.

However, those early successes in racing by the Appersons soon turned into bad luck for the car. In October, George Davis drove an Apperson Jackrabbit in the 200-mile Founders Day road race at Fairmount Park, Philadelphia. He was battling George Robertson's Locomobile for the lead when mechanical trouble ended his day. Lytle had his shot against Robertson the following season at the 395-mile Cobe Cup road race at Crown Point, Indiana. He brushed wheels when Robertson tried to pass him and ended up careening into a ditch.

The Appersons were also interested in events at the Indianapolis Motor Speedway because Carl G. Fisher was a friend of theirs. In 1909 when the track opened, the Appersons entered a Jackrabbit in a 300-mile race on August 15. Lytle was in second place for awhile before fading.

In September, Lytle raced in the

The Apperson Brothers Automobile Company employed these men as test drivers. (Courtesy of Howard County Historical Society, Kokomo, Indiana.)

Riverhead Motor Carnival in Long Island. He made the fastest lap in practice, but skidded into a tree. Mechanic J.F. Bates was fatally injured, while Lytle suffered critical injuries.

In October, Hanshue was back on the track in California. This time he drove a Jackrabbit to a victory in Oakland to capture the Portola Cup in a car owned by Leon T. Shettler. Hanshue also took victories at a hill climb near San Francisco and a 150-miler at Ascot Park, Los Angeles.

Also that month, Hugh Harding finished third in the 200-mile MacDonald & Campbell Trophy run in Farmount Park, Philadelphia. Poor luck struck him the very next race a couple of weeks later in Long Island. A steering knuckle broke on his "Big Dick" Apperson and he rolled it over. Fortunately, he was not hurt in the accident.

In November, Harding competed in the five-day meet that opened the new two-mile dirt speedway at Atlanta. He took a first and three thirds in his four starts against the fastest cars in racing.

1909 Models

Model I, 4 cyl, 35/40 hp, 128" wb
Touring, 5 passenger, $3,900
Runabout, 3/4 passenger, $3,900

Model K Jackrabbit, 4 cyl, 50/55 hp
Runabout (105" wb), $5,000
Touring, 7 passenger (123" wb), $4,200
Tonneau, (116" wb) $4,000
Roadster, (116" wb), $4,250

Model M, 4 cyl., 35/40 hp, 119" wb
Touring, 5 passenger, $3,350
Roadster, 2/3 passenger, $3,000

Model O, 4 cyl, 30 hp, 119" wb
Touring, 5 passenger, $2,400
Runabout, 3 passenger, $2,250
Roadster, 4 passenger, $2,250
Baby Tonneau, 5 passenger, $2,450

Model 6-40, 6 cyl., 128" wb
Touring, 7 passenger, $4,200

1910

By 1910, the plant employed 435 employees turning out 20 cars per week. Of course this was small in comparison with Ford, Olds, Buick and other manufacturers at the time, who were using assembly line techniques to turn out more than 20 cars per day. The men were working two shifts. Work on a third building to be used for testing began at the end of the year. In early 1910, a fire in a storehouse caused about $10,000 in damage, including several automotive bodies ruined, but the loss was covered by insurance and production wasn't hampered. The company had branches in Philadelphia, Chicago and Omaha. George Stout was hired as the sales manager and he launched a national advertising campaign.

On March 30, 1910, Harris Hanshue drove a Jackrabbit to a record run at the San Francisco Hill Climb. He negotiated the one and one-twentieth mile course in a minute and seven seconds to break the course record by five seconds. He also won the $4,000 and over stock car class. He was not so lucky in October at the Vanderbilt Cup classic on Long Island, where his Jackrabbit had carburetor trouble and he finished out of the money.

Better luck was had by Harry Ball in Denver. He won the 250-mile race at Cheyenne, Wyoming, with another Apperson finishing right behind him. Then, in Denver, he captured a three-hour track race by covering 167 miles.

The success of the Jackrabbit model enabled the Apperson Brothers to raise enough money incorporate for $400,000. This launched an extensive program to erect more buildings at Plant Two, located a couple of miles north of the original plant. The company began a national advertising campaign in November, featuring an

Apperson Motor Cars sign used by dealers.

advertisement for eight models ranging in price from $2,100 to $4,250.

1910 Models

Model 4-30, 4 cyl., 30 hp, 119" wb
Baby Tonneau, $2,100

Model 4-40, 4 cyl., 40 hp, 122" wb
Touring, 5 passenger, $3,000

Model 4-50, 4 cyl., 50 hp, 128" wb
Touring, 7 passenger, $4,200

Model 6-40, 6 cyl., 50 hp, 128" wb
Touring, 7 passenger, $4,200

Jackrabbit, 4 cyl., 50 hp, 116" wb
Roadster, 2 passenger, $4,250

Because of the popularity of the Jackrabbit, the company decided to use the name for all of its makes. Three models were offered: Model 4-30, 4-40 and 4-50. The cars all had four doors and a straight-line design, with prices ranging from $2,000 to $4,200. The Jackrabbit name was used for the next two years. A round radiator nameplate incorporated the Jackrabbit symbol. The company advertised the Jackrabbits as "The Car that Made the Rabbit Famous." To market its cars, the company published a catalog titled the ABC of Appersonism containing more than 50 letters from buyers of Appersons.

The Apperson team practiced at the Speedway three times in 1910, but never entered a car there in any races that year. The following year, they entered a car in the inaugural Indianapolis 500-mile race. The car, No. 35, was clocked on a quarter-mile straightaway at 91.83 m.p.h. and started 31st in the race; however, driver Lytle never finished the 500-mile race. Lytle had completed 82 laps before being knocked out by a horrendous crash in the pits. Harry Knight lost control of his Wescott entry and sailed into the pits, slamming into the Apperson entry, which then ran into Eddie Heare's Fiat. The Apperson Jackrabbit ended upside down like a dead rabbit. AAA referee A.R. Pardington didn't want to divulge the lap positions and lap times

The Apperson Company used an owner "interview" approach in this ad from 1911.

of the Apperson. "We consider it unfair to such as the Apperson which was withdrawn through no fault of its own," he declared. In fact, the first Indy 500 turned out to be quite dangerous, as one died and four were injured. "I didn't think anything was worthwhile if it meant risking my men's lives," Edgar Apperson said as the reason to quit racing at the Indianapolis Speedway after the accident.

1911

By 1911, the Apperson Brothers Company had three general distributors in California, Massachusetts and Oregon, and branches in Pennsylvania and Nebraska. The company also had dealers in the District of Columbia and 18 states: Arizona, California, Colorado, Connecticut, Iowa, Idaho, Maine, Massachusetts, Minnesota, Missouri, New Jersey, Ohio, Oregon, Pennsylvania, South Carolina, Texas, Washington and Wyoming.

1911 Models

Model 4-30, 4 cyl., 32.4 hp, 114" wb
Jackrabbit Touring, 5 passenger, $2,000
Jackrabbit Fore-Door Touring, $2,250

Model 4-40, 4 cyl., 40 hp, 122" wb
Jackrabbit Touring, 5 passenger, $4,200

Model 4-50, 4 cyl., 50 hp, 128" wb
Jackrabbit Touring, 7 passenger, $4,200

1912

While the company may have given up on racing itself, it still used speed as a way of marketing its Jackrabbit. The company emphasized that its 1912 Apperson touring car could do 65 miles per hour and averaged twelve miles per gallon of gasoline. Interestingly, speed limits in Indiana back then were 20 mph in the country, 15 in city limits and 8 in business sections. Prices dropped to below $2,000 for an Apperson car in 1912. The lowest priced Apperson was the Model 4-45 Touring car for $1,600. After five years with the company, A.G. Seiberling returned to the Haynes Automobile Company, so the Appersons hired Burtt J. Hubbard as chief engineer. The company was prospering, although its yearly sales rarely exceeded 1,000 units since 1906.

1912 Models

Model 4-45, 4 cyl., 45 hp, 114" wb
Jackrabbit Touring, 5 passenger, $1,600
Jackrabbit Roadster, $1,750
Jackrabbit Town Car, 4 passenger, $2,250

Model 4-55, 4 cyl., 55 hp, 118" wb
Jackrabbit Touring, 5 passenger, $2,000
Jackrabbit Special Touring (122" wb), 7 passenger, $3,000

Model 4-65, 4 cyl., 65 hp, 128" wb
Jackrabbit "De Luxe" Touring, 7 passenger, $4,200

The Apperson Company used several different jack rabbit emblems. The jack rabbit jumping through the eight represented the 8-cylinder engine.

1913

While the Apperson Brothers Company was no longer sponsoring race cars, some race drivers continued to use Appersons. Hanshue was

Limited Output—Limitless Quality!

This is the manufacturing policy of Elmer and Edgar Apperson. It means much to the buyer in comfort, confidence and cash. More keenly each day Apperson owners appreciate the power, speed, wear-resistance and low up-keep of the

Apperson "Jack Rabbit"
"The Wizard of the Hills"

Our production is limited. Never will it reach that point where *quality* suffers. Never will the "Jack Rabbit" lose its distinctiveness. *Quantity* can be had for the asking. *Quality* only by the stiffest effort intelligently applied.

The work of an entire "know how" organization is centered on the production of a relatively small number of *manufactured* cars. Each one, before it is delivered, passes test after test—by department foremen, final inspectors, superintendents—and last receives the personal inspection and O. K. of either Elmer or Edgar Apperson. No detail escapes them. Such personal attention from two of the best engineers the industry has known would be manifestly impossible were our output "mammoth," "stupendous" or "so many per minute." You know that.

Become acquainted today with the New "Forty-Five"—the twenty-first year tribute to the unerring motor car genius and instinct of Elmer Apperson. Personally, if possible; if not, through the medium of our De Luxe Catalog.

Prices—Based on a Profit of 9%

Including full equipment with positive electric lighting and electric self-starting system.

Light	4-45	. .	$1600—5 Pass. Touring
Light	4-45	. .	1600—2 Pass. Roadster
Standard	4-45	. .	1785—5 Pass. Touring
Light	6-45-58	. .	2200—5 Pass. Touring
Light	6-45-58	. .	2200—2 Pass. Roadster
Light	6-45-58	. .	2300—7 Pass. Touring

Apperson Bros. Automobile Company,
307 Main St., Kokomo, Ind.

(45)

Elmer and Edgar Apperson claimed that no detail escaped them in this 1912 ad. (Courtesy of the Wallace Spencer Huffman Collection, Indiana Historical Society.)

Part of the Apperson Brothers Automobile Company sat on the banks of Wildcat Creek, which flooded in 1913. (Courtesy of Howard County Historical Society, Kokomo, Indiana.)

back racing one in 1913 in the 443-mile Los Angeles-to-Sacramento road race on July Fourth. At one point he was thought to have died in a crash, but it turned out to be a blown tire and he went on to finish ninth.

Besides racing, the company took part in the Indianapolis to the Pacific Coast tour sponsored by the Indiana Automobile Manufacturer Association in 1913. Two Apperson automobiles made the two-month trip to demonstrate the performance of their vehicles.

The electric starter was first introduced in 1912 and the Apperson Brothers Automobile Company installed it in its cars the following year. The company charged customers an extra $100 if they wanted the starter and another $100 if they wanted five electric lights to go along with it. No longer would someone have to crank the motor to get it going. The change made it easier for a woman to drive a car. The company decided to drop its most expensive car in 1913, so models ranged in price from $1,600 to $2,250.

1913 Models

Model 4-45, 4 cyl., 45 hp, 114" wb
Jackrabbit Touring, 5 passenger,
  2,850 lbs, $1,600
Jackrabbit Roadster, 2 passenger,
  2,700 lbs, $1,600
Jackrabbit Coupe, 4 passenger, $2,100
Jackrabbit Town Car, $2,100

Model 4-55, 4 cyl., 55 hp, 118" wb
Jackrabbit Touring, 5 passenger,
  3,000 lbs, $2,000
Jackrabbit Special Touring, (122" wb)
  7 passenger, $2,250

1914

The Appersons realized that customers wanted more powerful machines and began offering six-cylinder engines in 1914.

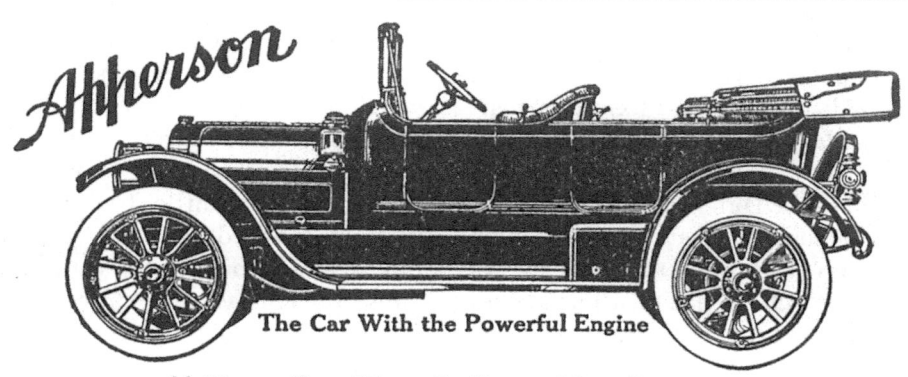

This 1913 advertisement was a general approach to the Jack Rabbit cars. (Courtesy of the Wallace Spencer Huffman Collection, Indiana Historical Society.)

The company offered two six cylinder motors: a T-head, 60 horsepower, and a L-head, 45 horsepower. The company introduced the new "light" four- and six-cylinder engine models at lower more popular prices—$1,485 to 1,785—in 1914. The price couldn't compare to the Ford Model T, which was selling for about $500 at the time, but the Appersons weren't marketing to the masses like Ford, which had half the United States car market. By this time, more than one hundred auto manufacturers were competing for customers in the United States. The light models featured a simple chassis that helped to lighten the model and keep the price down. Both were designed as convertibles with a fabric folding top that could be raised for protection from the elements. A brochure from the company boasted: "The car embodies advance principles of engineering and design found in no other car. The leverless gear-shift, which is mechanically controlled; the emergency brake operation from the instrument board; a driver's compartment that has no gear-shift or brake levers; the specially designed frame; the six-cylinder motor; and permanent top with side curtains stored in back of the front seat." The cars came in medium green and had vermilion wheels. While car makers began offering cars with left-hand drive in 1910, Apperson waited until 1914 to convert.

The 1914 Vanderbilt Cup race featured an Apperson Jackrabbit, which was the last appearance of a chain-drive car in a major U.S. event. Frank Goode was the driver. Sam Price finished in fifth in an

An overhead view of the Apperson Jack Rabbit. (Courtesy of the Haynes Museum.)

Apperson at a 150-mile race in Phoenix that year as well.

Production at the plant soon increased and the company began turning out a car per day. In late 1914, the company added 12 acres of space and production in order to produce 10,000 cars a year. Work was underway on plant number 2, and $200,000 was spent on new equipment.

In August 1914, Jesse Eccleston was appointed as the new general sales manager and J.H. Newmark as the advertising manager. Both had come from the Oakland Motor Company. Advertising in 1914 emphasized that Appersons were 95 percent Apperson-built and that the cars had more to offer at their prices than the competitors.

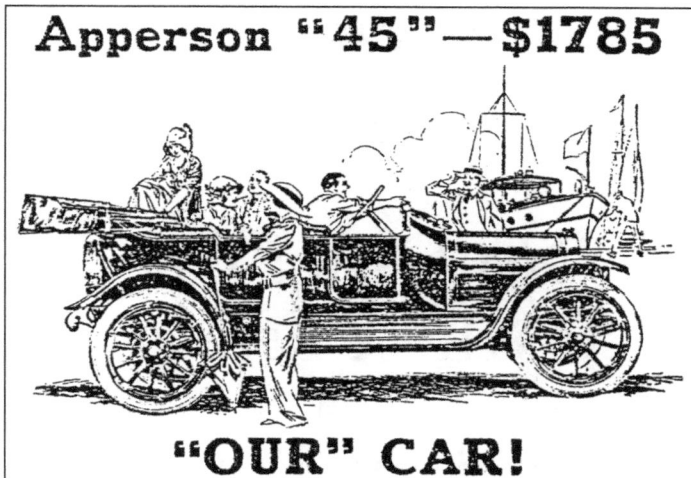

This ad appeared in *Motor Age* in 1914. (Courtesy of the Wallace Spencer Huffman Collection, Indiana Historical Society.)

1914 Models

Light 4-45, 4 cyl., 32.4 hp, 116" wb
Touring, 5 passenger, 3,290 lbs, $1,600
Turtle-Back Roadster, 2 passenger, 3,510 lbs, $1,600
Coupe, 4 passenger, 3,190 lbs, $2,350

Model 4-45, 4 cyl., 32.4 hp, 120" wb
Touring, 5 passenger, 3,360 lbs, $1,785
Sedan Limousine, 5 passenger, 3,648 lbs, $2,500

Model 6-45, 6 cyl, 29.4 hp, 128" wb
Touring, 5 passenger, 3,430 lbs, $2,200
Touring, 7 passenger, 3,530 lbs., $2,300
Roadster, 2 passenger, 3,300 lbs, $2,200

Model 6-55, 6 cyl., 43 hp, 128" wb
Touring, 5 passenger, $2,350
Roadster, 2 passenger, $2,350

1915

In 1915, the company began making completely equipped cars instead of requiring owners to purchase all the extras. The company also offered a 90-day warranty. Another technical marvel by the company in 1915 was the Model 6-60 Touring car. The six-cylinder car developed 60

No Other Car Has these Features

—a mechanical gear-shift which makes it impossible to "clash" the gears;

—a driver's compartment that is free from all levers;

—an emergency brake that operates from the instrument board.

But the dominant appeal of this Apperson lies in the inherent goodness of the car as a whole.

It is a car every member of your family can drive—with safety, comfort and absolute confidence. Drive it yourself today.

SIXES $1535 - $2200   EIGHTS $2800 - $3850

F. O. B. Factory

In the illustration, the driver's thumb is resting on the selector—the control of the new mechanical gear-shift. To operate you move this up into "first," with the thumb or forefinger, throw out the clutch and the gears shift automatically. You can go from neutral to high just as fast as you can move the selector and throw out the clutch— each shift is positive, instant and noiseless.

APPERSON BROS. AUTOMOBILE CO., KOKOMO, INDIANA

Member Kokomo Chamber of Commerce

Left: Apperson featured the mechanical gear-shift in its ads. (Courtesy of the Wallace Spencer Huffman Collection, Indiana Historical Society.)

Famous Apperson T-Head Six Cylinder Sixty Horse-Power Motor. Used in Standard Six-Sixty chassis. Right or Magneto Side.

Right: The Apperson T-Head Six Cylinder Motor, which was standard in the Six-Sixty chassis. (Courtesy of the Haynes Museum.)

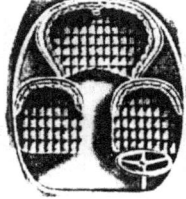

This ad was used to market the "Chummy" Roadster in 1915.

horsepower and sold for $2,350. The Appersons took credit for pioneering the float-feed carburetor, but A.L. Dyke also took credit for doing the same. The 1915 line featured a new water circulation system, modified streamline bodies and bijur cranking and lighting.

The company announced plans to expand the plant at the end of 1915 and to increase production to 10,000 cars year. However, they never achieved such lofty numbers.

On December 9, 1915, William Robertson drove an Apperson eight on a nonstop round-trip from Boston to New York City in 16 hours and 9 minutes. He drove the seven passenger car in high gear for the 488-mile trip.

1915 Models

<u>Model 4-40, 4 cyl., 25.6 hp, 116" wb</u>
Touring, 5 passenger, 2,760 lbs, $1,350

<u>Model 4-45, 4 cyl., 32.4 hp, 120" wb</u>
Touring, 5 passenger, 3,200 lbs, $1,685
Roadster, 2 passenger, 3,100 lbs, $1,685
Coupe, 4 passenger, 3,700 lbs, $2,350

<u>Model 6-45, 6 cyl., 29.4 hp, 122" wb</u>
Touring, 5 passenger, 3,000 lbs, $1,485

<u>Model 6-48, 6 cyl., 29.4 hp, 126" wb</u>
Tonneau, 7 passenger, 3,100 lbs, $1,585

<u>Model 6-60, 6 cyl., 43.35 hp</u>
Roadster, 3,300 lbs, $2,200
Touring, 5 passenger, 3,400 lbs, $2,200
Touring, 7 passenger, 3,500 lbs, $2,350

The Appersons then asked Hubbard to design and build a V-8 as soon as possible, because Cadillac was introducing an eight-cylinder engine. The first V-8 engines came from the French. In America, Buffum first offered a V-8 touring car in 1906. Hubbard developed an engine that included a thermo-syphon cooling system, a belt driven fan and generator combination. The Apperson V-8 first appeared in the 1916 models. Marketed as the "Eight with Eighty Less Parts," it proved to be quite popular among buyers. The slogan was used to refer to the engine's simplicity in comparison to other eights, like Peerless. While the use of a single camshaft eliminated some parts, the engine was not necessarily superior to the others of the day — the advertising just planted the idea that it was. Most other V-8s of the period used two camshafts, 32 cams and numerous push rods, followers and gears. The company also came up with other advertising slogans to sell their cars: "Drive an Apperson First, then Decide," "The Wizard of the Hills" and "Count the Rabbits on the Road."

In late 1915, the Apperson Brothers Company dropped the four-cylinder engine from its models and announced that its 1916 model would feature the eight-cylinder engine. The Apperson V-8 engine was put in the seven-passenger touring car and a four-passenger roadster called the Speed Boy for the sporty types. The Speed Boy was capable of hitting speeds up to 60 mph, and was also produced for fire-fighting purposes because of its speed and extra carrying capacity. The V-8 models

The Apperson V-8 was marketed as "the eight with eighty less parts." It was designed by Burtt E. Hubbard. (Courtesy of Haynes Museum.)

Burtt E. Hubbard designed the Apperson Chummy Roadster for four passengers. (Courtesy of the Haynes Museum.)

featured a V-shaped radiator as well, along with a three-speed gearset, floating axle and full electric lighting and starting equipment. The company also continued to feature cars with six-cylinder engines. To publicize the new V-8 engine, William Robertson drove an Apperson on his nonstop, New York City-to-Boston trip with three passengers to observe and check the results.

1916

On January 4, 1916, a patent was approved for the cloverleaf seating design for the Appersons. The design was Hubbard's idea. The individual front seats had an aisle between them for access to the back seat and it looked like a cloverleaf from above. The year turned out to be the best in company history, as 2,000 units were sold.

Hubbard also designed the Apperson Chummy Roadster with bucket seats in 1916, a forerunner to the convertible. The Chummy also had individual front seats with an aisle between to allow access to the rear seats, and gave the appearance of a three-leaf clover from above. A large, enclosed luggage compartment in the rear gave the car a streamlined appearance. The roadster had a 128-inch wheelbase and sold for $1,850. It was an immediate hit at the 1916 New York Automobile Show. This unique and popular model was protected by patent No. 48359. The Chummy Roadster's popularity led to a host of imitators from other companies, including a "So-Sha-Belle" by the Haynes Automobile Company.

On the racing scene, Sam Price entered an Apperson in the 1916 Corona road race. He and his mechanic were both injured during practice.

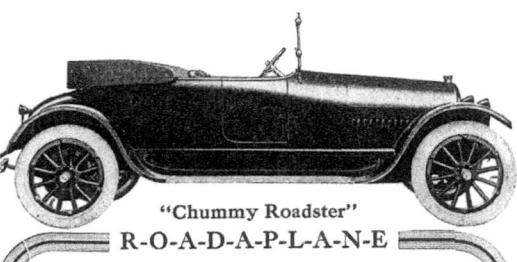

"Chummy Roadster"
R-O-A-D-A-P-L-A-N-E

It glides over the roads as the Aeroplane glides through the air, and hence its name.

Cutting Down the High Cost of Automobiling

THE Apperson Roadaplane has done more than merely prove itself an efficient performer under all conditions of service. That was to be expected, of course.

But the remarkable tire mileage and the equally remarkable saving in fuel consumption, due to proper balance, and light weight—3000 pounds—have added as great a measure of fame to this car as its beauty of lines, luxurious appointments and mechanical excellence.

The low operating costs experienced by owners are astonishing for cars of the size and power of the Roadaplane Sixes and Eights.

Again the supremacy of Apperson designing has been made manifest in this car.

The question of operating cost is one that vitally interests every car owner. It is one of the factors that has had much to do with the steadily increasing popularity of the car which rivals the Aeroplane in its smooth-riding properties.

Let us submit some tire and fuel records. You will find them an interesting and *helpful* guide in your selection of a car.

Six cylinder seven, five and four passenger, "Chummy Roadster" bodies. 130-inch wheelbase, 3000 pounds, 48 horsepower, $1690 and $1750.

Eight-cylinder 58 horsepower, $2000, f.o.b. Kokomo, Indiana.

Send for the Roadaplane Book.

Apperson Brothers Automobile Co.
Kokomo, Indiana, U. S. A.

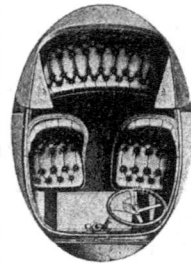

Seating Plan of the Chummy Roadster

APPERSON ROADAPLANE

1916 Models

Model 6-16, 6 cyl., 29.4 hp, 128" wb
Light Six Touring, 7 passenger,
   3,150 lbs, $1,550
Light Six Touring, 5 passenger,
   3,100 lbs, $1,485
Light Six Roadster, 4 passenger,
   3,050 lbs, $1,550

Model 8-16, V-8, 31 hp, 128" wb
Light Eight Touring, three or four
   door, 7 passenger, 3,200 lbs, $1,850
Light Eight "Chummy" Roadster,
   4 passenger, 3,200 lbs, $1,850
"Speed Boy" Roadster, 4 passenger,
   3,150 lbs, $2,000

1917

The increase in sales led the company to expand the next year with a new north-side plant with 500,000 square feet of floor space. This doubled the area available for manufacturing. The war years were good for the company, as it did some limited work for the government. Profits averaged some $200,000 a year. The company employed over 600 workers.

The Light models were dropped in 1917 in favor of Roadaplane models, a marketing idea of Elmer Apperson. He told the advertising and marketing department to come up with comparisons of the cars with airplanes in the literature. For example, the company touted the cars as giving the feeling of air support, or that the ride was as light as a ride in a plane. For example, "The Roadaplane floats over the roads as an aeroplane

The Apperson Brothers' approach to the Roadaplane didn't help sell the vehicle. (Courtesy of the Wallace Spencer Huffman Collection, Indiana Historical Society.)

floats through space." The company probably wasn't taking the poor roads at the time into consideration. The concept lasted only a year because it failed to show any significant increase in sales. Elmer also suffered a stroke and left the company. The models came with a six- or eight-cylinder engine. The six model, either the touring car or four-passenger roadster, featured a new block L-head engine, developing 48 horsepower, sold for $1,750—$200 more than the six the year before. The eight model, either touring car or four-passenger roadster, sold for $2,000—an increase of $150 more than the year before. The Roadaplanes had extra long springs and soft, luxurious Turkish-style leather upholstery. The cars came in blue, green or mouse gray.

1917 Models

Model 6-17, 6 cyl., 29.4 hp, 130" wb
Roadaplane Chummy Roadster,
  4 passenger, 3,100 lbs, $1,750
Roadaplane Touring, 7 passenger,
  3,200 lbs, $1,750
Beverly Light, 5 passenger, $1,690

Model 8-17, V-8, 33.8 hp, 130" wb
Roadaplane Touring, 7 passenger,
  3,290 lbs, $2,000
Roadaplane Chummy Roadster,
  4 passenger, 3,140 lbs, $2,000
"Speed Boy" Roadster, $2,000

1918

In 1918, the Appersons celebrated their 25th anniversary in the car making business with the Silver-Apperson, a V-8 with styling by Conover T. Silver, a New York dealer who later applied his styling talents to Kissel cars. Silver had come up with the design the year before when he made some unauthorized changes to his 1917 stock, because he thought they were drab in appearance. The Silver-Apperson sported bullet-shaped headlamps, a wedge-shaped bumper, modern body lines and wire wheels. The Anniversary model became an immediate success. The name was later dropped, but the design continued until 1923 because it was so popular. Equipped with the 60-horsepower V-8 engine, the Silver-Apperson came in custom-built bodies of special design or the regular Apperson body. The popular model could go 0–40 miles per hour in 40 seconds and stop at that speed in just four seconds in forty yards. At least that is what their advertisements boasted. For the special model, Edgar Apperson introduced the preselective gearshift on top of the steering wheel, the first successful one of its kind. Gears could be shifted with the touch of a finger on the short level. Of course, gears couldn't be changed without first engaging the clutch. Also for the first time, the Anniversary model included a V-type fan belt and pulley. The company paid little attention to its six-cylinder cars and gave them little mention in advertising, so they lagged behind in sales and were dropped the next year.

Sales brochures from the company featured some lovely ladies of the day. The brochures also boasted that a car could be driven "10,000 miles without removal of the spark plugs." The company also emphasized that it manufactured 99 percent of its cars.

1918 Models

Model 6-18, 6 cyl., 29.4 hp, 130" wb
Chummy Roadster, 4 passenger, 3,000 lbs,
  $1,990
Touring, 7 passenger, 3,250 lbs, $1,990

Model 8-18, V-8, 33.8 hp, 130" wb
Chummy Roadster, 4 Passenger, 3,150 lbs,
  $2,550
Touring, 7 passenger, 3,400 lbs, $2,550
Silver Special Touring, 3,469 lbs, $3,500
Sedan, 7 passenger, 3,600 lbs

Apperson Model 6-18 seven-passenger touring car from 1918. (Courtesy of the Haynes Museum.)

1919

The company dropped the six-cylinder models in 1919 in favor of a Standard Eight. The Standard was about $1,000 less than the Anniversary Eight. The Standard Eight lacked the sporting grace of the Silver specials and featured a horseshoe-shaped radiator.

By this time, several small automobile manufacturers had already gone by the wayside, and General Motors offered the Appersons a large amount of money to sell out. Elmer turned down the offer, which turned out to be a poor decision. By now the company employed some 600 workers and produced 3,000 units a year. That number would drop considerably the next year as the economy went into a recession and sales dropped accordingly. Misfortune continued as Elmer died on March 28, 1920.

1919 Models

Model 8-19, V-8, 33.8 hp, 130" wb
Tourster, 4 passenger, 3,400 lbs, $4,000
Anniversary Touring, 7 passenger,
   3,460 lbs, $4,000
Roadster, 4 passenger, 3,150 lbs
Sedan, 7 passenger, 3,600 lbs, $2,550

1920

The long-standing controversy—sometimes referred to as the "Battle of Kokomo"—over claims by both Haynes and the Appersons reached a peak in 1920. The company ran advertisements that were statements of who actually built the first mechanically successful American automobile. The advertisement pointed out that Elwood Haynes initiated the idea, but it was the Apperson brothers who helped carry it out. The brothers and their employees did

This Apperson of about 1920 may be familiar to those who know their Mack Sennett movies. The car's hood is decorated with World's Record figures, including 2,000 miles at 80.3 MPH and 1928¾ miles in 24 hours. The name Charles Basle is painted on the cowl — does anyone know the history of this car?

This 1920 Apperson was used in a Mack Sennett movie.

the actual mechanical work on the first car. The Appersons adapted clutches bought from a Dayton, Ohio company to the car. The reason for the advertisement was to set the record straight. The Appersons had been completely left off the placard at the Smithsonian Institution. The advertisement boasted that the Apperson Brothers were the first to build a double-opposed motor, first with a float-feed carburetor, first with electric ignition, and others firsts. Here is the advertisement as it appeared:

The Exact Facts Concerning Who Actually Built the First Mechanically Successful American Automobile. A Statement by the Apperson Bros. Automobile Co. The first mechanically successful American automobile.

Who built it?

This statement is to establish the true facts once and for all.

An erroneous impression has been gained by a few that a controversy exists relative to the 'First Car' matter.

We wish now to publicly announce that this is not true.

Here are all the facts— the actual facts— and nothing else.

In the early nineties, Elmer and Edgar Apperson operated a machine shop in Kokomo, Indiana.

At the same time Elwood Haynes was associated with the Natural Gas Company of Portland, Indiana.

This 1920 Apperson Model 8-21 four-passenger Sportster was formerly owned by Edgar Apperson and is being restored by the Auburn Cord Duesenberg Museum. (Courtesy of the Auburn Cord Duesenberg Museum.)

One day the thought came to Mr. Haynes that a gasoline vehicle, would have untold economic possibilities in America.

It should be remembered that certain inventors in Europe had already been at work on the idea of the gasoline automobile. For example, the famous Benz cars had been operating for quite a while.

Thus it was Elwood Haynes, who initiated the idea which developed into the first mechanically successful American made motor car.

However, the most important step of anyone who has found a new idea is to locate the brains and ability which will enable the development of the idea in a practical manner, so it can become a reality.

So in this instance the best and most practical mechanics were sought.

Messrs. Elmer and Edgar Apperson were selected as being the most competent.

At this time they owned the Riverside Machine Works, which was located on the site of one of our present plants.

It was here that the idea was discussed and developed by the three men.

The final outcome of these meetings was the building, by the Apperson Brothers for Elwood Haynes, of the car destined to become famous.

The actual mechanical work on this first car was done by the Apperson Brothers and their employees.

The motor was a small launch type, purchased from a marine motor company.

The speed transmission, which included four individual clutches, was of the ordinary lathe clutch type and was bought at Dayton, Ohio.

These clutches were adapted to the job by the Appersons.

It was at this time that the Appersons designed the first contracting band clutch, by means of which the power of the motor was applied to the driving mechanism. The car also was provided with compensating gears.

Today many of the fundamental units

and actions of this original car are still in use. Of course, they have been greatly refined, but the basic principles in many cases remain the same.

The point we wish to make — the point which we are entitled to make — the point, we believe, the public believes we are entitled to make, is that much of the initial engineering work, and actual process of building and assembling the car was done by the Apperson Brothers — by their own brains and with their own hands.

They were the engineers who designed and produced the first successful American made motor car of the internal combustion type.

That car — America's first car — was a success from the start. When it was pulled into the country for its trial trip, it actually ran!

Inasmuch as the material and labor entering into the construction of this car were paid for by Elwood Haynes, it became his property. He presented it to the Smithsonian Institution at Washington, D.C., where it is now on exhibit placarded as follows:

'Gasoline automobile built by Elwood Haynes in Kokomo, Indiana, 1893-1894. Successful trial trip made at a speed of six or seven miles per hour, July 4, 1894. Gift of Elwood Haynes, 1910, 262, 135.'

Yet in its issue of April 14, 1920, the New York Globe published the following:

"With the death of Elmer Apperson a short time ago the automobile industry loses a man who has been an important factor in its development from the very beginning.

"There has been some controversy as to whether Elmer Apperson or Elwood Haynes was responsible for the first American Automobile. Suffice it to say here, however, that no matter whether it was Elwood Haynes or Elmer Apperson who furnished the idea for the car now on exhibition at the Smithsonian Institution in Washington, labeled 'America's First Car,' there is no doubt that it was built by the Apperson Brothers in the Riverside Machine Works. Later the Apperson boys, in association with Elwood Haynes, formed the first American company for production of motor cars — the Haynes-Apperson Company. Later, the Appersons withdrew from the first organization and organized their own manufacturing company. Through all his life — and he was only fifty-eight years old — the soul of Elmer Apperson was in the building of automobiles. His death removes not only a pioneer of the industry but a useful citizen and an honorable man."

Also in confirmation of this same fact, Edward M. Souder, editor of the Kokomo Tribune, and boyhood playmate of the Apperson Brothers, in a "Memory" written at the time of Elmer Apperson's death, had the following to say:

"Elmer Apperson's business career had its real beginning in 1889 when he founded the Riverside Machine Works. That unpretentious plant became actually, though not in name, the first automobile factory in America, for it was there after plans suggested by Elwood Haynes, that he, in association with his brother, Edgar, built the first gasoline motor car constructed in this country. This car is in existence today comprising part of the mechanical exhibit in the Smithsonian Institution in the city of Washington."

With Elmer and Edgar Apperson there was associated with Elwood Haynes, John Maxwell, for whom some years later the now famous Maxwell automobile was named.

Thus we give all the facts concerning the conception, creation and construction of American's first mechanically successful motor car.

In 1898 the Haynes-Apperson Company was incorporated and a factory built to produce automobiles. This was the first regularly incorporated company in the United States for the manufacture of motor cars.

Elmer Apperson was General Manager of this Company and Edgar Apperson, General Superintendent.

This association continued for three years, at which time the Appersons withdrew to form their own company.

As time went on the Apperson Brothers gave to the world many notable engineering car improvements, the most noteworthy of which are as follows:

They designed and built the first double opposed motor;

Built the first car with a float feed carburetor;

Built the first car with electric ignition;

Built the first gasoline motor car engine to win an award in America;

Built the car that won the first American speed contest;

Built the car that made the first 100-mile non-stop run in America;

Built the car that made the first long overland American tour;

Built the two American cars that won first and second in the first Automobile Club of America tour;

Built their first four-cylinder car in 1903;

Built their first six-cylinder car in 1907;

Built their first eight-cylinder car in 1914;

Built and designed the first 'Chummy' roadster body;

Building now the first eight-cylinder motor with eighty less parts.

From this humble beginning in 1894 developed the present gigantic American automotive industry.

From this initial conception and creation, with cost about $750 to build by hand, we find today billions of dollars worth of automobiles in use in the Untied States.

Since 1893 and 1894 the Appersons continually and consistently have built better and better automobiles. They put into practice their basic and fundamental designs that are today in use by the entire automobile industry.

The purpose of making public this full announcement of all the facts is to make clear everyone's position.

Just as there can be no doubt as to who conceived the first car, neither can there be any doubt as to who created and constructed it.

"The Eight with Eighty Less Parts" was the theme of advertising in 1919. (Courtesy of the Wallace Spencer Huffman Collection, Indiana Historical Society.)

The Apperson advertisement was answered by the Haynes Automobile Company with "A Sworn Statement by Elwood Haynes," which was widely circulated. The statement included a further explanation of why the Appersons didn't receive credit. "It would have been practically the same machine if built in any other machine shop in the world or by any other workmen."

1920

The company exploded from one model and two makes in 1919 to two models and a dozen makes in 1920. The six-cylinder engine was dropped in favor of eights for all makes and models. Prices exploded as well, as they ranged from $2,950 to $5,500. Several of the models—Coupe, Cabriolet, Sedan, Limousine and Berlin—were enclosed. This reflected the shift in the automotive industry to more enclosed models. The company went as far as saying that the 1919 line was the "lineal descendant of the Jack Rabbit racers of the past," although the Anniversary Model showed no improvements. What were prices for parts like in 1920? According to a parts book from the Apperson Brothers, a radiator assembly cost $90. A motor went for $1,000, but a piston cost $8. A generator cost $80 and a fan belt cost $4. Distributors cost $25.

1920 Models

Model 1920, V-8, 33.8 hp, 130" wb
Touring, 7 passenger, 3,810 lbs, $2,950
Sportster, 4 passenger, 3,555 lbs, $2,950
Ace, 2 passenger, 3,290 lbs, $2,950
Sedan, 7 passenger, 4,020 lbs, $4,000
Sedanet, 4 passenger, 3,925 lbs, $4,000
Coupe, 4 passenger, 3,850 lbs, $4,000
Berlin, 7 passenger, 4,100 lbs, $4,000
Anniversary Model
Touring, 7 passenger, 3,810 lbs, $4,000
Tourster, 4 passenger, 3,750 lbs, $4,000
Sedan, 7 passenger, 4,225 lbs, $5,500
Cabriolet, 4 passenger, 3,880 lbs, $5,500
Coupe, 4 passenger, 3,975 lbs, $5,500

Sportster 4 Passenger

Touring 7 Passenger

1920 Apperson cars.

1921

Many of the models introduced in 1920 went the way of the dinosaur in 1921, and the company cut back to one model with five makes—three closed and two open. The Anniversary line was available in two models, a four-passenger and seven-passenger for the same price. Prices on other models were substantially lowered

THINGS · THAT · ENDURE

The works of man that endure are all alike and vitalized by the same spark. That spark is the striving for an ideal perfection that forgets immediate profit.

When the Apperson Brothers built with their own hands the first mechanically successful automobile, their goal was achievement of an ideal perfection.

And as Apperson has grown, this spirit has never changed. It has kept the Appersons breaking trail for more than a quarter of a century. It has endowed every Apperson car with enduring worth.

Appersons stay at their best a long, long time. Owners of old Apperson Sixes and Fours still drive them today,

finding it difficult to believe that the Apperson Eight can be an improvement.

Yet the Apperson Eight is a big advance. It has eighty less parts. Astonishing acceleration—from 1 to 40 miles an hour in 40 seconds. This shows the motor's flexibility and tremendous power. And the car is so perfectly balanced that the brake curbs the speed from 40 miles an hour to a dead stop in 4 seconds—40 yards.

These outstanding superiorities represent the excellence of the whole car and its every part.

And Apperson excellence endures. DRIVE an Apperson First—Then Decide.

APPERSON BROTHERS AUTOMOBILE COMPANY, *Kokomo, Indiana*

APPERSON
The Eight with Eighty Less Parts

The Apperson Brothers used this advertisement to sell their eight-cylinder car in 1920. (Courtesy of Howard County Historical Society, Kokomo, Indiana.)

In 1920 the Apperson Brothers came out with this Anniversary Special Sedan that accommodated seven passengers. (Courtesy of the Auburn Cord Duesenberg Museum.)

to make the autos more attractive to consumers.

1921 Models

<u>Model 8-21, V-8, 33.80 hp, 130" wb</u>
Open Sportster, 4 passenger, 3,550 lbs, $3,500
Open Touring, 7 passenger, $3,500
Anniversary Touring, 7 passenger, 3,810 lbs, $4,250
Anniversary Tourster, 4 passenger, 3,750 lbs, $4,250
Sedanet, 4 passenger, 3,925 lbs, $4,500
Ace, 2 passenger, 3,290 lbs
Sedan, 4,020 lbs
Coupe, 4 passenger, 3,850 lbs

At the end of 1921, an Apperson Standard Eight Tourster established a new 12-hour record for continuous running at the Beverly Hills track near Los Angeles. The test car averaged 81 miles an hour. As a result of the record, the company came out with the Beverly model at the New York Auto Show in January 1922. The model came in eight different makes with prices ranging from $2,620 to $4,195, a price reduction that buyers saw as a deal. In fact, the company lowered prices on all models some ten to twenty percent. The Sportster and Tourister came with a "tourequipt" accessory package that included sidemounts, wire wheels, six tires, windshield wipers, a compartmented trunk and other goodies for an extra $250.

The company continued to race their cars around the country. Charles Basile drove a Jackrabbit to a number of records at the Beverly speedway. Harvey Herrick was the manager of the car, which came from Harris Hanshue, the distributor of the Los Angeles Apperson Agency. The car

Top: This 1921 Apperson touring car had a powerful V-8 engine. (Courtesy of the Auburn Cord Duesenberg Museum.) *Bottom:* The Apperson Automotive Company used some pretty ladies to show off its 1922 V-8 Tourster. (Courtesy of the Auburn Cord Duesenberg Museum.)

was averaging 83.37 mph for the first 21 hours of the 24-hour race, but a pit stop resulted in poor gasoline with water in the fuel. This delayed the car for some time as the gas tank had to be drained and refueled. The car still ended up averaging over 80 mph for the entire race.

1922

The new Beverly models failed to spark more sales than the year before, as the company produced just over a thousand car, so an inexpensive six-cylinder auto was offered in November. Also in November, the Apperson Company was given $700,000 in a plan to re-finance the company in order to provide for production of a light car the following year. Profits began to dwindle and the company sustained a loss in 1921. The company then made a profit of $300,000 in 1922. Eventually, Edgar lost control of the company and was demoted to second vice-president. Don P. McCord was named as the new president. The board of directors met in December 1922, and decided to lower prices of the cars as low as possible to attract dealers and new customers alike.

1922 Models

Beverly Model, V-8, 33.8 hp, 130" wb
Sportster, 4 passenger, 3,550 lbs, $2,620
Touring, 7 passenger, 3,600 lbs, $2,645
Tourster, 4 passenger, 3,500 lbs, $2,995
Sedanet, 4 passenger, 3,900 lbs, $3,895
Sedan, 7 passenger, 4,000 lbs, $3,995
Limousine Sedan, 7 passenger, 4,100 lbs, $4,195
Sportster Tourequipt, 4 passenger, 3, 600 lbs, $2,995
Tourster Tourequipt, 4 passenger, 3,600 lbs, $3,245

Anniversary Model, 8 cyl., 33.80 hp
Touring, 7 passenger, 3,800 lbs.
Tourister, 4 passenger, 3,750 lbs

The 1923 Apperson could turn in a 38¼-foot circle. (Courtesy of the Haynes Museum.)

The Apperson Car, the Factory and the Policy

There is, to-day, no sentiment in the automobile business. If a dealer can't make money out of a car, he drops it. He is in business to make money—not to satisfy the sales ambitions of the factory or merely because it gives him prestige to represent a well known car—his job is to *make money*. Therefore, the intelligent, far-sighted dealer is, to-day, *thinking for himself*.

As a matter of self preservation he is sizing up his present line *and other cars* purely on the basis of how much money he can make in 1923—and thereafter.

He is vitally interested in the car, the factory and the factory policy. He knows that he has got to have a car that will sell—and stay sold. A car that will make a better demonstration than other cars; and then run longer, more smoothly and satisfactorily with less trouble and at less expense than other cars. A car that looks better and *is better*. A car that is so correctly engineered and conscientiously built that it does not eat up all the profit on service. Finally, he must have a car with a clean history—a car whose engineering record has no black spots on it. SUCH A CAR IS THE APPERSON.

Behind the car he must have a strong, clean, square-dealing factory, whose word is as good as its bond. A factory whose past calls for no explanations or apologies. A factory big enough to make all the cars he can sell and deliver them in A-1 condition ON TIME. SUCH A FACTORY IS BEHIND THE APPERSON.

The successful dealer must have a factory policy that is based on the one idea of the prosperity of the dealer. A factory policy that does not shove cars down his throat, does not ride him, does not make him stretch his financial facilities to the cracking point. Does not break him. A factory policy that backs him up and makes him strong with his banker. SUCH A POLICY IS THAT OF THE APPERSON.

These things being true of Apperson, this car, this factory and the Apperson policy commend themselves to those intelligent dealers who are out in 1923 to *make money*.

See the new Apperson Six and Eight at the New York Show, January 6th to 13th, in Space B-15, and at the Chicago Show, January 27th to February 3rd, in Space A-4 at the Armory.

APPERSON BROS. AUTOMOBILE CO.
Kokomo, Indiana, U.S.A.

This ad was used to attract dealers into buying 1923 Appersons. (Courtesy of the Wallace Spencer Huffman Collection, Indiana Historical Society.)

1923

Since the Beverly failed to boost sales, the name was dropped in 1923, but the eight was continued. The 1923 car featured two extra tires mounted forward, cowl ventilator, double spring-type bumper, sun and windshield wings. A company brochure stated: "To Apperson engineers belongs the credit for designing and building the first car in the world which has no levers in the driver's compartment." The six-cylinder engine was brought back in 1923 and put in a cheaper model. The Falls Engine was quite advanced for the period, as it featured overhead valves. A total of 640 of the six-cylinder Tourster models were made in 1923. However, sales were not dramatic enough to turn the company's financial troubles around, so feelers were extended to the Haynes company for a possible merger. Haynes, though, was in even more trouble than Apperson.

1923 Models

<u>Model 6-23, 6 cyl., 23.4 hp, 120" wb</u>
Tourster, 5 passenger, 2,885 lbs, $2,645
Sedan, 5 passenger, 3,250 lbs

<u>Model 8-23S, V-8, 33.8 hp, 130" wb</u>
Phaeton, 5 passenger, 4,050 lbs, $2,485
Phaeton, 7 passenger, 4,300 lbs, $2,485
Touring Sedan, 7 passenger, 4,500 lbs, $3,625
Sedan, 5 passenger, 4,380 lbs, $3,695

Two views of a 1923 Apperson Jack Rabbit on display at the Automotive Heritage Museum.

1924

The 1923 models were continued into 1924, as the company couldn't afford changes. Prices were also reduced in hopes of increasing sales. Apperson sixes sold from $1,535 to $2,100, while the eights sold from between $2,800 and $3,950. The failure of Falls Motors in 1924 only compounded Apperson's many problems as they provided the six-cylinder engine used in the 1924 model. The company was reorganized and the named was changed to

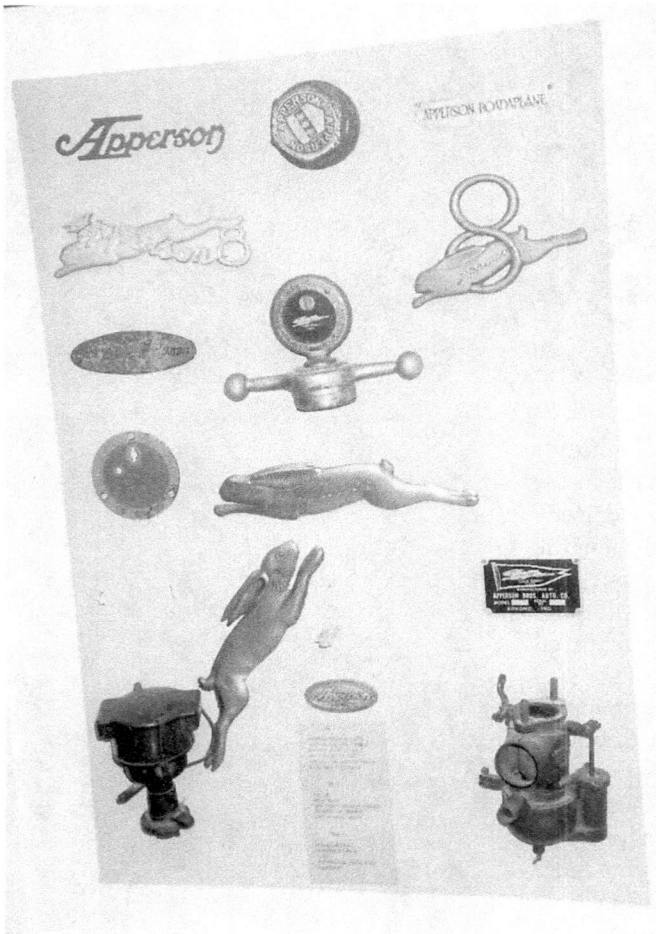

Apperson emblems grace a wall at the Haynes Museum.

Apperson Automobile Company during the summer.

1924 Models

Model 6-24, 6 cyl., 46 hp, 120" wb
Phaeton, 5 passenger, $1,395
Sport Phaeton, 5 passenger, $1,600
Sedan, 5 passenger, $1,995
Sport Sedan, 5 passenger, $2,100

Model 8-24, V-8, 70 hp, 130" wb
Phaeton, 5 passenger, $2,485
Phaeton, 7 passenger, $2,485
Sedan, 5 passenger, $3,385
Sedan, 7 passenger, $3,585

1925

In June 1925, the company announced it was coming out with fabric covered bodies, which would be a first in the automotive world. The "glove-finish" fabric would cover the cab frame and be durable. It would also help reduce the weight of the car, eliminate body squeaks and rattles and be inexpensive to replace. The company became the first to use Mertas-covered outer fabrics the following year. Front-wheel brakes were also introduced as the Lycoming straight-8 engine, which put out 65 horsepower at 3,000 rpm. Several other companies also offered straight eights. The "Eight With Eighty Less Parts" was finally phased out. Four-wheel brakes were added later in the year. By now, the company was purchasing most of its auto bodies from outside sources, which several other automakers did as well. The company did that to save money, but the effort wasn't enough to keep the company going.

1925 Models

Six, 40 hp, 120" wb
Sport Phaeton, 5 passenger, $1,650
Coupe, 2 passenger, $2.050
Sedan, 5 passenger, $2,095
Sport Sedan, 5 passenger, $2,100

Straightaway Eight, 60 hp, 120" wb
Sport Phaeton, 5 passenger, $2,485
Coupe, 2 passenger, $2,450

One of the last advertisements used by Apperson appeared in 1925 in the *Automobile Trade Journal*. (Courtesy of the Wallace Spencer Huffman Collection, Indiana Historical Society.)

Four-Door Brougham, $2,800
Sedan, 5 passenger, $2,850
Phaeton, 5 passenger, $2,485
Sport Phaeton, 5 passenger, $2,800
Phaeton, 7 passenger, $2,535
Sport Phaeton, 7 passenger, $2,900
Sedan, 5 passenger, $3,485
Sport Sedan, 5 passenger, $3,750
Sedan, 7 passenger, $3,585
Sport Sedan, 7 passenger, $3,850

1926

The 1926 coupe featured a glove-finish fabric body, which was advertised as being impervious to weather. The company gave way to the Pioneer Automobile Company, and the assets were liquidated in December 1925. In all, 17,087 Apperson automobiles were built by the company. An auction of company assets and property was held in July 1926. The real estate was appraised at $229,600 and the personal property at about $100,000, but the auction only resulted in everything being sold for the bargain basement price of $71,287.62.

1926 Models

<u>Six, 46 hp, 120" wb</u>
Phaeton, 5 passenger, $1,575
Sport Phaeton, 5 passenger, $1,650
Coupe, 4 passenger, $2,050
Brougham, 5 passenger, $2,050
Sedan, 5 passenger, $2,100

<u>Eight, 65 hp, 130" wb</u>
Sport Phaeton, 5 passenger, $1,995
Brougham, 5 passenger, $2,450
Coupe, 5 passenger, $2,450
Sport Sedan, 5 passenger, $2,495

The downfall of the Apperson Brothers Automobile Company was likely due to many factors. By the early 1920s, some 200 domestic manufacturers and a number of imports were competing for the luxury car market in which Apperson Company found itself. Competition was tough, and one mistake usually meant an end to a company. The death of Edgar Apperson was probably the first big blow. Elmer Apperson also had his sights set more on retiring in Arizona than leading the company. One mistake made by Apperson Automobile Company was the incorporation of four-wheel brakes. Apperson automobiles were somewhere between the cream of the crop and the low-priced, mass-produced automobile — not a good place to be. Only a few of the larger independents — like Packard, Hudson, Nash, Cord and Duesenberg — survived the Roaring Twenties.

4

The Haynes Automobile Company

The Apperson name was finally dropped in 1905. The reason the company held onto the Haynes-Apperson name for so long was Edgar Apperson's financial interest in the company. When that interest ended, so could the name. Elwood Haynes would have to rely on his own name to sell automobiles; however, that didn't seem to be a problem. The demand for the automobile was increasing, although by 1905 there was competition from 75 other automobile companies and only 150 miles of paved roads in the United States. While many companies made an effort to reduce prices to make the automobile more attractive to all Americans, the Haynes Automotive Company was more concerned with providing a better machine and charging more for it. The rich could afford to purchase the automobile and they wanted the convenience. That led Woodrow Wilson, then the president of Princeton, to say,

"Nothing has spread socialistic feeling more than the automobile. They are the picture of arrogance and wealth with all its independence and carelessness."

1905

The 1905 models were the first under the newly named company. A new roller gear and sprocket was introduced for all models. The long stroke motor was also adopted. The company inaugurated its first four-cylinder automobile—the Model K, which sold for $3,000, with a folding top for $200 extra. The new model could sit five passengers. The Haynes Automotive Company also offered two other models its first year: a two-cylinder runabout (Model L) and a surrey (Model M). The runabout sold for $1,350 and could seat two to four

The seat-over-the-radiator idea died hard. It was revived in the Haynes Model L produced by Haynes-Apperson in 1905. (Courtesy of the Haynes Museum.)

The Haynes Automobile Company was located south of the town center. (Courtesy of the Haynes Museum.)

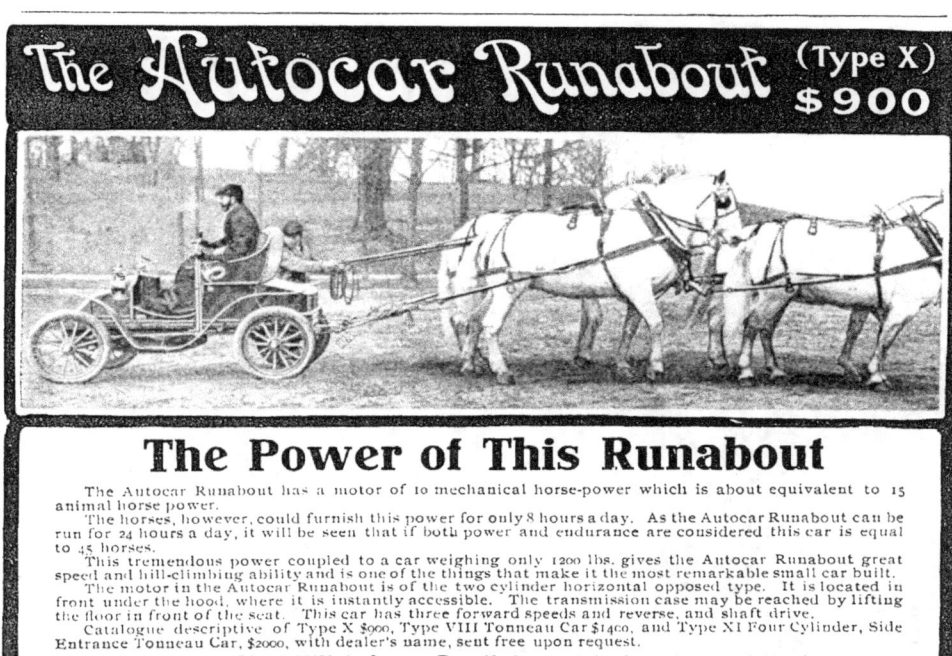

The Model K, advertised in *Musey's* magazine, was one of the first cars of the new Haynes Automobile Company in 1905. (Courtesy of the Haynes Museum.)

This was the first four-cylinder engine that powered the Haynes.

Haynes workers take a break from work for a portrait. This photograph was taken early in the history of the company. (Courtesy of Haynes Museum.)

people, as a back seat could be added. The model had an 81-inch wheel base, two-cylinder double-opposed engine, folding top and weighed 1,500 pounds. The surrey was a bit more expensive at $1,500 and could seat five people. The surrey also had an 81-inch wheel base. An advertisement boasted that the material used in the Haynes was the best money could buy, and that Haynes engineers took the greatest care in manufacturing.

1905 Models

Model L, 2 cyl., 16/18 hp, 82" wb
Stanhope, 16–18 Hp, 2-passenger, $1,350

Model M, 2 cyl., 16/18 hp, 82" wb
Light Tonneau, 4-passenger, $1,500
Tonneau, 5-passenger, $1,800

Model K, 4 cyl., 35/40 hp, 108" wb
King of Belgium Touring, $3,000

Racing Interests

The company's interest in racing dwindled after a bad experience in 1905. Chief engineer Frank Nutt drove a Haynes car, which was an exact duplicate of the 1906 Model R Touring car except for the racing body, to a fourth-place finish in the 113-mile qualifying run of the Vanderbilt Cup. He averaged 59.58 miles per hour on his last four laps and appeared to have qualified the car for the American team. However, race officials unexplainably decided to replace the third-, fourth- and fifth-place cars with more powerful entries. The Haynes car possessed a fifty-horsepower engine, which race officials thought was underpowered and would not fare well against the one hundred or more horsepower cars used by the Europeans. The company's new general manager, V.E. Minich, appealed the decision to race commissioners twice to no avail. He wrote, "In the name of fair play, as representative sportsmen, that we be given the place on the American team we so fairly deserve for the successful performance of our car." The following year, John W. Haynes drove a Haynes Cup Racer in the 1906 Vanderbilt Cup trials.

The company also participated in the famous Glidden Tours. Retired industrialist Charles J. Glidden of New England began the tour in 1904 and Elwood Haynes participated in the first run, which spanned over 1,000 miles from New York City to Bretton Woods, New Hampshire. The tours ran until 1914, with the Haynes Automobile Company partaking each year.

The company also participated in some other endurance and reliability contests. In 1908, L.R. Wagner drove the Model X to a perfect score for the second consecutive year in the Chicago Motor Club's 1,000-mile Reliability Contest.

Records claimed by the Haynes Automotive Company:

- Speed record, Louisville Track, 1895
- Speed record, Charles River Track, Boston, 1897
- Kokomo to New York City in 73 hours by the Phaeton, 1901
- Two first prize certificates in the New York-Rochester Endurance Contest, 1901
- First prize, Silver Cup, five-mile speed contest, Fort Erie Track, Buffalo, New York, 1901
- First prize, Silver Cup, ten-mile speed contest, Pointe Gross Track, Detroit, 1901
- Gold Medal, Pan-Am Exposition, 1901
- Blue Ribbon, Long Island Non-Stop Contest, April 1902
- Three 1st Class Certificates and Gold Medals in the New York-Boston-New York Reliability Contest, 1902

Elwood Haynes shakes hands with Charles J. Glidden, the industrialist who sponsored the Glidden Tours in which Haynes was proud to participate. (Courtesy of the Haynes Museum.)

- Two 1st Class Certificates in the New York to Pittsburgh Run, October 1903
- 1st Class Certificate, New York-Pittsburgh Endurance Run, 1904
- Gold Medal, White Mountain Road Test
- 1st Class Certificate, New York-St. Louis Tour, 1904
- Grand Prize, Louisiana Purchase Exposition, 1904
- Qualified for Vanderbilt Cup Race, October 1905
- 2nd Prize, Algonquin Hill Climb, Chicago, 1906
- 1st Class Certificate, Elgin-Aurora Endurance Run, 1906

The Haynes Automobile Company produced about 250 cars in 1905, its first year of production under the new company name. This was about the same number it had produced for the last three years.

1906

The two-cylinder models were dropped in 1906 and the company offered two models (O and R), both with four-cylinder engines. The Model O featured two different makes, a five-passenger touring car and a two-passenger runabout, both for the same price of $2,250. The Model R was a five-passenger touring car for $3,500. All models featured a shaft drive, vertical roller-bearing engines, a positive cooling system and selective sliding gear transmission that

Haynes tried to emphasize the transmission with this advertisement in 1906.

the company featured in advertisements. The advertising slogan used by the company was "The Car the Repairman Seldom Sees." Automobiles could be ordered in both Chicago and New York.

1906 Models

<u>Model O, 4 cyl., 30/35 hp, 97" wb</u>
Touring, 5 passenger, $2,250
Runabout, 2 passenger, $2,250

<u>Model R, 4 cyl., 45/50 hp, 108" wb</u>
Touring, 5 passenger, 2,750 lbs, $3,500

This 1906 Haynes was a great favorite with those sporty motorists who liked racy lines. (Courtesy of the Haynes Museum.)

1907

Early in 1907, the company lost the services of A.G. Seiberling to the Apperson brothers. Seiberling had been hired in the fall of 1905 as the superintendent, but he became disgruntled with Charles Haynes, manager of the Haynes Automotive Company at the time. Seiberling said Charles was trying to run the business along the same lines that he had to run his retail grocery business in Portland, and the company was going nowhere. So, Seiberling induced the Haynes board of directors to purchase his stock upon his departure to the competitor.

The company thought it would capitalize on the Vanderbilt Cup Race by offering a Vanderbilt Speedster, similar to the car it entered in the cup race. For the first time, the company also offered a five- or seven-passenger limousine in its three lines of cars in 1907. Prices of Haynes cars ranged from $2,400 for a runabout to $4,500

Wheel conforming fenders, front entrance handles and a spare tire carrier on the running board were introduced in the Model S in 1907. (Courtesy of the Haynes Museum.)

The Haynes Standard 50 H.-P. Touring Car for 1907, Model "T," the highest powered shaft driven car built.

Price, $3,500.00.

THE same attention to mechanical detail, the same care devoted to materials and style and luxury and convenience that has marked Haynes Models for the past thirteen years, is found in those of the coming season.

Exclusive mechanical features in 1907 as in 1906, make it the car of maximum road performance, dependable, reliable, the car the repairman seldom sees.

Send at once for full information and advance specifications, addressing Desk H 1.

In New York we shall exhibit at the Seventh National Automobile Show, Madison Square Garden, January 12-19, 1907.

Oldest Automobile Manufacturers in America
Members A. L. A. M.

HAYNES AUTOMOBILE CO.
KOKOMO, IND.

NEW YORK: 1715 Broadway   CHICAGO: 1420 Michigan Avenue

Ford made the Model T famous, but Haynes also had a Model T and used this ad to push it.

for a limousine. The Model T was advertised as the highest-powered, shaft-driven car built, also that it was dependable, reliable and a car the repairman seldom sees. Sales in 1907 amounted to $800,000.

1907 Models

Model S, 4 cyl., 30 hp, 103" wb
Runabout, 2 passenger, $2,400
Touring, 5 passenger, $2,500
Limousine, 5 passenger, $3,500

Model T, 4 cyl., 50 hp, 108" wb
Touring, 7 passenger, $3,500
Limousine, 7 passenger, $4,500

Model V, 4 cyl, 50 hp, 106" wb
Vanderbilt Speedster, $3,500

1908

By 1908, the company had increased production up to almost a car a day in its three manufacturing buildings. The company was the largest manufacturer in Kokomo with some five hundred employees receiving an annual payroll of more than $200,000. Of course this was small in comparison with assembly-line plants in Michigan, such as Ford, which was producing more than 10,000 vehicles a year. Still, Haynes ranked among the top 25 automobile manufacturers in America.

The Model W in 1908 could hold five passengers and sold for $3,000. The four-cylinder engine produced 45 horsepower. Buyers had a choice of dark green or red color. The touring model was featured as one of the leading types of 1908 automobiles by *Scientific American*.

The company entered two Haynes cars in the 1908 Glidden Tour, a 1,700-mile course from Buffalo to Pittsburgh to Albany to Boston, and both ended up with perfect scores.

The directors of the company decided to increase the capitalization and expanded production to plant capacity in 1908. Several Kokomo citizens were added to the list of stockholders and they took control of the plant for the next few years. This was accomplished through a trusteeship, with three trustees authorized to vote the majority of the stock as a unit for a period of five years. Plant size and productivity both increased as a result.

L.R. Wagner drove the Haynes Model X to a perfect score in Chicago's 1,000-mile Reliability Contest in 1908. (Courtesy of the Haynes Museum.)

The Haynes Model W was introduced in 1908. (Courtesy of Howard County Historical Society, Kokomo, Indiana.)

1908 Models

<u>Model S, 4 cyl., 30 hp, 102" wb</u>
Touring, 5 passenger, $2,500

<u>Model W, 4 cyl., 45 hp, 108" wb</u>
Touring, 5 passenger, 2,400 lbs, $3,000

<u>Model U, 4 cyl., 60 hp, 118" wb</u>
Touring, 7 passenger, $3,750
Roadster, 2 passenger, $3,750
Limousine, $4,750

1909

By early 1909 more than 250 automobile manufacturers were in business in the United States. They had built more than 52,000 cars the year before with a capital investment of about $200 million. Haynes had built about 350 vehicles the year before. More than 110,000 people were employed in the industry.

The 1909 Haynes Touring car still featured right-hand drive, but many companies were making the move to left-hand drive about this time. (Courtesy of Auburn Cord Duesenberg Museum.)

Top: A 1909 Haynes Touring car with the top up. (Courtesy of Auburn Cord Duesenberg Museum.) *Bottom:* Men stand with rifles in front of the Haynes Plant during troubled times prior to 1911. (Courtesy of Dave Griffey.)

Since Haynes didn't have a 6-cylinder motor in its cars, it used this 1909 ad to explain why its four was as good as a six.

In 1909, the company only offered the Series X, which came in five different models, all priced around $3,000 which didn't give customers much of a choice as far as price. The Series X was advertised as four cylinders giving six cylinder results in order to compete against those manufacturers offering a six. The advertisements said the six cylinders were too complicated to justify the conversion and would not offer a six until 1913. A 1909 Haynes touring car was featured by *Scientific American* magazine.

1909 Models

Series X, 4 cyl., 36 hp, 112" wb
Touring, 5–7 passenger, $3,000
X1 Runabout, 3 passenger, $2,900
X2 Baby Tonneau, 4 passenger, $3,000
X3 Double-seated Roadster, 4 passenger, $3,000
X4 Hiker, 2 passenger, $2,900

1910

With the alphabet running out on the company, a switch to numbers was made in 1910. The Model 19 was the first numbered model for the company and the only model in 1910 with two makes: a touring and a runabout. Former President Theodore Roosevelt ordered a Haynes Model 19. The increases in productivity soon showed up in sales figures in 1910, as the company sold about 1,000 automobiles—triple from what it sold the year before.

In 1910, advertisements gave emphasis on why somebody should buy a Haynes. The company tried to justify the price of the car by advising customers not to buy a cheap car because sooner or later they would be disappointed. The company said the car cost $2,000 because of its workmanship, mechanism and general quality. Therefore, a Haynes would last much longer than a cheap car. The Model 19 came fully equipped instead of charging for extras like it had done in the past. The Haynes came with full lamp equipment, a top, glass, speedometer, all tools, a jack and a tire repair kit.

1910 Models

Model 19, 4 cyl., 36 hp, 110½" wb
Touring, 5 passenger, $2,000
Runabout, 3 passenger, $2,000

The jump in sales may have been a result of the Haynes Automobile Company becoming the first company to equip an open car with a top, a windshield, head lamps and a speedometer as standard equipment. In 1911, the company also offered a Model Y, a seven-passenger touring car, for $3,000.

1911 Models

Model Y, 4 cyl., 40 hp, 125" wb
Touring, 7 passenger, $3,000

Model 20, 4 cyl., 28 hp, 114" wb
Suburban, 4 passenger, $2,100
Touring, 5 passenger, $2,000
Four-Door Touring, $2,100
Roadster, 2 passenger, $2,000

The Fire of 1911

The company suffered a huge setback at the beginning of 1911. The most disastrous fire in Kokomo's history destroyed several Haynes Company buildings on February 28, 1911, and claimed the life of an employee, John J. Briney. Fortunately, no completed cars were destroyed by the blaze. The fire did cause about $750,000 in damage and the company had only $240,000 in insurance, so about half a million was lost. The fire originated when an electric

The windshield was regular equipment on the Model 20 in 1911. (Courtesy of the Haynes Museum.)

light short-circuited and ignited a small pan of gasoline used to clean testing machines. The fire spread quickly to a paint room, which sent it out of control. Several workmen escaped from the upper floor by leaping from windows, while others used ladders during the daylight blaze.

Huge quantities of stock had been stored in tents and temporary structures outside the factory, so they were converted to production quickly in order to not lose manufacturing time. However, the company was already running 142 orders behind when the fire struck and this set them back further.

Company officials vowed to rebuild "a larger, modern and better equipped factory" on the same site. However, relocating the plant to another community was considered if local financing was not forthcoming.

The 1911 Haynes Runabout is on display at the Automotive Heritage Museum in Kokomo.

The Haynes Factory was devastated by fire in 1911. (Courtesy of the Haynes Museum.)

Haynes then announced his intention to stay. "Kokomo is good enough for us," he said.

The company of 500 employees decided to layoff some of its workers until it could get back on its feet, and a hundred were given temporary employment by the Apperson Brothers Automobile Company. The company found many other facilities around the city to start buildings its cars again until new building could be readied. By late summer, the company had rebuilt the buildings that were destroyed, and by September, the plant was back in full operation thanks to Haynes, who purchased enough materials himself to make 1,000 cars.

Rules and Regulations

The Haynes Automobile Company may have had the fire in mind when the rules and regulations were published for employees. Signs were posted in the company listing the following rules:

1. Employees must have parcels and tool boxes inspected upon entering and leaving the factory.
2. Employees must be at their places of employment ready to work when the whistle blows. There will be a 10 minute whistle blow two short blasts before regular starting time.
3. Employees must not get ready to quit work until whistle blows. Washing up, changing clothes, etc. will not be tolerated before quitting time.
4. Employees coming in after starting time will be required to wait 15 minutes in Employment Office or until even hour, when they may ring in and start work.
5. Employees who practice coming late to work will be discharged without notice.
6. Employees must make out accurate time cards for each day's work or for any part of the day.
7. Employees must ring clock on entering and leaving the factory and in every

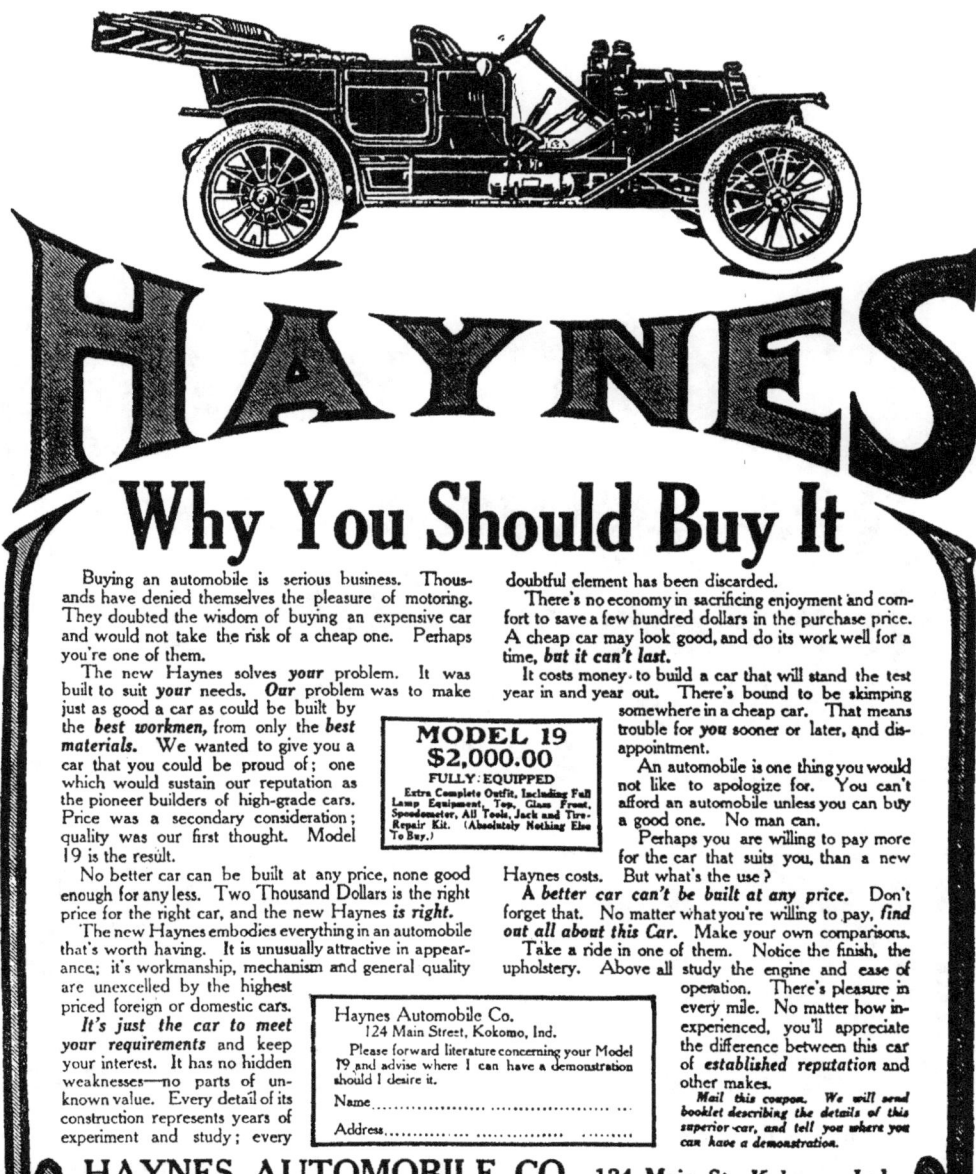

Haynes used lots of text to explain to customers why they should buy the Model 19 in 1910.

case, after ringing place card in rack. Under no circumstances will employees be allowed to destroy time cards.

8. Employees must remain in their respective departments at all times, only leaving on permission of foreman in charge. Visiting or loafing during working hours will not be tolerated.

9. Boisterousness, singing or whistling will not be tolerated.

Top: In the aftermath of the 1911 fire, the automotive bodies were spared from destruction. (Courtesy of the Haynes Museum.) *Bottom:* Work on the new Haynes body plant was rushed into completion after the fire of 1911. (Courtesy of the Haynes Museum.)

10. Conversation of private nature and not in connection with the work is prohibited.

11. All tools and jugs and items necessary to complete workman's outfit must be checked out of Tool Supply Department and returned when serving Company's employ.

12. Employees hammering or marring machinery, jigs or tools, etc. are subject to discharge without notice.

13. It is the duty of all foremen to keep their machinery well oiled and clean, ready for inspection at any time.

14. It is the duty of General Foremen and Sub-Foremen to keep close watch and see that machinery is safely guarded and that employees are thoroughly instructed as

Automotive bodies await painting in the paint shop of the Haynes Automotive Company. (Courtesy of the Haynes Museum.)

to the dangers of their occupations. Special attention must be given employees by foremen as to using ladders, belt shifters, and keeping gears covered; emory stands must be kept up to requirements of state inspector and not used until they are so protected.

15. Operators of machines are held responsible for the oiling of their machines each day.

16. Employees coming to work intoxicated or bringing intoxicants in the factory are subject to discharge without notice.

17. Foremen must see that their departments are supplied with fire extinguishers and that they are at all times in a usable condition.

18. Smoking in factory or in the Company property is prohibited.

19. Employees are requested not to carry matches in the factory.

20. Rubbish or waste must under no circumstances be thrown out of the windows or on floors but must be placed in cans in different departments for this purpose. Foremen must see that these cans or retainers are emptied each day.

21. It will be the duty of each foreman to see that the above rules and regulations are obeyed in his department.

While the company was becoming known for building a quality product that satisfied many of its buyers, there were a few unsatisfied customers as well as those who wanted to become dealers. Charles F. Pusch, a cigar manufacturer in Marysville, Kansas, wanted to sell Haynes cars there, but he wasn't happy with the Model X. He wrote a letter to the Haynes Automotive Company at the end of 1911, stating: "I have had more brakedowns (*sic*) with the Model X, on the level ground with low speed, than I ever had with the old Model K." He wanted to sell the models in Kansas, but they were more than $2,000, "while all the other factories were doing a satisfactory business on machines ranging from $1,200 to $1,600." The company wrote him back saying they could give him the new Model 20 for $1,800 to sell there.

1912

The company bounced back strongly in 1912, producing a dozen cars a day. The company decided to emphasize to dealers in *Motor Age* that there was no piece-work in the Haynes factory for the 1912 Haynes line. Up until that year, the company had purchased their car bodies from a company in France, a practice many companies followed. Advertisements also emphasized that Haynes workers were not paid on how much they could turn out, but on the basis of how well they work. The Model 21 came in four different styles: a five-passenger, four-door touring model for $2,100; four-passenger Suburban, $2,100; Colonial Coupe, $2,450; and Limousine, $2,750. The Model 21 came equipped with a 40-horsepower motor. The Model Y came in four styles: seven-passenger, four-door touring, $3,000; four-passenger Suburban, $3,000; Newport Limousine, $3,800; and Berlin Limousine, $3,900. The Model Y had a more powerful 50–60 horsepower engine. Regular equipment on both models included an Eisemann dual magneto, Strombery Model B Carburetor, silk mohair top, windshield, Prest-O-Lite tank, five lamps, Warner 60-mile Speedometer, extra Dorian Remountable Rim, and Tanner Automatic Gasoline

A Haynes was put on display in a roller skating rink at the Santa Clara County Fair on Sept. 5, 1912. (Courtesy of Haynes Museum.)

Top: The Newport Limousine, introduced in 1912, could hold seven passengers. (Courtesy of the Haynes Museum.) *Middle:* The Colonial Coupe looked a lot like its name and was introduced in 1912. (Courtesy of the Haynes Museum.) *Bottom:* The Model Y was introduced in 1912. (Courtesy of the Haynes Museum.)

The Haynes Company ran small ads like this for its 1912 model. (Courtesy of the Haynes Museum.)

Gauge. Electric lighting was added to all cars. Additional extras featured $25 for other paints, $50 for seat covers, $10 for enameled lamps and horn, and $75 for nickel plating brass parts.

1912 Models

Model 20, 4 cyl., 30 hp, 114" wb
Speedster, $1,650
Open Touring, $1.650
Roadster, $1,800
Fore-Door Touring, $1,800
Suburban, $1,800

Model 21, 4 cyl., 40 hp, 120" wb
Touring, $2,100
Close-Coupled Touring, $2,100
Coupe, $2,450
Limousine, $2,750

Model Y, 4 cyl., 60 hp, 127½" wb
Touring, 7 passenger, $3,000
Close-Coupled Touring, $3,000
Newport Limousine, $3,800
Berlin Limousine, $3,900

1913

A six-cylinder was first offered in Haynes cars in 1913, the year license plates were first required in the state. It was installed in the Model 23 touring car. The Model 22 was introduced, and it featured an electric starter that took an average of five seconds to fire up the car, an accomplishment in those days. The self-starter was first introduced in the Model 21 the year before, but the company didn't make it a selling point until it was sure the new device worked to their satisfaction. It did. The Model 22 also featured an Eisemann dual magneto, Stromberg carburetor and a Warner autometer. The cars featured better suspension than the year before to allow for a smoother ride.

1913 Models

Model 22, 4 cyl., 40 hp, 120" wb
Touring, 4–5 passenger, $2,250
Roadster, $2,250
Coupe, $2,750
Limousine, 7 passenger, $3,400
Berlin Limousine, 7 passenger, $3,500

Model 23, 6 cyl., 50 hp, 130" wb
Touring, 5 passenger, $2,500

Model 24, 4 cyl., 35 hp, 118" wb
Touring, 5 passenger, $1,785

The Model 21 featured a self-starter. (Courtesy of the Haynes Museum.)

This 1913 advertisement highlighted the Model 27.

The Complete Motorist

In 1913, the Haynes Automotive Company published a book called *The Complete Motorist*, by Elwood Haynes. The book contained the history of the Horseless Carriage created by Haynes and information about Haynes automobiles. Here is the introduction to that book.

An Introduction
— GEO. H. STROUT

Elwood Haynes is a young man. We have grown so rapidly into the automobile age that it is natural we should picture the "father of the automobile industry" as a venerable patriarch. But Haynes is young in heart, body and mind. His idea of making a gasoline-driven car was the inspiration that is the flower of youth. Always, from early boyhood, a person who "wanted to know" and "wanted to do," his inventive genius became second nature with him.

So today we take the automobile for granted. And too many of us take Elwood Haynes for granted. We do this just as we take Edison for granted, just as we accept Marconi's wireless as an everyday thing, just as we watch an aeroplane in a matter-of-fact way.

For what he gave America, Elwood Haynes is entitled to the honor Stephenson won with his locomotive and Fulton won with his steamboat.

The rude carriage that was a curiosity twenty years ago and less — the vehicle that vied with the two-headed calf and the wild man of Borneo at the county fairs — was the beginning of the greatest transportation aid since the birth of civilization. Because of it our standards of living have become higher. It has broadened the horizon of all of us.

Yet Elwood Haynes sits modestly at his desk in his office in Kokomo — dreamer still — and tells you of his invention of a new metal which is harder than steel. Some day — perhaps when you and I are gone — the Hall of Fame will hold a fair, broad tablet on which is carved imperishably the name of Elwood Haynes.

He is made in the mold of all great inventors — he can both dream and do.

From him the motorist of today may learn, as of old did they who sat at the feet of Gamaliel and garnered wisdom.

During the summer of 1913, the company received some good publicity when two of its cars traveled with a caravan of 22 Indiana-built cars and two trucks from Indianapolis to San Francisco. Elwood Haynes traveled in Car No. 12 with two company employees, Robert Crawford, the assistant sales manager, and L.R. Wagner, the designated driver. In Car No. 13 was George H. Strout, sales manager, W.J. Morgan, T.L. Tencher and F.R. Wagner. About the only bad publicity that the company experienced came at the end of the trip when L.R. Wagner struck and killed a small boy in Santa Barbara. The car was traveling at just ten miles an hour, but the child was accidentally pushed into the car's path. After the trip, the company launched an advertising campaign to take advantage of the publicity it had received on the trip. The company also began publishing a monthly magazine, *The Haynes Pioneer*. The magazine was published into the 1920s and provided retrospective views of the company. Haynes was a frequent contributor to the journal. A Silver Anniversary issue was published in July 1918, to celebrate 25 years of automobile manufacturing by the company.

The caravan to the West Coast was outdone by F.W. Hutchings, who made a coast-to-coast, border-to-border 15,000-mile trip through 34 states over every imaginable kind of road and trail. He went over mountains, across deserts, through sand, mud and snow in his Model 36 Haynes touring car. The Californian loaded the car with various camping equipment,

The Haynes Company entered two cars in the Indiana to Pacific Tour, including this No. 13 car. (Courtesy of the Haynes Museum.)

increasing the weight of the car to 4,510 pounds, but the Haynes motor pulled the exceptional weight every mile of the journey without once faltering. He began his trek in his home of Santa Cruz and went north through Oregon then east along the northern states all the way to Maine. With the coming of cold weather, he headed south to Bradenton, Florida. He then headed west and back home. "The Grand Canyon of the Yellowstone is a wonder in itself sufficient for a national park," he wrote the Haynes Company. "The tourist camp at Tampa, Florida, covers about three or four city blocks and has one to three thousand tourists a day." The long trips by Haynes and Hutchings did little to publicize the need for highway construction. Not until 1919, when Army Major Dwight D. Eisenhower led a military convoy from New York to San Francisco to publicize the need for highway construction, did the government get serious about paving roads. The first Federal Highway Act was passed then in 1921.

By 1913, the Haynes Automotive Company had branch offices—this was in the days before franchises were sold—in eight locations: New York City, Newark, Chicago, San Francisco, Sacramento, Los Angeles, Fresno and Oakland. 1913 also brought about a reorganization of the company, which helped Haynes divorce himself from management decisions. A.G. Seiberling was brought back after five years at the Apperson Brothers Automobile Company.

A.G. Seiberling was the general manager for the Haynes Automotive Company when this photograph was taken. (Courtesy of the Haynes Museum.)

He had been a superintendent from 1905–07 with Haynes. At Apperson, he became the secretary-treasurer, but Haynes gave him an attractive offer to come back as the factory manager then soon promoted him to general manager to succeed C.B. Warren. Replacing Seiberling as factory manager, was A.N. Wilhelm. Other personnel changes included R.T. Gray as advertising manager.

Advertising in 1913 stressed that the Haynes was America's first car and these other firsts:

- First two-cylinder opposed car built in the world.
- First to use aluminum in crank case.
- First to use nickel steel in axles.
- First side-door car.
- First to have the throttling carburetor.
- First to use the make-and-break spark and the first to use the jump spark.
- First to use electric ignition.
- First to use a magneto of any type.
- First to use the double independent system of ignition through two sets of spark plugs.
- First to use the electric gear shift.

1914

Electric shifting on the steering wheel was first announced in the summer of 1913 and it became standard equipment on all three 1914 models—Models 26, 27 and 28. Manual shifting was still available as an option, though for $200 less. The Vulcan Electric Gear Shifter still required a clutch for shifting and it cost $200 more than the hand shift. The operator would depress the clutch then push a button located in the middle of the steering wheel to make the shift in gears. A contact plate on the clutch permitted gear changes only when the clutch was disengaged. The gear shifter, like all Haynes parts, was thoroughly tested before it was made available to the public. "We have never experimented at the expense of our patrons," Haynes told his customers. "We have first made sure for ourselves and then have given Haynes owners the benefit of our experience."

Besides the electric gear shifter, Haynes

automobiles came equipped with parts that came from other manufacturers. For example, the Stromberg carburetor, American-Simms high tension magneto, Kingston air pump, Connecticut shock absorbers, McCue axles, Cleveland-Canton springs, Funck Q.D. rims, Warner speedometer, Union Rain-Vision windshield, United States tires, Bimel spokes, Fedders radiators and Timken-Detroit axles. The Haynes models could be serviced at Stromberg Service Stations, which were located in practically every city in the country, and service of the Stromberg carburetor was free.

Another item that became standard on Haynes autos was a hood ornament that read "America's First Car." This put a temporary end to the controversy between Haynes and the Appersons on whom should have the right to say they were the first. The open-body models came in two colors, Indiana-blue and Pacific-tour gray, with black gear, hood and fenders. The enclosed-body cars came in black throughout and Brewster Green, with black gear, hood and fenders. Each automobile body received 21 coats of paint.

The new electric gear shifter and the introduction of the new six-cylinder pushed sales figures of the 1913 model to 1,488 cars, which took the plant to capacity. Sales continued to grow into the 1914 model year as 1,700 models were sold.

1914 Models

<u>Model 26, 6 cyl., 50 hp, 130" hp</u>
Touring, 4 passenger, $2,700
Roadster, 2 passenger, $2,700
Touring, 5 passenger, $2,700
Coupe, 4 passenger, $2,700

<u>Model 27, 6 cyl., 50 hp, 136" wb</u>
Touring, 6–7 passenger, $2,785
Limousine, 7 passenger, $3,850

<u>Model 28, 4 cyl., 35 hp, 118" wb</u>
Touring, 4–5 passenger, $1,985
Roadster, 2 passenger, $1,985
Coupe, 4 passenger, $2,700

Note: the electric gear shift was $200 extra.

Do's and Don'ts

The Haynes Company advised its owners that its automobiles were easy to operate: "It is so simple — so easy to operate the Haynes car — that every motion comes almost as a reflex action — just as one eats when food is set before him." However, the company also published the following list of do's and don'ts:

- Don't try to see how long you can crank the engine with the starter, as you are liable to injure the battery. The starter is put on the car to start the engine and not to break records in cranking.
- Don't hold clutch pedal in starting position longer than necessary to start the motor. Be sure that ratchet gear on cranking motor is free.
- Be sure that starting switch is open when clutch pedal is in neutral position.
- Starting switch is operated with the same pedal that shifts the gears.
- Clean commutator on dynamo every thousand miles, using .00 sandpaper very lightly (not emery cloth). Keep dynamo clean on the inside as well as outside.
- Keep water in battery over plates.
- Use distilled water only (chemically pure), which can be purchased at any drug store.
- Don't take the starter apart every few days in order to find out how it operates. Let it alone. Should you get into trouble which you cannot locate with the above information, consult a mechanic or electrician, or the factor. Don't try and demonstrate to your friends how long an electric motor will drive an engine.
- Don't use starter with emergency brake set.
- Don't run with carburetor air valve closed after motor is warm.

Model 27 — 5-passenger Touring Car

Model 26 — 4-passenger Coupe

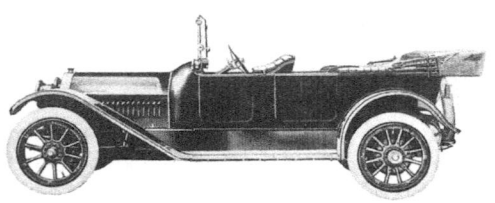
Model 27 — 7-passenger Touring Car

Model 27 — 7-passenger Limousine

Model 28 — 4-passenger Coupe

Model 28 — 5-passenger Touring Car

Model 28 — Roadster

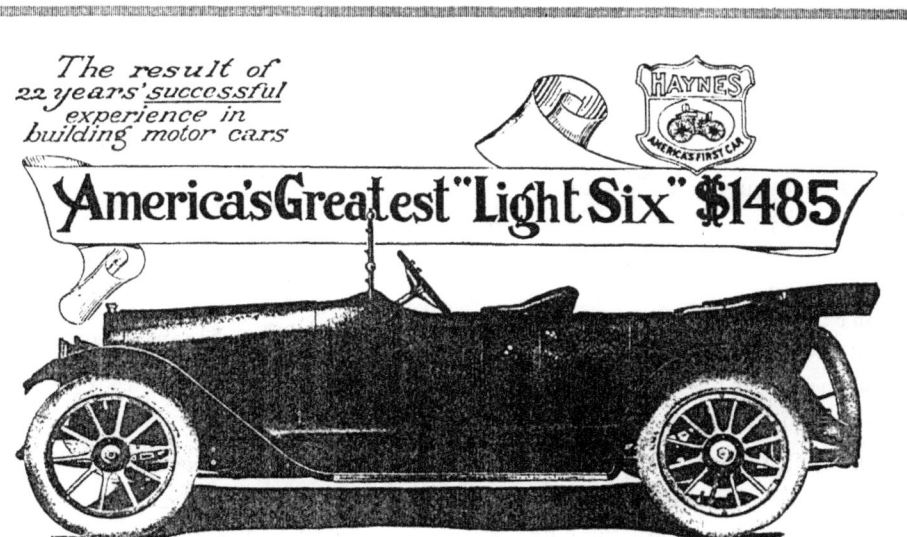

In 1914, Haynes thought highly of its Light Six and its price as evidenced by this advertisement.

- Don't run motor on dry cells.
- Don't race motor.
- Don't try to change gears too rapidly.
- Don't advance spark throttle too far on hard pull.
- Don't start your car in high gear.
- Don't shift from any forward gear to reverse without first bringing car to a standstill.
- Don't try to beat the other fellow to the next corner.
- Don't accelerate motor too rapidly.
- Don't release clutch pedal too rapidly.
- Don't apply service brake too rapidly.
- Don't coast down hill too fast.
- Don't leave car standing without first setting emergency brake.
- Don't run motor without a sufficient amount of oil and water.
- Don't slam your doors.
- Don't fail to look over your car at least twice monthly.
- Don't neglect your grease cups—they are put there for a purpose.
- Don't neglect your transmission and differential—they both need oil.
- Don't run over sticks, cans, glass, etc., in the road.
- Don't run on a soft tire.
- Don't run on a wet pavement without skid chains.
- Don't run on the battery.
- Don't fail to let the clutch in easily and gradually.
- Don't race the motor when shifting gears.
- Don't violate the unwritten laws of the road.
- Don't fail to carry necessary license numbers.
- Don't shift into or out of reverse when car is in motion.
- Don't start the motor until everything is in readiness.
- Don't drive fast on wet pavements—the car is liable to skid.
- Don't apply brakes with violence—it is very hard on the car and tires.
- Don't start on a trip without plenty of gasoline and oil.
- Don't allow the water in the radiator to freeze through neglect.
- Don't start the car with a jerk.
- Don't advance the spark too quickly.
- Don't overwork the motor on hills—shift gears.
- Don't turn corners too rapidly—it is hard on the tires.
- Don't forget to examine the car carefully after a very hard run.
- Don't start without a full set of tools and extra tire equipment.
- Don't run the car if you detect some unusual sound—investigate.
- Don't use the brake too much—slow down the car with the clutch and throttle.
- Don't change the adjustment on the carburetor until you are sure that it is at fault.
- Don't begin to make adjustments without searching carefully for the cause of the trouble.
- Don't forget to test your batteries once in a while to see that they are in working condition.
- Don't drive the car at high speed over bad roads—it is expensive.
- Don't run the car on partially inflated tires.
- Don't try to run the car with the emergency brakes set.
- Don't run your motor unless there is oil flowing through the sight feed.

Beside all the don'ts, the company had other advice for owners. For example, the company recommended that all gasoline should be strained through a clean chamois before being placed in the tank. If not, the dirt or sediment in the gasoline at the time would cause carburetor trouble. The company also recommended the regular systematic lubrication of the car. Engines then required a lot more oil than those of today. The Haynes engine took eight quarts compared to the five quarts most engines take today.

At the June 1914, Haynes Sales Convention, Elwood Haynes addressed his salesmen and gave them some advice to help them along in their endeavors:

> It will not always be an easy matter to sell cars, even with such a man to get it before the public eye. At times it will be discouraging and you may see the time that you will wish you had never seen an automobile, but these times will pass. They are simply moments of depression. The man who succeeds is the man who keeps at it all the time. When I think of discouraging times, and the old saying, "Keep a smile on your face," I always recall a story of a man in the South, in Arkansas, I believe, who was riding along in a soft part of the country, when he noticed what appeared to be a straw hat. Coming closer, this straw hat seemed to have a darkey's head under it, and he said to the old darkey, "Hello, Uncle Remus, you seem to have having a pretty hard time." Said the darkey, "I reckon I'se havin' a pretty hard time, Sah, but I'm not havin nigh as hard a time as this heah mule I'se a ridin'." There is always someone having just a little harder time than you are, so when you are having discouraging times, just think of the other salesmen who are having it just as hard. There is no excuse for a man, having a good car to sell, not selling it.

The Haynes Automotive Company factory in its heyday. (Courtesy of the Haynes Museum.)

1915

In July 1914, the Haynes Company dropped all of its four-cylinder models and began marketing its "Light Six" for the 1915 model year. The new Model 30 was offered at an attractive price of $1,485, which created some excitement. The Light Six could reach speeds of 60 miles per hour in high gear. It averaged 18 to 22 miles per gallon, a quart of oil to every 400 miles and 7,500 on a set of tires. Three colors were available: Indiana blue, black and Pacific Coast gray. Every 1915 Light Six was sold on April 1st with a third of the cars being sold to Hoosiers. The company sold about 2,000 models the first six months. The car proved itself in a number of tests. In one test, the new Light Six traveled 166 miles in low gear in eleven hours and seven minutes without a stop, averaging 15 miles per hour. Then in Pittsburgh, the Light Six set a new record in getting to the top of Heberton Hill, which ended at a 19-percent grade, at 30 mph from a standing start. Then at the Annual Thanksgiving Economy Contest, the car averaged 24.3 miles to the gallon. The Haynes Light Six Cabriolet sold for $1,750. The two-passenger vehicle had a collapsible top made of leather. The other Light Six was the Model 33, also referred to as the Kokomo Six, and it could carry four passengers. By the end of the model year, the company had sold all of its production and more than tripled sales figures, selling some 5,500 cars. The jump in sales figures put Haynes Automotive Company among the top 20 automotive manufacturers in the nation. The company also accounted for thirty-three percent of all cars sold in Indiana.

1915 Models

Model 30, 6 cyl., 55 hp, 121" wb
Light Six Touring, 5 passenger, $1,485
Roadster, 2 passenger, $1,485
Touring, 7 passenger, $1,550
Cabriolet, 3 passenger, $1,750

Model 31, 6 cyl., 65 hp, 121" wb
Touring, $2,250
Coupe, $3,000

Model 32, 6 cyl., 48 hp, 121" wb
Touring, $1,660
Coupe, $2,500

The company now had 646 new dealers seeking to sell the cars throughout the United States. One of the nearby dealers was the Heilman Motor Car Company in Cincinnati, Ohio. Said M.W. Jennings, the secretary and treasurer of Heilman:

> When we sell a Haynes, we do not feel our obligation is ended. In delivering the car we educated and instruct the buyer exactly how to drive it, giving him as many lessons as he'll take, because we have found that if a man thoroughly understands how to drive his car he enjoys it better and is much more satisfied. He naturally credits the car instead of himself. If he doesn't understand how to handle it properly he invariably condemns the car, not himself. The car being unable to talk has to take the blame. We also have the buyer go carefully and thoroughly over oiling and greasing the car. We urge him whenever in doubt regarding anything not to hesitate to call on us for help and information. Fortunately very little trouble is experienced with Haynes cars. We tell him we'll care for every complaint, small or large, and back this up to the last notch. We know the Haynes owners bring their cars to our place every four or five weeks for inspection. If between times any adjustments are necessary — they seldom are — our service department is open at all times and all adjusting and inspecting is done, no charge for one year. And Haynes owners get prompt, polite attention from good competent mechanics.

The Haynes Company bragged as much as possible in this ad that appeared in the *Saturday Evening Post* on June 19, 1915. (Courtesy of the Haynes Museum.)

The increase in sales required the company to expand its plants to keep up with demand. Building plans were first announced in April 1915. Six major buildings would be used to put together the Haynes automobiles. The different parts of the automobile would come together at the final assembly building, where the autos rolled slowly along a track so that final installations could be made.

In August 1915, the company issued a stock to raise $250,000 to enlarge the plant. A four-story machine shop, three-story paint shop and test barn were needed. Stock holders received a 22 percent dividend that year.

1916

Because of the popular demand for the Light Six, the 1916 model was developed and made ready ahead of time. The Light Six came in two models: 34 and 35. The Model 34 came in two body styles— a five-passenger touring car and a three-passenger roadster. Model 35 was a seven-passenger touring car. The same motor was used in both models. The five-passenger and seven-passenger styles featured an aisle-way between the front seats to make the rear more accessible, or it could be used to store a suitcase. Nowadays, the arrangement would be considered bucket seats with a gear shift in the middle, but the Haynes cars had the gear shifter located in the center up by the dashboard. The top on these models could be raised by one person. The clutch and brake pedals were adjustable to suit the individual driver, which was a rare convenience. The front seats also were adjustable. Each Light Six went through three exhaustive tests. The motor was block tested then torn down and inspected. The entire chassis was given a searching road test. The finished car then was given a final road test before shipment. However, the tests didn't always catch problems, as evidenced by one buyer of Haynes cars. F.J. Davies of the *Evening Herald* in Shenandoah, Pennsylvania, received a "lemon" from the company and wrote Elwood Haynes about his dissatisfaction: "On opening up the transmission box today, it was found in such condition that it was a surprise it was permitted to leave the shop, and that it was doubtful if it ever would work properly and should be replaced with a good one." He paid $1,765 for the seven-passenger vehicle and wanted the company to do something about his problem. How the company resolved the situation is unknown.

In addition to the Light Six, the Haynes Automotive Company introduced the Light Twelve model. The Light Twelve was so named because it was powered by a 12-cylinder, V-shaped, valve-in-head, 365.3-cubic-inch motor that was much more powerful and speedier than the six-cylinder model. The motor was introduced at the New York Automobile Show in January 1916, but production didn't begin until August. The motors carried a 90-day warranty. The 1916 closed models could readily be converted to an open car. The glass panels slid out and went into a specially designed and out-of-the-way compartment. The upper sections of the door hinged over and fastened securely. The change took about a minute. The Light Twelve came in two models: 40 and 41. The Model 40 came in two styles— a five-passenger touring car and a three-passenger "So-Sha-Belle" Roadster — each costing $1,985. The Model 41 was a seven-passenger Touring car for $2,085. The year 1916 turned out to be the apex for the company when 7,100 autos were sold. However, the company

The Haynes Company used this ad to advertise its Light Six and Light Twelve in the *Saturday Evening Post* in 1916. (Courtesy of the Haynes Museum.)

felt it could produce some 12,000 a year with increased capacity. The company declared a 108 percent stock dividend after earnings of $1.6 million.

1916 Models

<u>Model 34, 6 cyl., 55 hp, 121" wb</u>
Roadster, 3 passenger, $1,485
  Light Six Touring, 5 passenger

<u>Model 35, 6 cyl, 55 hp, 127" wb</u>
Kokomo Six Touring, $1,495

<u>Model 40/41, 12 cyl., 60 hp, 127" wb</u>
Roadster, $1,595
Touring, 5 passenger, $1,885
Touring, 7 passenger, $1,985

Demountable sedan and coupe tops for all open models was $275.

To promote the new Light Twelve model, the company ran a series of advertisements in an effort to find the oldest Haynes car still in existence. They offered to exchange a new Light Twelve for the oldest Haynes auto found. The contest was won by Edward J. Howard, the president of the Howard Shipbuilding Company, who owned an 1897 Haynes-Apperson that he had bought from the company in the summer of 1897. The exchange of the 1897 car for the new Haynes Light Twelve was made at the Indiana Fair Grounds in Indianapolis on Good Roads Day. President Woodrow Wilson was the speaker of the day. Light Twelves were built through 1922, although only 650 were sold. The six-cylinder Haynes was the mainstay of the company and was built up until the end of the company.

In late 1916, the Haynes Company announced that it would increase floor space

Percy Ford piloted a "Light Twelve" Haynes racer to victory in the 100-mile Chicago Dealers' Race in June 1917 with an average of 89 mph.

by some 12–15 acres by building a new plant. This would allow the company to produce as many as 100 vehicles a day. However, the United States' entrance into World War I slowed the growth of automobile sales. Growth in the automobile industry was just 20 percent in 1917, compared to 80 percent in 1916.

1917

The Light Six was refined with many changes when Models 36 and 37 were introduced in January 1917. The Model 36 came in two styles—for the five-passenger Touring Car or three-passenger "So-Sha-Belle" Roadster—each costing $1,485. The Model 37 was a seven-passenger Touring Car that went for $1,585. The alterations included seat covers, aluminum pistons, improved body lines, gypsy curtains, hydrometer and a cigar lighter. The motor developed more horsepower than the previous models to provide more flexibility, hill-climbing power and get-away ability. The new motor allowed the car to reach 30 miles per hour in just seven-and-a-half seconds and 60 miles per hour at the top end. The car averaged 15 to 22 miles to a gallon of gasoline and 400 miles per quart of oil. A set of tires averaged 8,000 miles.

1917 Models

Light Six — Model 36, 6 cyl., 29.4 hp, 121" wb
Touring, 5 passenger, $1,485
Roadster, 4 passenger, $1,585
Touring, 7 passenger, $1,585
Sedan, 5 passenger, $2,150
Sedan, 7 passenger, $2,250

Light Six — Model 37, 6 cyl., 29.4 hp, 127" wb
Roadster, 4 passenger, $1,485
Touring, 7 passenger, $1,585
Sedan, 5 passenger, $2,150
Sedan, 7 passenger, $2,250

Light Twelve, 12 cyl., 36.3 hp, 127" wb
Touring, 7 passenger, $2,085
Touring, 5 passenger, $1,985
Roadster, 4 passenger, $2,085
Sedan, 5 passenger, $2,650
Sedan, 7 passenger, $2,750

Another effort to promote the Light Twelve came in 1917 when Percy Ford won the 100-mile Chicago dealer's race in June 1917, with an average speed of 89 miles per hour. The Haynes car was the only vehicle to complete the race without a stop.

The year 1917 also marked a change in marketing. The company began running advertisements in women's magazines, trying to lure female buyers. An ad in the *Ladies Home Journal* read, "Why not drop a hint that you would like to have them investigate the Haynes." Another advertisement said the Haynes was "gentle in a lady's hands, as an old carriage horse."

The driver of a Haynes car would check the temperature of the car from this thermostat on the 1918 model.

The Haynes Fourdore was very popular. (Courtesy of the Haynes Museum.)

The Haynes Fourdore was billed as "The Prettiest Four-Passenger Roadster" in this ad in the *Saturday Evening Post* on January 19, 1918. (Courtesy of the Haynes Museum.)

1918

The prosperity the company experienced up until 1917 was soon replaced by austerity when the nation became involved in World War I. Sales figures in 1918 dropped to 2,200 cars. The company did get involved in the war effort when Seiberling went to Washington and obtained a contract from the government to build four thousand truck motors for the war effort. This helped a little in offsetting the drop in sales. A typical worker with the company was paid $13 to $17 a week.

Few changes were made in the Haynes line in 1918. One of those changes was the introduction of the Fourdore, a four-door, four-passenger roadster. The Fourdore was advertised as the prettiest roadster around, with comfortable cushioned French pleated seats that allowed enough room for "six-footers." The auto also featured a watertight luggage compartment. That feature was probably attractive, since it would keep out the rain — or a river if the car were to get off track. The buyer could choose either the Light Six or Light Twelve engine for the Fourdore. Three finishes were available: deep carmine, beige brown or royal green.

The drop in sales by all manufacturers near the end of World War I spelled the end for many small car manufacturers, but the Haynes Company had grown to producing forty cars a day and plant space had increased to 400,000 square feet. Capitalization had grown to $3.5 million. The boom of 1919 resulted in increased demands for the automobile.

1919

In January 1919, the company undertook a world-wide advertising campaign to carry its product into every country of the world, from Norway to Siam. Even such distant countries as Tasmania, Greece, Indo-China and the newly made Czecho-Slovakia were not overlooked, as the company's efforts went to some 65 countries. Orders began coming in for the Haynes cars soon after. The company executed trademark registrations in 23 foreign countries.

The company also launched advertising campaigns in many foreign countries to support the effort. The advertisements emphasized the four characteristics that go into the manufacturing of Haynes cars — beauty, strength, power and comfort. Cars were upholstered in genuine mohair velvet with the rare Mount Vernon pattern carried out in the silver fittings, frosted rosette light-dome and quarter-lights and a smoking case of solid mahogany. These touches were used to appeal to fastidious and discriminating patrons.

At the end of 1919, the company had exceeded $9 million in sales. All Haynes workers were given Christmas bonuses ranging from $5 to $40,000 in cash, depending on length of service.

1918/19 Models

Light Six Model 38, 6 cyl., 29.4 hp, 121" wb
Touring, 5 passenger, $1,725
Touring, 7 passenger, $1,825
Sedan, 7 passenger, $2,585
Coupe, 4 passenger, $3,250
Fourdore Roadster, 4 passenger, $1,825

Light Six, Model 39, 6 cyl., 29.4 hp, 127" wb
Fourdore Roadster, 4 passenger, $1,825
Touring, 5 passenger, $1,725
Touring, 7 passenger, $1,825
Sedan, 7 passenger, $2,585
Coupe, 4 passenger, $2,535
Town Car, 5 passenger. $3,250

Light Twelve, 12 cyl., 36.3 hp,

127" wb
Town Car, 5 passenger, $3,985
Fourdore Roadster, 4 passenger, $2,785
Sedan, 7 passenger, $3,385
Coupe, 4 passenger, $3,335
Touring, 5 passenger, $2,785

In 1919, a severe housing shortage had plagued Kokomo, so the Haynes Company decided to have 42 cottages built for some of its workers. "I have been watching the housing condition in Kokomo for a long time with increasing disquietude and apprehension and this feeling has been made stronger by the knowledge that our big new factory building will be ready for work in the near future," said vice president A.G. Seiberling. "Of course this means that many hundreds of new workers will have to establish their homes in Kokomo, and when we consider that each man has an average family of a wife and at least one child, you can see that it means new homes must be provided." The company only required a small down payment.

In 1919, the company issued $1.6 million in 7 percent convertible serial gold notes in order to raise money for plant improvements and increase production to 50 cars a day. Within a week the notes were oversubscribed, so some checks had to be returned. "The eagerness with which Haynes stock was sought by substantial business men all over the country is significant of the fact that Haynes cars and the Haynes Automobile Company are in popular favor not only from the automobilists' standpoint, but also from the viewpoint of astute financiers," declared Seiberling. The money was used to finance new factory additions so that the company could produce 15,000 automobiles annually. The company also declared a dividend of 1¾ percent upon preferred stock on Sept 1, 1919.

The year 1919 also brought about a new advertising program and Gilbert U. Radoye was hired to lead the ambitious effort. His motto was: "Early to bed, early to rise, demonstrate every hour — and advertise." He fashioned an advertising campaign in 1920 that stressed Haynes autos as "Cars of Character" to appeal to the upper middle class. The ads stressed that the company sold cars with "Beauty, Strength, Power and Comfort." For example, an ad on the new Brougham stated that the car conveyed "an expression of richness, exclusiveness and dignity." The Haynes Creed was: "To build well, to build faithfully, to create intelligently; to hold character above every other consideration; these are the ideals expressed in the Haynes. And of them and upon them we achieve the four essential factors of car character: Beauty, strength, power and comfort." The 1920 seven-passenger limousine catered to brokers, lawyers, bankers and other merchants who could afford such social attainment and a chauffeur. The limo featured seating for five in the rear, as two auxiliary seats were available. The back was also equipped with a chaufphone, vanity case, flower vase, smoking case and clock. Gray silk curtains on quick-acting rollers were adjustable against the sun's rays or for privacy. Cord Tires and Wooden Wheels came as standard equipment.

1920

The Haynes Company was leaning more toward marketing to the rich, although Seiberling had recommended a smaller, cheaper car. He felt the company could sell a car for $985 and still make a profit of $50 per sale. He had gone as far as buying a location for a new facility, purchasing the equipment for $75,000 and designing the car before Walter Haynes killed the deal. The vice president later blamed the downfall of the company on not taking his advice to produce a cheaper model. Instead of offering a cheaper car, the company upped prices by $200 on all new 1920 models to pay for advances in the cord tires and rising costs of manufacturing. The question of prices came up in 1920 and Seiberling answered the question this way: "My straightforward reply is that the prices of automobiles will not come down for some time." The company's high-priced inventory as well as an expansion in 1920 would haunt them later.

Apparently, Haynes executives didn't think the readjustment in the automobile industry would affect them. They thought the company was big enough to survive the fallout, but competition from Detroit was strong. Small automotive companies were beginning to fall by the wayside. The expansion in 1920 was the building of a new four-story assembly building, 500 feet by 150 feet, with a moving assembly line in the 110 block of South Home Avenue. At one point, the assembly line reached a maximum production of 60 cars per day. The company also began building its own automobile bodies then boasting that its cars were at least "90 percent Kokomo-made"—because most of the parts were made right there in Kokomo, where hundreds of companies made automotive parts.

1920 Models

Light Six, Model 45, 51 hp, 127" wb
Touring, 7 passenger, $2,685
Roadster, 4 passenger, $2,685
Coupe, 4 passenger, $3,300
Sedan, 7 passenger, $3,550
Limousine, 7 passenger, $4,200

Light Twelve, Model 46, 62 hp, 172" wb
Touring, 7 passenger, $3,450
Roadster, 4 passenger, $3,450
Coupe, 4 passenger, $4,000
Sedan, 7 passenger, $4,200
Limousine, 7 passenger, $4,950

The Story of America's First Car, a film about Elwood Haynes, premiered on May 17, 1920, in Kokomo. Hundreds of people

Like many factories in those days, the Haynes Automobile Company had its own baseball team.

The Newest HAYNES Model 22
Electric Starting and Electric Lighting

FOR the twentieth year of the Haynes Automobile, we announce the complete, perfect motor car. Haynes Model 22 has every mark of the fine construction that has distinguished the Haynes car so many years; it has all the beauty of design that has made Model 21 so popular; it has such roominess as you never saw in any other automobile; comfort to please those who seek *luxury;* and *an electric starting and electric lighting equipment of utmost simplicity and absolutely 100 per cent efficiency.*

It is fitting that America's first car—in point of years—should now be America's unquestioned *first car* in point of perfect, efficient completeness. And the price for touring car models is but $2250, f. o. b. factory. We *hope* we shall be able to build enough cars to fill our dealers' orders.

A Starting Device That is *Not* an Experiment

When so many manufacturers were loudly announcing "self-starters" last year, some people wondered that we said *nothing* about self-starters. But Haynes owners and Haynes dealers and everyone else who knew Haynes history did not wonder. They knew that when a *real starting* device was perfected, one that would start a car every time and never allow any possibility of injury to the motor—*the Haynes would have it.* We were working toward such a device then, an electric cranking device. It was *perfected* six months ago. But still we waited. We wanted to be *very sure.* That's Haynes policy. In these six months, the first Model 22 test cars, equipped with this device, have been put through *thousands* of tests in the shops and on the road, and the starter has *never* failed.

Hundreds of these tests have been made under unfavorable conditions which could not arise in an owner's experience, and we couldn't *make* the starter fail. It *cannot* fail. And the equipment is so free from complications, so very simple, that if any trouble ever should appear, the car would *not have to be sent back to the factory.* Any electrician in America could make wiring repairs on either the motor (starting device), or the dynamo (lighting device). Consider that point carefully. The average time of 10,000 Model 22 starts has been *5 seconds.*

Need We Speak of Haynes General Construction?

Everyone who knows automobiles at all knows that the Haynes name is a guarantee of the best materials, correct design, excellent workmanship. Other than for its electric starting and lighting equipment, Model 22 does not differ greatly from the construction of recent Haynes models. The car is roomier. Upholstery *twelve inches deep* and of fine hair. Motor 4½ x 5¼ inches, 40 h. p.; wheel base 120 inches; tires 36 x 4½ inches. Equipment *complete,* including Eisemann dual magneto, Stromberg carburetor, Warner autometer, demountable rims, top, windshield, etc. You will find the new Model 22 at your Haynes dealer's *now.* Go see it, or write us for catalog and full details of starting system.

HAYNES AUTOMOBILE COMPANY, 20 Union Street, KOKOMO, INDIANA
1715 Broadway, NEW YORK   510-512 N. Capitol Blvd., INDIANAPOLIS   1702 Michigan Ave., CHICAGO
Van Ness Avenue at Turk Street, SAN FRANCISCO

This 1920 ad emphasized four vital factors in the Haynes: beauty, strength, power and comfort.

swarmed into Victory Theater to see the movie. The Haynes Company maintained a baseball team during its reign, too. The company turned a "fine profit" in the first half of 1920, according to Haynes, but the second half results were dismal, and 1921 didn't start out much better for the company.

1921

Before 1921, stockholders enjoyed phenomenal returns on their stock and investments with the Haynes Automotive Company. A stockholder from 1915 enjoyed 224 percent in cash dividends and 566 percent in stock dividends. Some stockholders and directors made a killing if they could see the writing on the wall and the decline of the small manufacturer, like the Haynes Company.

In April 1921, the company was still prospering as demand for the new Model 50 was so strong that dealers were coming to Kokomo to pick up cars rather than wait for regular shipment by rail. The 1921 line featured longer wheelbases and larger engines. The Model 47 was powered by a six-cylinder engine and cost between $2,935 and $4,250. The Model 48s were more luxurious and powered by the twelve-cylinder engine. The models ranged in price be-

The Haynes Special Speedster came out in 1921 and was aimed at the sportsman and racing types.

A 1921 Haynes Model 47 on display at the Automotive Heritage Museum in Kokomo.

tween $3,450 and $4,950. These cars were all finished in coach green, except for the bright red Special Speedsters.

1921 Models

<u>Light Six, Model 47, 50 hp, 132" wb</u>
Touring, 7 passenger, $2,935
Tourister, 4 passenger, $2,935
Speedster, 2 passenger, $3,500
Brougham, 5 passenger, $3,950
Sedan, 7 passenger, $4,250
Suburban, 7 passenger, $4,250

<u>Light Twelve, Model 48, 70 hp, 132" wb</u>
Touring, 7 passenger, $3,635
Tourister, 4 passenger, $3,635
Speedster, 2 passenger, $4,200
Coupe, 4 passenger, $4,350
Brougham, 5 passenger, $4,650
Suburban, 7 passenger, $4,950

Haynes came out with the Special Speedster in 1921. The two-seater was ideally suited to the sportsman, the clubman, the golfer, the salesman and the athletic type, according to the company. In fact, the car came equipped with a special storage compartment just behind the door for a set of golf clubs. The top was made of a durable khaki and Spanish leather was used for the upholstery. "Beauty, Strength, Power, Comfort," was the advertising slogan used to promote the automobile. The company also advertised the Haynes 75 Speedster as, the car you want if you want to go 75 miles an hour. The six or twelve-cylinder car with a light-weight aluminum body could actually go faster. Howdy Wilcox, the 1919 winner of the Indy 500, took the car for a spin on the Motor Speedway on March 9, 1922. "I attained speeds ranging from seventy-four to eighty miles an hour," Wilcox said in an advertisement. "It is the sturdiest and fastest stock sport car I have ever driven to date." The car could also cover a mile in 48 seconds. In 1923, the Model 75 Speedster was renamed as the Haynes 77 Blue Ribbon Speedster.

1922

1922 Models

<u>Model 48, 12 cyl., 70 hp, 132" wb</u>
Touring, 7 passenger, $3,635
Tourister, 4 passenger, $3,635
Speedster, 2 passenger, $4,200
Brougham, 5 passenger, $4,650
Sedan, 7 passenger, $4,950
Suburban, 7 passenger, $4,950

<u>Model 55, 6 cyl., 50 hp, 121" wb</u>
Touring, 5 passenger, $1,785
Roadster, 2 passenger, $1,835
Sedan, 5 passenger, $2,835

<u>Model 75, 6 cyl., 75 hp, 132" wb</u>
Touring, 7 passenger, $2,485
Tourister, 4 passenger, $2,485
Speedster, 2 passenger, $2,685
Brougham, 5 passenger, $3,185
Sedan, 7 passenger, $3,485
Suburban, 7 passenger, $3,485

The postwar boom coming to an end in 1921 began to create a severe crisis for the automobile industry. For the first time in automotive production history demand was less than what was being produced. Competition for customers also came from a growing used car market. However, the Haynes Automotive Company was not immediately impacted by the slowdown in the economy.

The company met the slowdown in the economy by reducing the price of the new Model 55, which replaced the Model 50, by $200. The 55 models had a 121-inch wheel base and were equipped with a light six motor. The touring car carried five passengers and featured genuine leather upholstery. While the 55 two-passenger roadster featured a light six motor, the 55 sedan was an all-purpose car and the 55 Coupelet was much like a roadster, carrying three passengers.

The Model 75, which featured a size option, succeeded both Models 47 and 48. The 75 models had a 132-inch wheel base and were equipped with a more powerful motor that produced 70 horsepower. The new six-cylinder motor was equipped with a new Haynes volatilizer, which insured greater motive power with fuel consumption and increased motor life. The volatilizer was demonstrated at Uniontown Mountain near Pittsburgh. The touring car topped the summit of the mountain at a record breaking 42 mph. The 75 touring car could carry up to seven passengers. It carried two spare tires. A trim looking trunk covered with moleskin was carried on a trunk rack over the gas tank at the rear of the car. The 75 Tourister carried four passengers. The 75 Special Speedster carried just two passengers and was the sports car of the Haynes company. The 75 also had a Brougham, Sedan and Suburban. The Sedan and Suburban were upholstered in genuine leather. Silken curtains on quick-acting rollers protected passengers from the glare of the sun. The Sedan and Suburban were capable of carrying seven passengers, while the Brougham sat five.

The new 1922 models started off as good sellers and a production schedule of 30 cars was set up for January, with the company lowering prices some 10 percent in January in order to attract buyers. First quarter sales of 1,177 cars was a 68½ percent rise over first quarter sales a year before. By the end of the year, 5,915 cars were sold, which generated a gross income of about $9.5 million. The company realized about $400,000 on the year, but the company was still in the red.

America's Blue Ribbon Sport Car
The HAYNES 75 SPEEDSTER

"*On Thursday, March 9, 1922, I drove a strictly stock Haynes 75 Speedster over the Indianapolis Motor Speedway course at Indianapolis, Indiana. I attained speeds ranging from seventy-four (74) to eighty (80) miles an hour. The speeds were clocked officially by the Indianapolis Motor Speedway electric timing machine. In my opinion, the Haynes-built 75 six cylinder engine is a remarkable stock motor. It has the necessary speed, stamina and getaway to meet the requirements of the most exacting motorist, and at topmost speed it showed a decided lack of motor vibration. It is the sturdiest and fastest stock sport car I have ever driven to date.*"

(Signed) "Howdy" Wilcox

POWER, BALANCE, SPEED — a Mile in 48 Seconds

When Howard Wilcox established the performance record for the strictly stock Haynes 75 Speedster, he demonstrated the worth of the high quality of steels and other materials used in the manufacture of this fast sport car.

The mechanical reasons which enabled Mr. Wilcox to attain an average speed of seventy-five miles an hour, are the same which give any owner of a Haynes 75 Speedster dominance on the road.

With a car of such phenomenal power and stamina, only a very small portion of its capacity is employed in ordinary driving. This means that the Haynes 75 blue ribbon Speedster will give more satisfactory service for a greater number of years than the car whose maximum power is required for every day's use.

The liberal use of tested steels and drop forgings makes this car safe at the high speeds the Haynes 75 blue ribbon Speedster will naturally be driven by its enthusiastic owner. The blue ribbon award for speed, stamina, power, reliability and endurance, to the Haynes 75 Speedster, is a fitting tribute to the famous Haynes engineers who alone have the distinction and honor of designing and perfecting automobiles for more than a quarter of a century.

The Haynes 75 blue ribbon Speedster is a strikingly beautiful car in appearance; its owners are deservedly proud of it.

In its class it may unhesitatingly be said to be the greatest value possible. See it at the nearest Haynes dealer's showroom and place your order at once, so that you may secure delivery in plenty of time to enjoy the Haynes 75 blue ribbon Speedster through the season. Descriptive literature will be mailed promptly on request.

$2395
F. O. B. FACTORY

The Haynes Automobile Company, Kokomo, Indiana - Export Office: 1715 Broadway, New York City, U. S. A.

The new, improved Haynes 75 blue ribbon two-passenger Speedster is equipped with individual steps and individual fenders, and two extra wire wheels. Wind deflectors, rear vision mirrors, windshield cleaners, exterior side cowl lights, and searchlight type head lamps are also furnished at no additional cost.

Haynes used race driver Howdy Wilcox to promote its 75 Speedster in this full page ad. (Courtesy of the Haynes Museum.)

In December 1922, the company an- nounced a new sales policy in an effort to

Top: A 1922 Haynes Model 75 on display at the Automotive Heritage Museum in Kokomo. *Bottom:* Haynes factory workers put the final touches on autos on the assembly line in 1922. (Courtesy of the Haynes Museum.)

raise sagging sales. Prices were cut and a number of new dealers and outlets were obtained. The touring car was reduced to $1,595 and the seven-passenger touring car went for $2,395.

1923

The company announced a projected increase in sales to 9,000 cars in 1923. The opposite turned out to be the case. Sales dropped 30 percent in 1923! 1923 cars were similar to the year before, except for the addition of four sport models: sport roadster, sport coupe and two sport touring models. The 57 line featured a five-passenger touring car, a five-passenger standard sedan, a five-passenger sports sedan and a two-passenger roadster. The touring car was a few inches longer and wider to provide better comfort. The 77 models included a seven-passenger sport touring car, a five-passenger sport Brougham, a blue ribbon speedster and a four-passenger sport tourister. Some of the 1923 models featured a Burgundy Wine color that was produced by Haynes' chemists. Coach blue was used for other models.

1923 Models

Model 57, 6 cyl., 55 hp, 121" wb
Touring, 5 passenger, $1,595
Sedan, 5 passenger, $2,595
Sport Touring, 5 passenger, $1,850
Sport Sedan, 5 passenger, $2,695
Sport Brougham, 5 passenger, $2,395

Model 77, 6 cyl., 70 hp, 132" wb
Touring, 7 passenger, $2,395
Brougham, 5 passenger, $3,095
Sedan, 7 passenger, $3,395
Sport Touring, 7 passenger. $2,550
Blue Ribbon Speedster, $3,250
Suburban, 7 passenger, $3,395

The company boasted that its cars were 95 percent Haynes built in 1923. The company came up with the slogan to assure its customers of quality and to boast that "the Haynes is the greatest automobile value on the market today." Ford went a step further by trying to provide cars that were 100-percent made by the company. Some 1,200 workers were employed by the Haynes factory, which was less than half of what the company employed during its heyday. The assistant general manager, C.W. Crick, told the city of Kokomo, "In our opinion the most crying need at the present time of the city of Kokomo is better housing conditions, extension of water and gas lines to outlying districts and extension of car lines."

A Haynes Model 75 from 1923 on display at the Automotive Heritage Museum.

Top: The 1924 Haynes Model 60 featured doors that opened opposite ways. *Bottom:* The Model 75 Speedster was renamed the Haynes 77 Blue Ribbon Speedster. (Courtesy Stan Mohr Local History Library of the Howard County Historical Society.)

The company decided a merger with some other automotive companies was necessary to survive. The proposed merger with Winton of Cleveland and Dorris of St. Louis would result in Consolidated Motors Corporation, with a capitalization of $19 million. The Haynes and Dorris company stockholders agreed to the proposal in June 1923, but the Winton Company delayed and the plans were abandoned. The merger would have probably not got the companies out of the quagmire in which they were stuck. With the merger off, the Haynes Automobile Company began planning to refinance, as creditors were nipping at their heels. Some lawsuits had already been filed and others were being threatened. Bankruptcy was certain if creditors didn't back off, and bankruptcy is where Dorris and Winton ended up after the proposed merger died. Nearly 50 American automobile companies died on the vine in 1923.

1924

The financial crisis forced the company to tighten its belt and let some highly paid personnel go in an effort to cut expenses. Vice president A.G. Seiberling and advertising manager Gilbert U. Radoye were shown the door as well as some others. Seiberling would later lose everything when the company failed. The company also turned to a refinancing plan that called for the citizens of Kokomo to purchase a million dollars' worth of Haynes Automobile Company bonds. Company directors pledged to raise another half million in bonds. The effort was dubbed "Save the Haynes" and a bond campaign committee was organized with headquarters in the YMCA building. The enthusiastic citizens of Kokomo and 1,300 workers at the plant responded enthusiastically, but fell just short of raising a million dollars in bonds by the end of the year. The goal was finally reached two days into 1924 and a gala was held to celebrate. The celebration was a great night for Kokomo. The

A 1924 Haynes Model 60 on display at the Automotive Heritage Museum.

company took the occasion to name its new general manager, Hayden Eames, a graduate of the Naval Academy.

The Model 60 was introduced in 1924 in an effort to get the company out of the hole it was digging. It was priced attractively at $1,295 in an effort to compete with some of the bigger auto makers. However, Buick came out with a small model that sold for $1,200 a week before, so the strategy didn't work.

1924 Models

Model 60, 6 cyl., 50 hp, 121" wb
Touring, 5 passenger, $1,295
Special Touring, 5 passenger, $1,395
Roadster, 2 passenger, $1,695
Sedan, 5 passenger, $1,895
Special Sedan, 5 passenger, $1,945

The financial crisis was temporarily averted and orders for cars flooded in right after the celebration, but the enthusiasm soon wore off as the new Model 60s did not sell well. The advertising manager, S.E. Burke, tried a hard-sell approach that emphasized that Haynes was the first car. The campaign fell short because of the high price of the automobiles. Only 1,500 models sold on the year. More bond sales were required in April to keep the company afloat.

The summer of 1924 turned out to be a hot and long one for the Haynes Automotive Company. Eames turned out to be less than satisfactory as the new general manager and left the company in July. A Chicago firm that Eames had hired and two minor creditors filed suit in federal court seeking receivership for the Haynes company. As a result, the Haynes plant ceased all manufacturing on September 2. The company declared bankruptcy on October 22, with liabilities listed at $3,619,000 and assets at $1,684,000. Some 35 automotive companies closed their doors in 1924.

A meeting of Haynes Company creditors was held on September 5. After a discussion of a merger with the Apperson Automotive Company that went nowhere because of the sad state of affairs there as well, the suit for receivership went ahead. The company was declared bankrupt in October. Robert L. Tudor was appointed by the court to handle company affairs.

Tudor supervised the liquidation of the manufacturing stock, which included the assembling of two hundred more Model 60s in December and January from the materials on hand. The cars were exhibited at the National Automobile Show in January, but not the Chicago show.

1925

A sale of these assets was set for January 22, but all bids received were rejected because they weren't high enough. The sale was rescheduled for February 19, and the bondholders then bid the amount of their bonds and acquired the plant for $750,000. They also paid $125,000 in cash for inventory and materials not covered in the mortgage. Their efforts to operate the plant, however, failed as well.

1925 Models

Model 60, 6 cyl. 50 hp, 121" wb
Touring, 5 passenger, $1,600
Brougham, 5 passenger, $2,200
Sedan, 5 passenger, $2,300

The board of directors from the Haynes Company had to pay off about a half million dollars in company loans which had been guaranteed by them. The preferred and common stock of the company became worthless. Haynes said in the letter that he lost the $60,000 of his preferred stock and all of his common stock of over $250,000

The preferred stock of the Haynes Automobile Company eventually became worthless to stockholders.

when the company failed. He expected to receive 10 cents on the dollar when the plant was to be disposed of by the bondholders. "The cause for our present failure dates back to 1920 when we loaded up with high priced material that we obliged to sell later at a heavy loss, due to the price cutting of our various competitors," he explained in correspondence.

Haynes also received a letter from Dr. W.C. Horn asking for some compensation for the losses. "I sure feel bad to think we have had such an utter failure when uncalled for if properly managed," Horn wrote. He had purchased some $9,000 in stock for Mollie Horn, his elderly wife, who was disabled by a broken hip. Haynes replied to Horn: "The Directors not only lost all their holdings in the company, but had to pay in addition over $400,000 of the company's notes, on which they were endorsed. Besides this, a number of us lost heavily on money which we had loaned to the company, and which they were unable to pay." Haynes also received a letter from H.S. Worcester of Huntington, Indiana, asking for a car in exchange for the worthless Gold Bonds he had in his possession. He had purchased $1,300 in bonds.

The Haynes Automotive Company lasted much longer than other companies in the United States. More than a thousand automotive companies, 500 of which were in Indiana, went out of business before the Haynes Company or, for that matter, the Apperson Brothers Automotive Company. So both companies were successful for more than a quarter of a century, quite a feat for that era.

Haynes Automobile Company Sales, 1906–24

Year	Sales
1906	300
1907	300
1908	350
1909	350
1910	1,000
1911	1,000
1912	1,200
1913	1,400
1914	1,700
1915	5,500
1916	7,100
1917	5,500
1918	2,200

5

Aftershocks

As soon as the Haynes and Apperson companies went out of business, their vehicles depreciated as quickly as stocks did in 1929. Ten years after their demise, the vehicles were worth about $100 in the Blue Book. However, those same vehicles are now more than 75 years old and worth some $30,000 or more because they are so rare.

Haynes Automotive Company

Most of the Haynes plants lay dormant for a decade, but their existence laid the groundwork for a return of the automotive industry in Kokomo. Crosley Radio renovated the Haynes Auto body plant in 1936. Delco Radio Division of General Motors purchased the facility eight months later. A year later they introduced the first push-button car radio. The name of the company changed to Delco Electronics in 1970. Today, as Delphi Electronics, it continues to be an innovative supplier to the automotive industry, offering such new technologies as Forewarn collision warning systems, Eye Cue heads-up displays, Telepath navigation systems, night vision, keyless entry, intrusion sensors, adaptive cruise control and premium auto systems.

The Chrysler Corporation opened its first Kokomo facility at another old Haynes Auto plant, at 1100 Home Avenue in 1937, to produce manual transmissions. Chrysler remained in the building until it could build a new plant in 1965. Chrysler's continuing confidence in Kokomo is manifested by its construction of a new $1.3 billion state of the art transmission plant and the continual reinvestment in the present facilities. Kokomo produces all Chrysler three-speed and four-speed electronic front-wheel drive transmissions and all rear-wheel drive transmissions.

Vernon Garves purchased the main Haynes building in 1977 and began storing wrecks there for parts. He renovated the building by putting on a new roof and replacing windows. The Warren Auto Parts and Salvage Company now occupies the old plant.

Top: The main building of the old Haynes plant is now used by Warren Auto Parts and Salvage to store its relics. *Bottom:* The Haynes Administrative building is now used as an apartment building.

The Haynes Assembly Building came down in 1998. (Courtesy of Dale Etherington.)

The Haynes administrative offices were turned into apartments and are still in use today as such. Across the street was the assembly plant, which is gone. And south of the assembly plant was the paint building, which was used by the Kolex Sign Company for awhile before it was torn down. Also gone is a body plant that Haynes built in 1924. Ironically, the body plant was never used as the company went bankrupt.

Apperson Automobile Company

The Apperson Automobile Company plant went out of business in 1925 and the buildings were sold off. An unknown automotive supply company moved into the building that replaced the Riverside Machine Works. The Northern Indiana Supply Company then purchased part of the plant in 1935 and has been there ever since. Another of the buildings in the complex of five, three-story factories is being used by Allen Enterprises. Two of the buildings were once connected by a walkway, which has since been torn down. An old Interurban rail station sits by the building. It was in use earlier in the 1900s and provided rail transportation to Indianapolis. The other Apperson plant on North Washington was bought by the Reliance Company, which made garments and parachutes during World War II. Later General Motors bought the building and used it for production until the early 1990s. The building was torn down in 1993. The Apperson headquarters building was last used by the Veterans of Foreign Wars before it was torn down in 1999. The city now owns the property, which lies vacant.

The Northern Indiana Supply Company now calls the old Apperson plant home.

Pumpkinvine Pike — the road used by Elwood Haynes on his first ride in the Pioneer — has been straightened. It used to be a curvy road located in the country. Progress and city expansion doomed the road, which was straightened out and renamed as the Boulevard. If Elwood Haynes were still alive, he would have never recognized the street, which is now flanked on one side by automotive plants and on the other side by homes. The street was supposed to be renamed in his honor, but that has never come to fruition. Although the city approved the measure at the time the Haynes mansion was purchased, the change never came about for some unknown reason. Ironically, the city did rename a street in honor of the Apperson brothers. Apperson Way was dedicated on Oct. 22, 1955.

The home where Elwood Haynes created his first car still stands today, but in another location. The home was set on rollers and moved to an out-of-the-way part of town in the name of progress. So instead of becoming a historic landmark, it became just another house occupied by an average citizen.

Haynes Stellite Company

The Haynes Stellite Company was purchased by Union Carbide Corporation in 1920 and was not in the black until 1925. The company weathered the depression by selling "Haystellite" rods to East Texas oil fields. Oil field operations boomed during the depression years and Stellite concentrated on this field to good effect. With the worst of the depression behind, the plant expanded in the late 1930s.

The war was a boom to business as the company became a major supplier of parts for the military and commercial air-

Elwood Haynes' first home in Kokomo, which was provided by the gas company, still stands today.

craft. The wartime workload at Stellite was extremely heavy, with around-the-clock production. All of the valves used in aircraft engines had seating surfaces of Stellite welded onto an alloy steel body, which gave them a tremendous increase in life and efficiency. Another military use was reflectors for search lights on naval vessels. Stellite was the only alloy with a combination of hardness to resist scratching, strength to resist breakage and high reflectivity. A modified Stellite alloy was found to give marvelous results as a liner for machine gun barrels. Aeroplane engines used superchargers and the most efficient supercharger could be driven by a turbine running on engine exhaust. Naturally, the turbine blades became heated to a high temperature and after hundreds of tests a Stellite alloy was the best for the jobs. Production was as high as 2,200,000 a month at the Kokomo plant.

Then the Korean War and the evolution of the jet engine brought about the production of turbine blades and vanes for military jet aircraft. Much of the blading of the J-33 and J-40 gas turbine engine, which powered the jets in the war, were of Stellite alloy. To produce the turbine blades and vanes, the company opened a plant in Alexandria, Indiana. It was owned by the Air Force and operated on a cost-plus basis. The Alexandria plant closed in 1958 when national developments in defense shifted from planes to rockets. A major market was lost, so the company had to change its focus.

The space age and the Vietnam War brought about new applications for stellite. The metal was used to produce alloy rotor shields for helicopters to protect them from debris encountered while landing on unpaved sites. Other alloys were used in helicopter and jet aircraft engines as well as for gun barrel liners.

In 1965, J.J. Phillips of the Stellite Division of Union Carbide had the following to say about Haynes:

> Of the many industrial and social contributions by Mr. Elwood Haynes, perhaps the most significant may be his invention of the basic cobalt-base alloys. As a perpetual living memorial, his alloys are in use today. The need was so urgent and his provision was so complete that, in many applications, no improvements have been necessary in his alloys after over 60 years of effective and valuable use.
>
> The alloys known as "Stellite" alloy No. 4, "Stellite" alloy No. 6 (also 6B and 6K), "Star J" Metal and 98M2 alloy are produced today, throughout the world, exactly as invented by Ewood Haynes as early as 1899, and described in his patents granted in 1907 and 1913. These alloys continue to be valuable for use as cutting tools, well and mine drilling bits, bearing materials, and hardfacings for articles that must endure severe wear conditions: tractor plowshares, discs, machinery parts and the like. Several original Haynes alloys are in use in many modern severe-service applications: jet aircraft, nuclear energy installations, rocket motors and others.
>
> Elwood Haynes provided the earliest and most practical superalloys with his invention of the binary cobalt and chromium alloys and alloys containing a cobalt-chromium base with tungsten, molybdenum, and/or other elements. In some cases, the basic alloys have been modified for use in specific applications. His alloys provided the strongest foundation of the entire superalloy industry as we know it today. The later modifications—containing such elements as vanadium, zirconium, boron, tantalum, columbium, etc.—became the superalloys of today, for example, HAYNES alloy No. 25.
>
> The class "superalloys" is generally the unsung hero and workhorse of metallurgy. The inherent excellent physical, chemical, and mechanical properties of these alloys made them eminently suited for service under severe conditions of high heat, corrosion, stresses, and endurance. In many critical applications, superalloys are successfully used after all other classes of metals have failed or are otherwise unsuited to serve as rocket engine components, jet and gas turbine engine parts, nuclear processes parts and other modern sophisticated ware.
>
> In 1911, Elwood Haynes discovered some valuable properties in stainless steels and made significant improvements and advancements in the art. Granted in 1915, his patent based on his stainless steel improvements, was a foundation of the American Stainless Steel Corporation (about 1920) in Pittsburgh, Pennsylvania. The entire stainless steel industry has advanced to its present position by the efforts of many pioneer enterprises and experimenters, such as the American Stainless Steel Corporation, with Mr. Elwood Haynes' contributions.
>
> In keeping with his characteristics as a benefactor and teacher, Mr. Haynes shared his knowledge and discoveries by publishing many technical papers disclosing his contributions to metallurgy.

A major transformation went about in 1970 when the Stellite plant was purchased by Cabot Corporation. As the war in Vietnam came to an end, the company turned more towards space. Nearly 14 tons of alloys and 2000 investment castings were used in each Apollo vehicle.

The Haynes International plant in Kokomo now specializes in making heat treating metal for aerospace, nuclear, chemical, electronic and transportation industries.

Haynes and Apperson Automobiles

Haynes and Apperson automobiles are now like some endangered species. The rare, treasured vehicles are worth thousands of dollars to collectors. Of course some of the collectors live in or near Kokomo.

Bob Gollner of Kokomo owns several

Bob Gollner showed off his 1918 Haynes Model 34 R Cloverleaf Roadster during the car show at the Haynes-Apperson Festival in 2001.

Apperson and Haynes automobiles. He still drives a 1918 Haynes Model 34 R Cloverleaf Roadster and takes it to car shows. He bought the vehicle in 1992 for $22,000 from the Spencer Huffman estate. Gollner, who is in the midst of restoring another Haynes, owns a 1923 Apperson Jackrabbit that sits in the Automotive Heritage Museum in Kokomo.

Another vehicle on display at the museum belongs to Dave Griffey, whose father worked for the Appersons back in 1923. The vehicle is a Haynes Model 75 Roadster, which Griffey purchased in 1984 from the second owner of the car in Chicago Heights, Illinois. He paid $35,000 for the vehicle, which had a rotted out roof. He first became interested in Haynes cars at an early age. "I was assigned to do the biography of Elwood Haynes in the fifth grade," he explained. He was able to interview Haynes' daughter, Bernice, but Haynes' son, March, refused to cooperate.

One more Haynes automobile sitting in the museum belongs to Dale Etherington. He purchased the 1922 Touring Model 75 in 1997 for $28,000 from a man in Quakertown, Pennsylvania. "I always wanted a Haynes," the retired Chrysler worker explained. He doesn't drive the car any longer because it has a leaky gas tank.

And yet another car in the museum, a Haynes Model 47 Touring car, belongs to the Morris Family of Kokomo. The Mervis Family, also of Kokomo, own a 1921 Haynes Model 47 Touring car. Also, the Carr Family of Westfield own a 1924 Haynes on display at the Automotive Heritage Museum.

In Pennsylvania, Alvin Fox of Souderton owns a 1923 Haynes. He bought the car in 1975 at a junkyard in Wilmington, Delaware, for a mere $3,000. He found out that the original owner of the car was one Willard Naughton in Ashland, Pennsylvania, which is in the coal region. "I restored it a little at a time," he explained. After

Top: Dave Griffey stands by his 1923 Haynes Model 75. The vehicle now sits in the Automotive Heritage Museum. (Courtesy of Dave Griffey.) *Bottom:* Alvin Fox of Souderton, Pennsylvania, has fully restored a 1923 Haynes. (Courtesy of Alvin Fox.)

Russ Haines of Tallahassee owns a 1917 Haynes. (Courtesy of Russ Haines.)

finishing it, he showed it off in parades and car shows. Like Elwood Haynes, he has even taken it on the Glidden Tour, which is celebrating its 100th anniversary soon. Fox thinks his Standard Touring Model 60 is now worth about $35,000.

In Florida, Russ Haines owns a 1917 Haynes that is worth at least $50,000, judging from the fact that he's been offered that price three times. But he's not selling the Model 37 Cloverleaf just yet. Haines used to work for Bell Telephone, which had its headquarters in Kokomo, so he decided to buy a Haynes because it came from Kokomo and because of the closeness to his own name. He found one in Georgia that needed a lot of work and he told the owner, "I need to be the owner of that car." The owner finally decided to give up on the restoration project and sold it to Haines for $8,500 in 1990. Haines worked furiously on the restoration because he wanted to drive the car to the 100th anniversary of the first car in Kokomo in 1994. He made the deadline and took it to Kokomo for the centennial. The car doesn't have all the original parts anymore because Haines had so much difficulty with them, so he has done some replacement with newer parts. For example, he uses a carburetor from a Chevrolet and a clutch from a Ford. The original price for the car was $1,725.

Once in awhile, an Apperson, Haynes or Haynes-Apperson car ends up on the auction block. In 1991, a 1910 Haynes Boottail Wicker with a four cylinder, 30-horsepower engine was auctioned at a Barrett-Jackson Classic Collector Car Auction. The car went for $25,000. More recently, a 1902 Haynes-Apperson Roadster was auctioned off for $24,000 at The Auction in Las Vegas in 2000. However, most car sales are private in nature between collectors.

6

Honoring Haynes and Apperson

Elwood Haynes was bestowed many honors while he was alive. After his death, the honors continued. On the 75th anniversary of his birth — October 14, 1932 — the city of Portland honored the inventor with an impressive ceremony and erected a marker on the site of his birth. President Herbert Hoover sent a message that was read at the ceremony. Haynes' older brother, Sumner Haynes, spoke at the ceremonies, which was attended by some 3,000 people. He related a story about his brother during the speech: "One of the five-gallon cans that had contained linseed oil used about the painting of the new house, which was being built two squares away, was used by my brother as a boiler in which to make steam to run a little engine that he had constructed, and as was usual, he had quite a company of boys around him and with no steam gauge on the boiler, he could not tell when the limit of pressure had been reached. The result was that the boiler exploded and the oil went out with a great spray covering some of the boys' faces and hands and clothes. It happened that no one was seriously hurt."

The two-ton marker at the site of his birth contains a bronze plate carrying a replica of the Pioneer. The inscription reads: INVENTOR OF STELLITE, INVENTOR OF STAINLESS STEEL IN COMMEMORATION OF ELWOOD HAYNES, THE INVENTOR OF AMERICA'S FIRST SUCCESSFUL AUTOMOBILE, THIS TABLET MARKS THE LOT WHERE ORIGINALLY STOOD THE HOUSE IN WHICH ELWOOD HAYNES WAS BORN, OCTOBER 14, 1857. DONATED BY NELSON R. WILLIAMSON AND SON.

The problem with the marker and bust of Haynes was that it was now located on the property of a funeral home, which had taken over the property in 1906. In the late 1950s, the owner of the Williamson & Spencer Funeral Home decided that he needed the space for a parking lot, so he donated the bust to the Jay County Public

This plaque honors the birthplace of Elwood Haynes in Portland, Indiana.

Library and buried the stone under the pavement. The plaque was thrown in the garage along with other relics. About 30 years later, Jane Spencer came across the plaque and thought it was a shame that the bronze plaque honoring a famed Hoosier was disposed of like yesterday's newspaper. The fourth-grade teacher told her husband she was putting the plaque back on a rock and displaying it again in a garden setting for all to see. "It's part of learning about Jay County history," said the former elementary school teacher. Now third and fourth graders visit the plaque while studying Indiana history.

During World War II, the S.S. *Elwood Haynes* from the Permanent Metals Corporation was commissioned near San Francisco. The vessel was a 10,500-ton "Liberty Ship." Calvin Haynes christened the ship in January 1944.

In 1954, Haynes was honored with the building of the Haynes-Beckert Research Library at the laboratories of Union Carbide Corporation in Niagara Falls. The following year the Elwood Haynes Elementary School was dedicated in Kokomo. The school was built at a cost of $660,000 and stands at Markland Avenue and Cooper Street. Opened in the fall of 1955, the school was attended the first year by 168 students in grades one through eight.

In 1957, on the 100th anniversary of Elwood Haynes' birth — October 14, 1857 — Haynes and Apperson employees gathered for a huge picnic in Highland Park, which sits next to the Haynes Museum. The picnic later became an annual affair.

Then, when the city of Kokomo celebrated its centennial in 1965, the famous first test ride of the Pioneer was re-enacted on Pumpkinvine Pike on July Fourth. A restored 1897 Haynes-Apperson car owned by Jack A. Frost of Detroit, Michigan, impersonated the history-making run.

Haynes and Apperson company workers came together in Highland Park for a reunion in 1957 on the 100th anniversary of Elwood Haynes' birth. (Courtesy Howard County Historical Society, Kokomo, Indiana.)

Haynes Museum

The former home of Elwood Haynes was purchased by the city of Kokomo in 1965 from General Motors Corporation, which had purchased the home from March Haynes and used it as a residence for its high-priced employees. Work began immediately on the three-story home to transform it into a museum. Nearly two years later, on May 28, 1967, the Elwood Haynes Museum was dedicated.

The museum, which is owned and operated by the Kokomo Parks Department, has that old home feel as the floors moan to the weight of the several thousand visitors that come each year. Attendance has decreased through the years because of high gas prices, according to curator Kay Frazer, who has managed the museum for more than two decades. The museum still gets many groups of school children out on field trips, but there are days when no visitors come to see the museum because of its out-of-the-way location. The museum, which charges no admission but accepts donations, is open from 1 to 4 p.m., Tuesday-Sunday, and is closed on holidays.

The basement of the old estate, which was built in 1915, has been turned into a home theater with room for about 50 people, and an outdated black-and-white film about automobiles informs visitors on how automobiles began in this country. Elwood Hayes' accomplishments are recognized at the beginning of the old movie. Years ago there was a tunnel in the basement that Haynes would use to get to his laboratory located across the street, catercorner from the home. The old lab is now privately owned and used as a home.

The first floor of the museum features

Top: The Elwood Haynes Museum in Kokomo was originally his home and is now owned by the city of Kokomo. (Courtesy of the Haynes Museum.) *Bottom:* Curator Kay Frazer explains the Haynes Museum to a couple of visitors.

A 1905 Haynes-Apperson is lifted to a platform so it can be wheeled into the Haynes Museum. (Courtesy of the Haynes Museum.)

a 1905 Haynes automobile that was brought in through a window, which was quite a feat. The living room shows off much of the history of the Haynes Automotive Company. The room once contained a pipe organ when Haynes lived there, but it is no longer there. Knowing of his religious convictions, the organ was likely donated to a church after his demise. The dining room contains the china that the Haynes owned

A 1923 Haynes Roadster is one of three vehicles in the garage at the Haynes Museum.

as well as paintings of the couple. The stairways leading to the upstairs are littered with photos from Haynes' automotive background. The second floor contains the history of the Stellite plant which Haynes founded and samples of his work on metallurgy. Some Apperson items are also contained on the second floor. The third floor is used as a residence by the curator. Three Haynes automobiles are stored in the garage behind the home. They are no longer used in parades and act as static displays. In 1985, the American Society for Metals designated the Haynes Museum as a historical landmark to commemorate Elwood Haynes' achievements.

The Elwood Haynes Museum was designated as a historical landmark by the American Society for Metals in 1985.

Automotive Heritage Museum

Another museum in Kokomo has even more Haynes automobiles than the Haynes Museum. The Automotive Heritage Museum displays more Haynes and Apperson automobiles than any other museum in the world. The museum opened on January 1, 1997, in a building was previously housed a Big R Store, which was downsizing to a smaller store. Big R sold the building to the not-for-profit group for $1.5

Top: On display at the Automotive Heritage Museum in Kokomo is an automobile incorrectly dubbed the "Pioneer II." The vehicle is more likely a replica of the first car, the Pioneer, which is on display at the Smithsonian. *Bottom:* Apperson Way and Haynes Avenue come together inside the Automotive Heritage Museum.

million, although the property was worth much more. Located at the northern approach to Kokomo on U.S. 31, the museum features about a dozen automobiles from the Haynes and Apperson companies. One of the automobiles on display is called the Pioneer II, which Paul Isgrigg of Columbus claims as the second vehicle built by Elwood Haynes and the Appersons. The second vehicle was, in fact, called the Trap and carried four passengers which sat back-to-back from early photos. If anything, the Pioneer II is a replica of the first car built by the trio, which is on display at the Smithsonian. Isgrigg refused to comment on the replica.

The Haynes and Apperson display is the centerpiece to the museum and graces the front of it. The exhibit includes a replica of the facade of Haynes' first home in Kokomo, the one the gas company allowed him to live in. Other interesting exhibits in the museum include a 1930s gas station and a 1950s diner. Cars, motorcycles and the first motorized firetruck are exhibited as well. The museum is open 10 a.m. to 5 p.m. daily, but is closed on Thanksgiving, Christmas and New Year's Day. Admission is charged. In 2000, about 4,000 visitors from some 25 countries visited the museum.

Auburn Cord Duesenberg Museum

Haynes and Apperson automobiles are also on display at the Auburn Cord Duesenberg Museum in Auburn, Indiana. The museum has an exhibit that covers the entire automotive history in Indiana, and a 1923 Haynes is on display along with the history of the Haynes Automotive Company. A Haynes-Apperson is on display in the Alcoa exhibit, because the 1901 model

The Auburn Cord Duesenberg Museum features this Haynes-Apperson Model A, on loan from the Henry Ford Museum.

features an aluminum crankcase. The car is on loan from the Henry Ford Museum. The museum also possesses a 1920 Apperson, which was once owned by Edgar Apperson. It was in storage and will be restored at a later time.

Other Museums

The result of Haynes Automobile Company selling overseas has shown up with a 1918 Haynes shown at Svedino's Automobile and Aviation Museum in Sweden. The Haynes on display is a Model 45, Type T, seven-passenger touring car. It has belonged to the museum since the late 1950s. The museum has some 140 cars on display.

Haynes-Apperson Festival

Kokomo began celebrating the accomplishments of the automakers on July 4th, 1975, with the annual Haynes-Apperson Festival. The festival evolved from a car show that was held the previous year by Haynes-Apperson Chapter of the Pioneer Auto Club. The car club ran the festival until 1982, when it was turned over to WWKI, a local radio station. The annual weeklong festival, which began as a two-day event, features a car show, parade, games and a carnival downtown. The grand marshal of the parade in 1984 was Wilma Rudolph, an Olympics track star. In 1990, the festival committee paid $75,000 to Paul Isgrigg for a restored 1902 Haynes-Apperson. By 2001, only one Haynes automobile was brought out for the car show and none appeared in the parade. Regardless, the festival is a time for celebration in the City of Firsts.

Other Celebrations

The famous first run by Elwood Haynes and the Apperson brothers has

Mamie Doud Eisenhower purchased a 1902 Haynes-Apperson, and the car now rests at her birthplace in Boone, Iowa. (Courtesy of the Haynes Museum.)

Right: The oldest vehicle in the Haynes-Apperson Festival was this 1928 pickup truck. No Haynes or Apperson cars were entered in the 2001 parade.

Jack Frost and his mechanic took the helm of a Haynes car for the rerun of the original test drive during the centennial of the incorporation of Kokomo in 1965. (Courtesy of Howard County Historical Society, Kokomo, Indiana.)

been re-enacted several times in history. In May 1960, a re-enactment of the historic run was made by Jack A. Frost of Detroit in an 1897 Haynes-Apperson. On July 4, 1994, Howard County celebrated its sesquicentennial and re-enacted the historic drive on Pumpkinvine Pike 100 years earlier.

Then, on November 3, 1995, the Post Office issued a 32-cent stamp honoring the 1894 Haynes. The following year, the postmaster of the U.S. Postal Service in Kokomo presented a reproduction plaque to Congressman Steve Buyer on July Fourth, the anniversary date of the first ride in the automobile.

ANTIQUE AUTOMOBILES
1894 Haynes and 1898 Columbia

America's automotive pioneers were a unique group of risk-takers. Intrigued by the idea of transportation that did not depend on animals or rails, they tinkered and experimented continuously. They then set up companies to manufacture automobiles, and sold the idea of the motorized carriage to a skeptical American public.

One such businessman was Elwood P. Haynes (1857-1925). In 1893, Haynes purchased a single-cylinder two-stroke marine engine with the express purpose of using it in a car. Within a year, his automobile was ready for the road. It debuted July 4, 1894 in Kokomo, Indiana, traveling at six or seven miles per hour.

In 1898, Haynes joined with Edgar and Elmer Apperson to form the Haynes-Apperson Automobile Company. Their partnership was short-lived, lasting only until 1902. Haynes then struck out on his own. To help promote his new company, he donated his prototype 1894 car to the Smithsonian Institution in 1905. His claim that it was America's first gasoline-powered car was successfully refuted by Charles Duryea. It is, however, the oldest American car still in existence.

One of Haynes' most innovative contemporaries was M.I.T.-graduate Percy Maxim (1869-1936). The genius behind the Columbia automobile, he headed a successful auto manufacturing firm in Hartford, Connecticut. His inventive ideas included replacing the tiller with a steering wheel and moving the engine to the front, where it was mounted on springs. In 1896, Maxim oversaw development of the Columbia electric-powered car, of which 540 were produced in the first two years.

Columbias were America's top selling automobiles at the turn of the century. The company built 2,000 cars for use as taxicabs in major U.S. cities. A Columbia subsidiary, the Electric Vehicle Company, held the patent to the gasoline engine. By enforcing the patent, the company was able to collect royalties from most other car manufacturers.

The 32¢ U.S. stamps picturing the 1894 Haynes and 1898 Columbia were designed by Ken Dallison of Toronto, Ontario, Canada.

The 1894 Haynes was included in a series of stamps honoring antique automobiles that was issued on Nov. 3, 1995.

Reunions

Former members of the Haynes and Apperson Brothers Automobile Companies began holding yearly reunions in 1951. The first reunion brought together 509 former employees for the first time in many years, to remember the days when women screamed and horses bolted at the sight of a horseless carriage. Thirty-five of the vintage automobiles were on display at the first reunion. As the years passed, their numbers dwindled and by 1979 fewer than 100 former employees were still alive. The last picnic was held in 1998 when three former workers came to a picnic at Dale Etherington's home. Today, there may be none left.

Models

Although the Haynes-Apperson was one of the first vehicles in America, the car has never been die-cast. Companies like the Franklin Mint, Lilliput and Hot Wheels have ignored the car though the Franklin Mint did do a model for the 1896 Ford Quadricycle.

Avon came out with this glass model of the 1902 Haynes-Apperson. It carried after-shave lotion.

7

Elwood Haynes

By the time Elwood Haynes was born on October 14, 1857, in Portland, Indiana, the small town had fashioned a tannery, wagon-shop, blacksmith shop and an ashery (a shop where pearl-ash was made by leaching wood ashes). Elwood's roots went all the way back to the Massachusetts Bay Colony, where his relatives landed in 1698 from Wiltshire, England. His great-great grandfather fought in the Revolutionary War. His father, Jacob, was one of a dozen children fathered by Henry Haynes, who manufactured weapons during the War of 1812 in Massachusetts. Jacob decided on a legal career and headed west in 1843 to Indiana and opportunity. He married Hilinda Sophia Haines of Ohio. By the time Elwood was born, Jacob had already distinguished himself as the Jay County school commissioner and examiner, as well as being elected as the judge of the court of common pleas for Jay and Randolph counties.

Elwood, the fifth child of his family (the family grew to a dozen before his mother was finished delivering ten babies), was born during a turbulent time in American history. Tensions were rising to a fever pitch and soon turned to America's bloodiest war, the Civil War. Some of Elwood's earliest recollections involved Union soldiers gathering in Portland to go off to war. The Haynes family lived in a two-story frame house with only two rooms on each floor.

When Elwood was nine, the family moved to a new house in Portland, which was located on 35 acres of land. Elwood loved to search the woods around his log cabin in Portland for game with his bow and arrow. "Squirrels were so plentiful that at times they were hardly considered worth the ammunition required to kill them." When he wasn't roaming the woods, he was digging into books.

First Vehicle

His first experiments with a vehicle may have been when he was 12. He built it principally from parts of abandoned threshing machines. It was used on the nearby

Elwood Haynes in his childhood days. (Courtesy of the Haynes Museum.)

Judge Jacob Haynes, Elwood's father.

railroad and was propelled by hand. According to a letter by Frank, his brother: "This car seemed to arouse the ire of the section foreman, and he would pursue us with dire vengeance, but was unable to overtake us as Elwood had so constructed the car that the bearings were open and the frame light, so that we could easily take to the fields with the frame and axles where we could not be pursed. We made the mistake of running at night, and stopped on a bridge where the section crew was hiding. The car was destroyed and thrown in the creek. He made many mistakes and received many hurts."

Education

As a youth, Elwood also had a keen interest in old McGuffey readers as well as some serial stories from magazines. He took a particular liking to "Principles of Natural Philosophy." He also developed a passion for courses in chemistry and science, which led him to perform his first scientific experiments at the age of 14. He didn't possess any test tubes, so he developed a clay vessel with a cover instead. He then made a small furnace for heating to start experimenting. After he finished elementary school, he continued his education on his own, as no high school existed in Portland.

Then in 1876, the community opened a high school and Elwood went back to formal education at age 19. When he finished high school two years later, he — like many teenagers — still had no clear career path in mind. Because of his success in school, his parents enrolled him at Worcester County Free Institute of Industrial Science (later named Worcester Polytechnic Institute), Massachusetts.

Class Ode
by Elwood Haynes

Now Classmate's bonds must sever,
Perhaps, alas! forever:
Life's conflicts just before us,
Dark clouds seem hov'ring o'er us,
And we must march to meet life's foes,
Must feel and bear its hardest blows.

But there's no time for weeping,
An unseen eye is keeping
Guard, that naught shall befall us
In marching where He calls us.
To help us conquer all our foes,
And bravely bear life's hardest blows.

We'll gird hope's armor tighter,
Our hearts will all beat lighter.
There's music in the rattle
Of life's great storm battle,
And in our hearts we'll give three cheers,
And smiles will take the place of tears.

An early photo of Bertha Lanterman Haynes. (Courtesy of the Haynes Museum.)

Haynes worked hard at his studies in mathematics, science, language and drawing classes. "My occupation is a little monotonous," he wrote in a letter to his girlfriend, Bertha Lanterman. "Nothing but Study! Study! from one week's end to another." He entered Worcester badly handicapped because of back-wood schooling. Mathematics proved very difficult, but he pressed on doggedly. As a night custodian at the Worcester Free Public Library, he developed a tenacity of purpose without which his scientific discoveries would never have been perfected. The older-than-average student was popular with classmates and they elected him to president of the class. For recreation, he played football during the fall.

In his third and final year he studied metallurgy, ore analysis and assaying. "This school requires almost as much of its students in three years as is usually required in four," he wrote Bertha. He worked diligently on a research project that led him to the making of razors. His graduation thesis was titled "The effect of Tungsten on Iron and Steel." While the paper attracted no attention at the time, it laid down the germ idea of at least two important discoveries and laid down laws which became universally accepted by the world of science. At that time, nobody knew much about tungsten, iron or steel, but Elwood saw possibilities which had been overlooked. With eager enthusiasm, he began to experiment in making an improved steel through the introduction of elements other than carbon. This had resulted in the making of a steel which contained tungsten alloyed with iron in various proportions. He had also added chromium to the tungsten and iron alloys, making a combination of three metals. Out of this he made several razors, which appeared to demonstrate that at least he had a good idea if it were put to practical use. He graduated fourteenth in a class of twenty-one in 1881.

Elwood Haynes in his college days. (Courtesy of the Haynes Museum.)

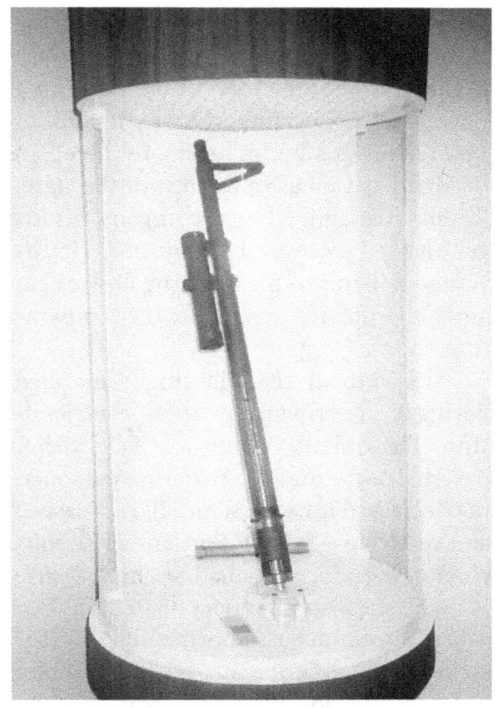

Haynes' discoveries in metal eventually led to weapons like this M-60 machine gun.

After graduation, it didn't take him long to find employment. He took on a teaching position in Jay County schools. The job paid just $1.35 a day, but he accepted, even though he had to walk five miles in the morning and evening the first week. Then he found a place within a mile and a half of the school house. It was a poor job for a brilliant young scientist though he soon took a liking to teaching. By 1883, he was named principal of Portland High School, though it was still more of a teaching position in those days. More importantly, it gave him an opportunity to teach science. Saving every cent of money he could, he attended Johns Hopkins University the following year, where he studied chemistry under Dr. Remsen and biology under Dr. Martin, both remarkable professors from whom the young scientist could learn more. Haynes learned new experimental techniques and valuable laboratory procedures that would help him in later years. He failed to finish his second term at the Baltimore institution because he left early when his mother passed away in May 1885. He became a science professor at the newly established Eastern Indiana Normal School in Portland. His wages were $1.40 a day.

The winds of change came in Elwood's life in 1886. His schooling had prepared him for it. The discovery of natural gas in Jay County interested him and he offered his services to drillers. They accepted. He analyzed soil samples in Findlay and Lima to help determine tables of the underlying strata. The teacher was beginning to become a businessman. Haynes delivered a public lecture on the subject of natural gas and oil, listened to with marked interest by a large audience, many of whom had made the subject of geology a study. Haynes computed the pressure of a well, estimated the number of stoves it would heat, then solicited the citizens of Portland to organize a company to pipe it to the city and use the gas in their homes. The Portland Natural Gas and Oil Company was soon organized. The stockholders in the company elected Jacob Haynes, his father, to the board of directors, who then elected Elwood as a superintendent by the fall of 1886. The "gas boom" soon followed in Portland as well as in the rest of the state. Besides managing the gas company, his ingenuity led to several inventions. He invented a meter to measure the flow of gas and a thermostat to regulate the temperature.

In October 1887, he finally married Bertha B. Lanterman after a ten-year friendship. The quiet wedding was held at her parents' home and the two honeymooned in Cincinnati for a weekend. Bertha served as a church organist in Portland. The couple soon produced their first child, Marie Firth Haynes, born January 28, 1889. When asked about his newborn child, he responded, "A mighty fine little girl! Lung pressure six pounds to the square inch, and I'm on my way to the office to get a regulator for it." However, the joy quickly turned to sorrow when the infant daughter died within six months, as did their second child, a son, born a year later. The Hayneses accepted the tragedies as the will of God and went on with their lives. As an elder of the First Presbyterian Church of Portland, Elwood was a highly religious man.

In the summer of 1890, Haynes accepted the challenge of constructing the nation's first long-distance, high-pressure natural gas pipeline from northern Indiana to Chicago. He and his wife moved to Greentown where he became a field superintendent for the Chicago company to oversee the drilling of new wells. He found that the pipeline carrying gas to Chicago would freeze up in the winter, so he decided to dry the gas to prevent the trouble. His ingenuity solved the problem. He worked long hours, and on the weekends, but he also enjoyed what he was doing.

One day a farmer with a strong German accent came into the office and asked him if it was time to drill a well on his land; calling his attention to the lease, he said, "Der party of der first part, dats de company, aind it? — agrees to drill a veil widin one year — dats tomorrow?" Haynes asked him for the lease and read the same passage he had quoted, but proceeded a little further in his quotation: The party of the first part agrees to drill a well within one year or thereafter. "Oh," said the old farmer, "or thereafter — that thereafter is quite a word, aind it?"

First Automobile

In December 1892, the Haynes moved to Kokomo when Elwood was named supervisor of the Kokomo branch of the Indiana Natural Gas & Oil Company. They moved into a home belonging to the gas company on North Washington Street. Days later Bertha gave birth to a daughter, Bernice, who would be the first to survive infancy.

In his new position, Elwood had more free time for other endeavors, such as a road vehicle to replace the horse, which he had begun to think about for several years. Then in the summer of 1893, he attended the Chicago World's Fair and came across the gasoline-powered Sintz engines. He decided then and there it would be the engine for his invention.

The $225 one-horsepower marine upright, 2-cycle, gasoline engine arrived along with Harry Kraft, a trouble shooter from Sintz. Haynes mounted the 180-pound engine on sawhorses in his kitchen, because he lacked anywhere else to experiment at the time. After cranking the engine several times, it finally started. However, it ran with such intense vibration that it pulled itself from its attachments. Fortunately, one of the battery wires was wound around the motor shaft and thus disconnected the current. The experiment tore up the kitchen floor, so to further test the engine, Haynes made arrangements with Elmer Apperson, who owned and operated the Riverside Machine Shop. It was agreed that work on the vehicle would be done after hours and that the Apperson brothers wouldn't be responsible for the outcome. He would pay them 40 cents an hour. Haynes drew up the plans for the vehicle and the Appersons, along with their workmen, built it. In order to provide against the vibration, he designed a frame of hollow steel tubing and used bicycle tires for its wheels. The weight of the machine would be over 800 pounds.

After months of work, the vehicle was ready for a test ride on July 4th. A big celebration was planned for the city and the Appersons let the public know about the test ride. When the vehicle — named the "Pioneer"— was rolled out that afternoon a crowd immediately gathered out of curiosity. "The moment it [the car] appeared, a crowd gathered as if by magic, forming a circle of not over twenty feet in circumference," the inventor explained. "I deemed it unwise to start the machine under these conditions as none of us had ever seen a machine of that sort, much less operated one. It was therefore attached to the rear of a horse carriage and hauled about three miles into the country, where a start was made on Pumpkinvine Pike." The motor started right away. Haynes took the driver's seat, while Elmer Apperson and Warren Wrightman rode. The new contraption coughed like a long-time smoker and moved along the road at around seven miles per hour, about as fast as a human jogging. After about 15 minutes of chugging along, Haynes stopped the vehicle and the men turned it around manually, since there was no reverse gear. Haynes decided to drive the vehicle all the way back to the machine shop. On the way back, he was convinced that there was a future for his horseless carriage. As the machine entered the town, it was greeted by a bevy of girls on bikes. They gazed wide-eyed in amazement of the vehicle which moved as fast as them. The Pioneer sputtered and quit as it came to a stop in front of the Riverside shop. After that, Haynes began driving his wife around at night when the streets were quiet.

While the test run of the Pioneer was a success, Haynes was not very satisfied with the results. He was unhappy with the steering, the engine and other things on his first design. It was back to the drawing board.

A 1901 Haynes-Apperson is now on display at the Auburn Cord Duesenberg Museum in Auburn, Indiana.

The steering was controlled with a vertical rod that had a horizontal handle attached to it, making it look like an L. The driver moved the stick forward to turn the vehicle to the right and back to turn left. It was awkward and dangerous. A muffler was also added to quiet the engine. The engine was too weak, so Haynes wrote the Sintz company for a better engine. He wanted them to lend him an engine, but he had to settle for trading in the old engine for a new two-horsepower model. The second engine proved to be too difficult, so he and Elmer Apperson decided to build their own engine for a second automobile model. To lighten the engine, Haynes introduced aluminum into the crankcase. The alloy for the crankcase was 93 percent aluminum and 7 percent copper.

Haynes-Apperson Company

Haynes and the Appersons agreed to incorporate the company in 1898. Elwood became one of the five directors in the corporation as well as its president. His brothers—Walter M. and Calvin—also purchased shares in the company. Elwood continued to work for the gas company, so he was a very busy man, but he still found time for his family, which had grown to four when his son, March, was born on January 3, 1896. As an elder in his church, Elwood usually attended services twice a week. During his leisure hours, he liked to read and formed the Gentlemen's Literary Club. He especially loved poetry and often committed numerous stanzas to memory. Singing was another of his many interests. The family drank Coca-Cola when it was new to the market, and oleomargarine was always on the table.

Elwood received permission from the gas company to turn a room over the kitchen into a laboratory to continue metallurgy experiments. The lights in his new laboratory flickered far into the night as he shaped the various metal combinations. In 1899, he succeeded in forming an alloy of pure chromium and pure nickel, which not only resisted all atmospheric influences, but was also insoluble in nitric acid of all strengths. Later that year he succeeded in forming an alloy of cobalt and chromium, and an alloy of the same metals containing a small quantity of boron. Those alloys were extremely hard, especially that containing boron.

In July 1899, Elwood decided to join Edgar Apperson in an important delivery. The two journeyed more than 1,000 miles to Brooklyn, New York, to deliver an auto to Dr. Ashley A. Webber, a physician. The leisurely trip took 21 days and only one problem occurred—a flat tire. "We have every reason to feel fully satisfied with the machine," Haynes told New York reporters. "The test was made solely to prove the durability of the carriage. Had we desired to make high speed we could have come through in half the time."

Around the turn of the century, Bernice Haynes convinced her father she was ready to drive one of his automobiles. He let her drive a two-cylinder runabout out to the country. She was eight. The next year she wanted to go farther and go it alone. Elwood finally gave her permission to drive around the block by herself. She did it a great many times and sometimes with other children from the neighborhood in the car. She would drive at the slowest speed. Driver's licenses had not yet been invented, but when they were, she reportedly became the first female licensed driver in the state in 1929—but the Indiana Bureau of Motor Vehicles couldn't verify that information. Driver's licenses did not exist in the state until 1929.

Top: Bernice Haynes learned to drive at an early age. (Courtesy of the Haynes Museum.) *Bottom:* The Haynes family, minus Elwood, goes out for a Sunday drive. (Courtesy of the Haynes Museum.)

Haynes Automotive Company

In late 1901, the Appersons decided to leave to form their own company. This moved forced Haynes to resign from the gas company so he could devote more time to the automobile company. With the Appersons gone, he began to make some changes to his models, making them more innovative. One of his innovations was a tilt steering wheel that allowed the driver and passenger easier access to the vehicle. He also took over writing advertisements for the company. In the ads, he featured technical improvements in the new models. He also teased readers for more by adding, "Watch this space for the good points of the Haynes-Apperson." The company wasn't renamed until 1905.

Haynes soon turned over the day-to-day operations of the automobile company to V.E. Minich, so he could concentrate on his experiments with metals. However, he continued to research problems with the automobile and wrote about the impurities in gasoline for the *Horseless Age* in 1906. The article, titled "Sulphur in Gasoline," examined the problem of clogged fuel lines and offered a solution to it. He also wrote an article in the same publication the following year tracing the development of new alloys for use in automobiles. He sedulously pursued lighter, sturdier metals for the automobile.

At the urging of his wife, he discovered a way to impart stainlessness to steel to be used for silverware. He was the first to apply for a patent on stainless steel in America. However, he allowed his patent to be assigned to the American Stainless Steel Company to manufacture and market stainless steel products. He then received royalties of most of the stainless steel produced in the United States for the 17-year life of the patent.

Another of his inventions has had even more far-reaching applications. His continued experiments with hard metals resulted in an alloy that he named "stellite." He first discovered the alloys while he was searching for suitable contact points on spark plugs. The original stellite was a combination of cobalt and chromium and was patented December 17, 1907, at a cost of $20. He continued modifying the metal to produce products for different industries. It was not until 1910 that he announced his discoveries to the scientific world at the American Chemical Society's San Francisco convention. He was a member of the society as well as the International Congress of Applied Chemistry and American Institute of Metals. At the convention, he read a paper titled "Alloys of Nickel and Cobalt with Chromium." The announcement helped to stir interest in the new metal. The chromium he developed was much more expensive than brass and nickel, so he didn't use it in his automobiles. Chrome wasn't used in cars extensively until the 1920s.

In April 1908, Haynes was invited to New York City to lead a parade of 2,000 cars down Broadway. Haynes was chosen to lead the evening parade because he was generally recognized at the time as the first American automobile inventor. The celebration was designed to commemorate the first decade of the automobile in New York. Elwood led the parade in his Pioneer followed by nine other Haynes automobiles, one for each year of the decade.

By 1910, the Haynes Automotive Company was turning out more than 1,000 autos. The company was on a pace to exceed that figure when a disastrous fire destroyed several buildings of the Haynes company in February 1911. An employee died in the blaze, but no completed cars were destroyed. Haynes again took an active role with the company to get it back on its feet until the company got back into full production in September. He even used his own money to purchase materials for 1,000 vehicles. Then he returned to his laboratory. To help out with his experiments on various alloys, he hired Harry Lanterman, his brother-in-law.

Haynes Stellite Company

In early September 1912, Haynes learned that his tool metal patents made with the stellite alloy had been allowed, so he purchased property near his automobile plant to start a new plant. He built a small cement block building and began to manufacture products commercially before the end of the year. The Haynes Stellite Company grew slowly — grossing only $7,000 in 1913, $11,000 in 1914 and $48,000 in 1915. Haynes was more interested in continuing experiments than turning a profit. The alloys he produced were valuable for use as cutting tools, well and mine drilling bits, bearing materials and hard facings for articles that had endured severe wear conditions. Then in October 1915, Haynes decided to incorporate the company with the help of two other gentlemen, Richard Ruddell, a Kokomo banker and industrial promoter, and James C. Patten, Ruddell's son-in-law and an aggressive businessman who took over the active management of the company. After that the company grew so quickly that a 10 percent dividend was being paid monthly. A new addition was made to the original building, new equipment was ordered and more employees were hired. Elwood also put his son March to work at the company to handle some of the finances. March would later become a bank director.

Caravan

Another one of Haynes' interests was improving roads in America to accommodate his automobiles. He accepted the chairmanship of a local Good Roads Committee in 1912. Then in 1913, the automotive leader made a last-minute decision to take a vacation from his business interests and travel to the west coast in a caravan to emphasize the need for road improvements. The caravan of twenty-two Indiana-built cars and two trucks, two of which belonged to the Haynes Company, left from Monument Circle in Indianapolis on July 1. Haynes was joined by C.A. Branston of London, England, Robert Crawford, advertising and publicity manager, and other company employees.

The caravan crossed eight states and endured temperatures ranging from below freezing to 115 degrees as they passed through plains, gorges, mountains, and deserts. They experienced blinding rains, tornadoes, floods and a burning sun. Automobiles encountered poor roads, knee-deep mud, steep mountain grades and treacherous mountain passes. The tour experienced some problems in Utah and Nevada, turning into more of an "endurance contest" for awhile until it could regroup in California and finish as one group in San Francisco.

After passing up Berthoud Pass leading to the summit of the Continental Divide, Haynes wired the factory: "I was enabled to observe our cars working on varying grades of five to twenty-five per cent, and was highly pleased to witness them vindicate their calculated power. The Six in which I rode weighted with its load to over 5,250 pounds, yet it was always able to maintain a speed of at least eleven miles per hour on the steepest grades under the worst conditions." Haynes sent telegrams each day during the trip to keep the factory appraised of the daily progress.

Some states actually constructed roads in preparation for the trip and the caravan was the first to use them. The governors of various states escorted the cars across their state. When the caravan arrived in San Francisco, it was greeted by banners streaming, horns blowing and huge automobile parades. A parade in San Francisco included a couple of hundred Haynes cars to mark the moment.

The trip turned out to be great publicity for Haynes and his company, and he turned out to be the star attraction. A reporter on the trip noted, " 'The Father of the Automobile,' as he is called, has addressed many audiences throughout the tour and his presence has added weight. His picture has appeared in almost every paper in every city through which the party has passed, and he has been honored as no other man on the trip." After the trip Haynes said, "The performance of Indiana machines was highly creditable, and I feel compelled to say in all sincerity that Indiana has established a great prestige in the minds of the people along this road regarding the character of its products. My cars have proved to the world that their efficiency is incomparable, that their construction is so sturdy that no passable roads, or continuation of difficult roads, will ever halt a Haynes. Never in automobile history, and I have kept close watch upon progress I assure you, have cars borne up so perfectly, so splendidly and with such absolute efficiency as have these two regular stock Haynes cars out of our factory. It seems as though automobile buyers need no further assurance from us that their Haynes cars can at a moment's notice master the worst roads with which it is in the power of Nature and man to endow any country in the world."

In 1914, Haynes let his customers know what the Haynes automobile meant to him. He wrote: "You see, the Haynes is not a commercial proposition with me — it is my contribution, as a man, to the great work of the world. It means to me what the phonograph meant to Edison; what the steamboat on the glorious Hudson meant to Robert Fulton; or what the first spasmodic tickings, coming over miles of wire, meant to Samuel Morse; what the first weird message of the human voice, coming from one end of a tin can and being heard at the other end of a line, meant to Alexander Bell; or what the majestic sweep of the soaring man-made machine meant to Wilbur Wright."

Prohibitionist

For a long time, Elwood Haynes supported prohibition. He took exception to fellow classmates drinking alcohol early in life. Haynes spoke to youths on the evils and dangers of drinking alcohol. He also had been a friend and supporter of J. Frank Hanly, who had been governor of the state from 1905 to 1909. Hanly became the presidential candidate for the Prohibition Party in 1916 and convinced Haynes to run for the Senate on the prohibition ticket. But Haynes would not wage a statewide campaign. He did support the party's fundraising efforts with thousands of dollars and loaned the party a new Haynes automobile, dubbed the "Prohibition Flyer." Haynes received fewer votes than the other Prohibition Party candidate and both were far behind the two major parties in the election. His political aspirations ended there, but he continued to support the party with donations. Indiana finally prohibited alcohol in 1918. After prohibition came to an end, Elwood became a Republican.

Elwood Haynes parks one of his automobiles at his mansion. (Courtesy of the Haynes Museum.)

The supporter of prohibition was named to a federal grand jury, which was to hear several prohibition cases, in December 1920. Haynes sat on the jury for three months. His role as a prohibitionist was best described years later in a speech by C.V. Haworth: "One of Elwood Haynes' outstanding characteristics was his strong convictions, and no matter whether his views met with popular favor or not, he was willing to accept leadership and shoulder the burden of any cause that he considered vital and important to the State and Nation. He felt it the duty of every citizen to participate in its public affairs, and when he was chosen to be the standard bearer of his party, he accepted that challenge and carried on a vigorous campaign in a dignified manner in accordance with good ethical procedure. Always an ardent advocate of prohibition, yet tolerant of the views of others, he worked to the end that it be brought through education. So highly was he respected by his fellow citizens, that when he was a candidate for high office, many citizens, regardless of party affiliations, supported him."

In 1916, he also bought a large property on Webster Street and built a three-story brick house with a full basement for his laboratory. The mansion would eventually become the Elwood Haynes Museum.

The following year the United States was drawn into the world war and demand for efficient machine tools to produce war materials increased tremendously. For example, the Lincoln Motor company ordered 300 pieces of stellite alloy so it could machine steel cylinders for Liberty Aeroplane engines. Machines equipped with stellite also turned out most of the shells used by American forces in World War I. Field hospitals were also equipped with scalpels made by the company. The Stellite Company sold more than $1 million worth of stellite in 1916, and by 1918 profits exceeded a million dollars. Haynes became a millionaire that year and his refusal to give substantial year-end bonuses to his workers resulted in alienating many of them. He reasoned that, "it doesn't pay to give the working man too much money — it makes him independent." The result was that Haynes paid the federal government a half million in taxes. Besides being a millionaire, Haynes was also a philanthropist. He gave money to the Presbyterian Church, the Worchester Polytechnic Institute and the Prohibition Party. He was also generous to struggling young churches of all denominations, small colleges and students needing assistance. Although the Haynes had lots of money, he continued to act like an ordinary citizen. He was friendly, went to church every Sunday, did chores around the house and had a keen sense of humor. He was never snobbish.

Another metal product that Haynes discovered was stainless steel, but he decided not to produce and market it like a fellow founder, Harry Brearley, in Great Britain. Brearley was the first to produce stainless steel cutlery on a modest basis and bring it to world attention. Instead Haynes allowed his discovery to be made by the American Stainless Steel Company. He was added to the board of directors in 1918, along with his son, March, and received an interest in the company.

After the war concluded, Haynes turned his attention from tools to making tableware, pocket knives and jewelry at the Stellite plant. Besides changing what the company produced, the ownership changed hands to Union Carbide on April 10, 1920. Haynes received some 25,000 shares of Union Carbide stock, worth about $2 million. He would make another half million in dividends before he died.

In 1919, Haynes was elected as president of the Young Men's Christian Association. He had helped establish the YMCA in Kokomo and had spoken to children on a regular basis for years. He agreed to another term in 1920 and held a successful membership drive. Then his company treated 175 boys to a swim, meal and movie on Thanksgiving Day.

Elwood left his cars behind in 1919, taking a ride in an Curtiss aeroplane to dedicate the new Haynes Aviation Field. The Army got involved because Haynes built the field for any Army aeroplanes that might wish to visit Kokomo. Lieutenant Henry Boonstra also took Vice President A.G. Sieberling on a ride. In 1919 Elwood headed one of committees to raise money for the Roosevelt Memorial Association, to raising $5 million for a monument in the former president's honor.

The following year the governor of Indiana appointed Haynes to the state board of education. He had been an advocate of education at all levels and the appointment gave him the opportunity to do something about it. He served on several committees and became the chairman of the committee on vocational training. Haynes also served on the board of trustees for two institutions: Western College for Women at Oxford, from which his daughter had graduated, and Taylor University.

In April 1920, Haynes decided to sell the Haynes Stellite Company to the Union Carbide Corporation, which became a major supplier of metal-cutting tools.

The postwar boom fizzled out and the automobile industry began to suffer in 1921, including the Haynes Automobile Company. The company got behind in its debts, so Haynes had to dip into his own money

Elwood Haynes rocks on his porch with his dog, Duke, at his mansion. (Courtesy of the Haynes Museum.)

and loaned the company $25,000 out of his own pocket to help out. Also during that year, Haynes was named to two boards: the Indiana Board of Education and the Indiana State Library Board. His special field was vocational education.

Perhaps in an effort to diversify, Elwood Haynes began a new company with the Hunt brothers called Hunt Porcelain, Inc. The company would manufacture everything in the way of porcelain insulation for electrical wiring and appliances. The company would also make spark-plug cores and eventually spark plugs. Elwood was the president, while his son, March, would help with the finances. J.F. Hunt was the secretary and general manager.

Besides education, Haynes was an advocate of the metric system and supported a move to have the United States adopt the system. He testified before the Senate on October 12, 1921, and even demonstrated the difficulty in not using metrics to determine cylinder volumes. "Ten times as many figures were needed with our present system," Haynes reported. The desired law never materialized.

Year of Award

The year 1922 was one of awards for Elwood Haynes. He received the prestigious John Scott Medal for his discoveries in stainless steel, stellite and other metals. The medal was the highest award given to a scientist of the United States. Indiana University also conferred an Honorary Doctor of Laws Degree on Haynes in recognition of his distinguished attainments and achievement. On July Fourth, the Haynes Monument was dedicated on Pumpkinvine Pike in an elaborate ceremony by the Indiana Historical commission and Hoosier State Automobile Association. A crowd of some 7,000 showed up to listen to the music of the local Chamber of Commerce and to watch both Battery A of the 150th Field Artillery Union of the National Guard firing a twenty-one gun salute and an airplane demonstration. Also at the ceremony was Haynes' first car, the Pioneer. The car was shipped by train from the Smithsonian for the special occasion. The ceremony was filmed by Pathé News and shown in theaters throughout the country. President Harding sent a message on June 23 that was read to the crowd: "My Dear Mr. Oliver: Your message telling me of the plans to celebrate the anniversary of the first successful operation of an automobile of American production has greatly interested me. It may be doubted if in all history of invention so striking a revolution has been effected in any department of human activity in so short a time as has come through the development of the automotive car. It is an anniversary well worthy of commemoration, and I am most appreciative of your invitation to participate."

While Haynes received some awards during the year, he also received a nasty letter from Charles E. Duryea, dated August 20, 1922, accusing him of "making statements about the first car you built which mislead the public and cause those who know the facts to believe you are intentionally misleading them." For years Haynes had advertised that he was the inventor of America's First Car because Duryea's car was nothing more than a motorized buggy. Both of their first cars sat side by side in the Smithsonian.

Duryea must have let bygones be bygones, as he sent Haynes another letter a few years later proposing that they start a company, together to build a rotary valve engine. He needed about $100,000 from Haynes to get the company going. Duryea would be content being second fiddle in the company as he proposed calling it the

A vast crowd of people came to see the dedication of the Haynes Monument on Pumpkinvine Pike on July 4th, 1922. The monument commemorates the first mechanically successful automobile. (Courtesy of the Haynes Museum.)

Top: **Thousands of automobiles carried the crowd of more than three thousand to the elaborate dedication ceremony. (Courtesy of the Haynes Museum.)** *Bottom:* **Elwood Haynes (right) along with his brother March and their wives came out to the dedication ceremony. (Courtesy of the Haynes Museum.)**

Haynes-Duryea Company. The letter came after the Haynes Automotive Company went bankrupt, so Haynes was in no position to help the other automotive founder. March Haynes replied to Duryea because his father was vacationing in Florida the month before Elwood's death. He referred him to Mr. William Robert Wilson who was trying to reorganize the Haynes Automotive company.

Top: Immediately following the dedication address, the American flag was hoisted to bring the ceremony to a climax. (Courtesy of the Haynes Museum.) *Bottom:* The Haynes Monument.

Haynes built this laboratory diagonally across from his mansion. The two were connected underground. Since then the tunnel has been filled in and the laboratory is now a home.

Haynes returned to his laboratory for awhile until his automotive company ran into further financial problems in 1923. He considered a merger with two other troubled automotive companies, Winton of Cleveland and Dorris of St. Louis. However, Winton delayed and the merger plans were abandoned. Haynes then had to turn to refinancing the company. He became the treasurer of the "Save the Haynes" effort, launched in 1923 to raise one million dollars for the company. The goal wasn't reached in 1923, but it was by the second day of January in 1924, and a gala was held to celebrate the moment. When speeches were requested by the crowd, Haynes responded: "Words are inadequate to express my fullness at the consummation of this greatest achievement. Nothing in reason is impossible in the community. You have demonstrated it. I thank you one and all from the bottom of my heart."

Financial woes continued, however, and Haynes had to dip into his own savings to rescue his automobile operations. He also called upon his brother, Calvin, to come back to Kokomo to help out in the crisis. The San Francisco resident, who had once acted as the general manager, declined. "I know my limitations better than anyone else," he reasoned.

More money was needed and times were getting desperate, so Haynes approached Henry Ford about a merger. Ford declined. In the final moments of the company, Haynes proposed a merger with the Apperson Brothers Company, which was also in deep financial trouble. The company declared bankruptcy in October 1924. Haynes was responsible for $94,774 in

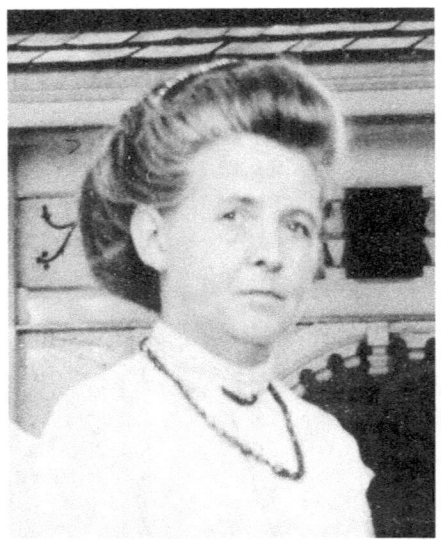

Bertha Lanterman Hayes. (Courtesy of the Haynes Museum.)

Elwood Haynes just before his death. (Courtesy of the Haynes Museum.)

company loans. He also lost some $60,000 in preferred stock and all of his common stock, valued in 1920 at $275,700. He also lost a substantial amount on the bonds he purchased in the bond drives of 1923 and 1924.

Gold Medal

On January 6, 1925, Haynes was honored with several other automobile founders with a gold medal at a New York City dinner, by the National Automobile Chamber of Commerce. Also on hand were two others who helped build Haynes' first car: Edgar Apperson and J.D. Maxwell. Others decorated at the dinner included R.E. Olds, A.L. Riker, John S. Clarke, Rolling H. White, H.H. Franklin, Charles E. Duryea, Charles B. King and Alexander Winton. The dinner was held in conjunction with the New York Automobile Show. Upon return from New York, Haynes was exhausted and came down with the flu.

Because of his sickness, he could not attend a committee meeting in January to erect a State Library, and he began missing many meetings.

In March, he received a letter from Purdue University saying that he had been placed on a committee to consider the "Relation of Chemistry to National Defense." He declined the offer, saying he could not serve on any committee "which contemplates a subject involving a hostile attitude toward the nations of the world." He said he wasn't a "pacifist," but he did say that he did not believe that world wars were necessary.

He decided to travel to Jacksonville, Florida, in March to enjoy some warmer weather and rest from his illness. His son, March, took care of his business interests. March lived three blocks away from the Haynes mansion, while his daughter, Bernice, lived a block away. His brother, S.W. Haynes, was part of a law firm, Haynes & Jenkins, in Portland, Indiana.

Elwood never recovered from the disease and died of congestive heart failure on April 13, 1925. DePauw University was poised to award him a degree, but his death came before they could bestow it.

Although he had lost hundreds of thousands during the demise of his automotive company, he left behind an estate still worth a lot of money. He had other substantial stock and bond holdings.

A year after Elwood died, his daughter gave birth to a son, whom she named Elwood after her father. However, her mother didn't like the name being said, so Elwood was given the nickname of "Bud." The same held true when Haynes' son named his son after the inventor. Elwood March Haynes earned the nickname of "Woody."

Bertha Haynes lived for another eight years after her husband died before passing in August 1933 at age 75 from a stroke. After she died, March Haynes moved from his home three blocks away and took ownership of the mansion. He later sold the home to General Motors and moved to California, where he died at age 72 in 1968.

8

Elmer Apperson

Elmer Apperson was the older of the two brothers and became the brains of the family business, while Edgar was more of the brawn. Elmer was born three miles southeast of Kokomo on August 13, 1861. He was the great-grandson of the famed Daniel Boone from Kentucky. His ancestors first came to America in 1668, and Dr. James Apperson settled in the county of New Kent, Virginia. His parents, Elbert Severe and Anna Eliza (Landon), were pioneer residents in that part of the county since the 1840s. He attended district schools in Taylor township, grade school in Kokomo and Normal school at Valparaiso. Early in life he exhibited a marked interest and extraordinary aptitude in mechanics. During his boyhood, he roamed the woods and hunted with his dog and gun.

After his formal schooling, Elmer became a machinist apprentice and worked briefly in the railroad shops in nearby Peru. He then went to work as a mechanic at the Star Machine Works. He also earned additional money during harvests by working as a machinist on threshing crews in the northwest.

In 1888, he decided to break out on his own and opened the Riverside Machine Works in Kokomo. A year later he relocated the business on the south side of town along Wildcat Creek. His brother, Edgar, soon joined him to help out, along with about a dozen other workers. The company worked on general repair of mechanical items for the farm and produced some items for lumbermen, including saw wedges, which were later patented.

Along came Elwood Haynes in the fall of 1893 to change the future of the business. Elmer was 31 and conservative, so he thought Haynes' project was a bit extravagant at first. He later warmed up to the fact and when the first test ride was made, he was one of the passengers in the car.

The first car had its problems though, so Elmer helped Haynes design a second, more powerful car that would be run in the first automobile race in America. The second automobile was powered by an Apperson designed 2-cylinder double opposed engine. After the race, Elmer decided to enter the business of automobile manufacturing. The trio built a third car, called the Trap, in 1896 and Elmer became the driver of the vehicle, which was featured by the Robinson and Franklin Circus. He drove the car around the Midwest and when he arrived at a baseball game in Evansville, he caused such a stir that the game was called after three innings.

The following year orders began coming in for more cars and work at the Riverside company turned more and more to automobiles. Then in 1898, the Haynes-Apperson Automobile Company incorporated and Elmer became the secretary. He was also a member on the board of directors and owned 29 percent of the company. In the factory, Elmer served as manager of the manufacturing operations.

In the summer of 1899, Elmer went to lunch with Mary Landon and told her, "I want you to drive the auto back after lunch." She became the first woman to drive a Haynes-Apperson automobile and she believed she was the first woman to drive a horseless carriage in the country.

Although Edgar was the racer in the family and for the business, Elmer sometimes drove cars as well in the endurance contests of the times. He finished second behind his brother in the New York to Buffalo Pan American Exposition race on October 10, 1901.

Later that month, Edgar decided to quit the company. Elmer told him, "Make drawings for a new and better car. I'll be along soon." By the end of the year, Elmer called it quits as well. Elmer suggested equal shares for the new company with his brother, but Edgar refused because Elmer was providing the capital. They settled on two-thirds for Elmer and one-third for Edgar, but later they became equal partners. While Edgar was usually involved in racing company cars for publicity, Elmer drove an Apperson to victory in a three-mile race in July 1903, in Marion, Indiana.

The company was making slow prog-

Elmer Apperson. (Courtesy of the Haynes Museum.)

ress the first few years until Elmer decided to adopt a jack rabbit as the name and logo for the company in 1906. The company built a racing model and the Jackrabbit soon became a popular car. In fact, the company adopted the name for the whole line of vehicles for a time. Then in 1917, he came up with the idea of naming the Appersons as Roadaplanes, but that model wasn't as embraced as much as the Jackrabbit.

The Appersons weren't big on applying for patents, but Elmer did have a patent approved on an electric ignition in 1908. The patent was later violated by several companies, and the Appersons threatened lawsuits before settling out of court with a couple of firms.

In 1917, Elmer suffered a mild stroke and decided to take it easy after that, but he still retained the title of president. However, he turned the active control of the company over to Edgar. He reflected in an interview: "As a boy, I was very proud and happy with Kokomo, the scene of all my youthful joys and sorrows. Later after traveling the country over during my manhood and visiting most of the important places, I found it impossible to find another community with exactly the same appeal as this city or ours."

Early in 1920, Elmer traveled to California to spend the winter and open a new building that would act as a factory branch for the company. He was attending a car race at the Beverly Hills Board Track on March 28, 1920, with his wife when he suffered a massive heart attack and within a few minutes he was dead. He was 58. The Republican and Presbyterian was married to Catharine Elizabeth Clancy of Chicago. She was his third wife. His first wife, whom he wed around 1895, passed away and he divorced his second wife, Olive Edwards. He had no children from either marriage.

A funeral was held in Kokomo for the automotive founder. Edwin M. Souder, editor of the *Kokomo Tribune*, spoke at the funeral: "The name Apperson has become a familiar one in many lands and is synonymous with good workmanship wherever motor cars are known." Burial was in Crown Point Cemetery and one of the pallbearers was Jonathan D. Maxwell, who had helped build the original Pioneer car. Besides his wife and brother Edgar, he left behind a brother, Oscar W. Apperson.

Beside the Apperson Brothers Company, Elmer served as a director of the Curtiss Indiana Company and the Kokomo Trust Company.

9

Edgar Apperson

Edgar Landon Apperson was born on October 3, 1869, in the same house as his brother. Like Elmer, he too was educated in the public schools. When he was not in school, his father would take him out hunting. His first rifle was made in 1811 and was used by his grandfather in the War of 1812. The first kill with that rifle was a squirrel that he shot through the body. His dad dressed him down for spoiling the meat. After that he shot game in the head.

While attending high school, he served an early apprenticeship in Elmer's Riverside Machine Shop. After his schooling was over, he began making and fixing bicycles at his own bicycle shop. He also worked for his brother. Then he met a lady, Laura Pentecost, and they were wed on April 12, 1892. They lived with Apperson's mother at first. Their marriage would later end in divorce. He provided quite adequately for his wife as he sold all he and his three men could make, but he was tired of the same limited problems. Then along came Elwood Haynes and changed all that. Edgar went from two wheels to four wheels and many more challenges that came with making a buggy run without a horse.

Because Elmer was so busy, he turned the Haynes automobile project over to Edgar to work on when he could. First, Edgar had to finish fixing some threshing machines before he could devote any time to the "horseless carriage." He had to work from some very rough ideas that Haynes had. He contributed much on the wheels, tires, axles and steering of the first car. He later claimed that he designed and built the car without much help from Elwood Haynes, but he was known to stretch the truth quite a bit, so exactly how much he contributed is up for speculation. Regardless, he did a lot and at odd times, because he worked on his bikes and other things in the shop during regular hours.

After eight months of work, Edgar and his brother finally finished the car on the night of July 3. Elwood wanted to take the car out the next day, although it was a holiday. The car was towed out of town and Edgar cranked the motor. After it started, Haynes got the first drive before Edgar got

Edgar Apperson. (Courtesy of the Haynes Museum.)

a chance to maneuver the four-wheeled motorized buggy. It ran without difficulty.

The engineer and builder was instrumental in producing the second car for Elwood Haynes. It was to run in a race in Chicago, but an unfortunate accident on the way to the starting line put the second car out of commission. Edgar wasn't in Chicago for the race; he was off buying a houseboat for him and his wife.

The following year, Edgar helped prepare a third vehicle, which was leased to the circus. Soon, orders for more cars were coming in and Edgar took on the responsibility for delivering them to owners. When more orders began coming in for their automobiles in 1897, Edgar quit his bicycle business. He spent much of the summer touring the Midwest and New England for P.C. Lewis, the first buyer of Haynes-Apperson cars. Lewis purchased three of them.

The year 1898 brought about incorporation for the company and Ed, as some called him, became the chief engineer and designer for the Haynes-Apperson Automobile Company. He continued to deliver what was built because owners had no idea how to drive or maintain the new vehicles, so he was much more than a delivery boy. If the order came from afar, the vehicles were usually shipped there by train. But Edgar delivered a car all the way to Saratoga Springs, New York, to the son-in-law of Commodore Cornelius Vanderbilt. He was put up in the mansion for two weeks while he taught Vanderbilt how to drive the car. "Each day I'd teach him to drive, but it was slow work," Edgar later told a writer. "Once he drove the car into its place in the carriage house, stepped on the throttle, yelled, 'Whoa!' and went through the rear wall. When I left he gave me a twenty-year gold pass, Pullman fares included, for myself and family on the New York Central System." When Edgar delivered a car, he would be responsible for picking up the remaining half owed on the car. The first half was paid when the vehicle was ordered.

Edgar was also often sent out when owners ran into trouble, because there were no local mechanics or repair shops in those days. One day he got a call from a department store in Fort Wayne that their car wouldn't start. Edgar traveled all the way to Fort Wayne to find out that the only problem with the car was that it had run out of gasoline. There were no gas stations in those days, either. Gas was sold at the local hardware or grocery store. He continued to help farmers with their threshing machines as well.

In 1899, he was assisted by Haynes for one important delivery. The two men decided to drive to Brooklyn, New York, to deliver a car to Dr. Ashley A. Webber. The trip would be the longest cross-country venture up to that time and span more than 750 miles. On their way to New York, they scared quite a few horses. In one instance, a startled horse pulling a wagon of girls jumped over a stone wall. The young ladies screamed in surprise, but the horse jumped back and proceeded down the road without any harm. On another occasion, they came across an Irish woman driving a load of vegetables to market. She called for them to stop and motioned wildly with her hands. She told them, "I would not have asked you to stop, sir, but the horse is blind, sir." They took great pains to explain that the horse had nothing to fear. When they passed, the horse paid no attention to the horseless machine.

The pair took their time getting to Brooklyn. The leisurely trip took 21 days, 10 of which were spent on the road. They experienced no engine trouble and only a flat tire. Ironically, Dr. Webber couldn't master the new contraption and later brought it back to the company.

When he wasn't delivering cars, Edgar drove in a number of races that helped publicize the company and their cars. In his first race, he drove the two-passenger high-speed model, which could master a top speed of 30 miles per hour, to victory at the Charles River track in Worcester, Massachusetts. The track was used for bicycle races and was just a third of a mile. "We didn't go so fast, but we made an awful lot of noise," Edgar said. He also drove to a perfect score in a 100-mile non-stop contest on Long Island, New York.

In April 1901, Edgar drove in the Long Island test run and won a blue ribbon. He covered the 100 miles without any problem, using five gallons of fuel. The four of them were splattered with mud as the wet weather made the road sloppy. Edgar also won the New York to Buffalo Pan American Exposition race, stopped before the scheduled end because of the assassination

Edgar Apperson drives a 1903 Apperson in front of the company with Clyde Spraker and two ladies in the back. (Courtesy of the Haynes Museum.)

of President McKinley. He had a perfect score and his brother finished second in a Haynes-Apperson as well. Later in the year, Edgar won a race in Detroit on October 10. He covered the 10-mile course in 17:43, for a speed of 34 miles per hour.

After he returned to Kokomo, Edgar decided to quit the company because he was only being paid $20 a week. He also had a difference of opinion on what cars the company should be building. He began making plans for a new and better automobile for a new company to be formed by him and his brother.

Although he was busy with the new company, he always had time for his favorite game — baseball. The 200-pound switch hitter played on the Kokomo Elks team. He once faced Hall of Famer Christie Mathewson of the New York Giants, who happened to be a Fort Wayne Elk. "When I went up in the last inning, Mathewson smoked two past me," he later related. "I was batting right-handed. I could place 'em better there, but I could hit 'em farther from the other side. No rule against it then, so I switched over. Mathewson smoked his third pitch in, and I laid it outside the park."

Edgar continued his racing ways to help promote their vehicles, which were considered the hot rods of the era. He won three consecutive hill climbs in Altadina, California, which led to him winning permanent possession as nobody would compete with him after that. His chief competitor at the time was famed race driver Barney Oldfield. Edgar performed the feat by designing an Apperson Jackrabbit fitted with a new carburetor, new cord tires and extra-strength axles. The developments allowed him to leap a wooden bridge at full speed while other drivers had to slow down.

Edgar built a race car that became known as the "Big Dick." He drove it to victory in Savannah, Georgia, among other races. Then he won the Pasadena Hill Climb two years in a row with the Apperson Jackrabbit. He used a French-type carburetor and a 5 × 5 four-cylinder engine. He decided to quit racing in 1912 after an Apperson crashed at the Indianapolis 500.

Besides racing, Edgar developed many practices that became common in automotive manufacturing. Yet, he took out only one patent during his lifetime. That came in 1907, when he was the first to use

Edgar Apperson drove one of his models in the Vanderbilt Cup Races in Chicago in 1904. (Courtesy of Howard County Historical Society, Kokomo, Indiana.)

a German magneto. Long after he retired, he was called as a witness in a patent suit.

But many times he never bothered to apply for a patent because he was so busy building cars to fuss with it. "It happened this way," he explained later in life. "When we built our early four-cylinder motors we worked on the principle that a curved manifold would give freest passage from carburetor to cylinders. The manifolds, of brass, bent beautifully. All car makers used them, but I discovered the middle cylinders were starved. That didn't seem reasonable, so I studied it and figured the passage to the end cylinders was too easy. I decided an almost square turn was needed. The in-rushing charge of gas would be slowed down and the two middle cylinders would have a chance to get their share. So I built a manifold along those lines and, by measuring the length of the exhaust flames—the only test we had in those days—found each cylinder was getting the same charge."

However, Edgar continued to run the cars around Kokomo, as he road tested all the cars that the company made up until 1915. To demonstrate the quality workmanship of the Apperson cars, he once laid an expensive Persian run in a showroom window, drove a car on it and ran the motor for days. Not a drop of oil fell on the rug. "My brother and I had one central, dominating thought—to make cars that were mechanically perfect," he said in the 1914 catalog. Edgar strived for perfection, but in those days perfection was tough to achieve because of the lack of technology.

Once he was driving five miles an

Edgar Apperson owned this home in Kokomo before moving to Arizona. (Courtesy of Howard County Historical Society, Kokomo, Indiana.)

hour in downtown Salt Lake City, Utah, when he was stopped for speeding. He pleaded guilty and paid a $10 fine. He later said it "was damn fine advertising."

In 1916, he visited Thomas C. McReynolds, Sr., in Phoenix. McReynolds was a boyhood friend who helped finance the Apperson Brothers Company. Edgar made a second visit a year later. He liked the area so much that he bought some property there for his retirement years, which would come sooner than he probably thought.

Elmer suffered a stroke in 1917, so Edgar took over effective control of the company and became the general manager. When the Press Club of Indiana honored the Appersons, Edgar had to accept the award of a bronze tablet for his sick brother. The tablet said they were being honored for "their achievement in building the first practical commercially successful American automobile." The Presbyterian and Republican also served as a bank director for the Howard National Bank.

In 1918, Edgar began work on the Anniversary Model to celebrate 25 years in automotive production. The model employed a V-type fan belt and pulley for the first time. He also came up with a gearshift on top of the steering wheel instead of on the floor.

When Elmer died in March 1920, while watching a car race in Los Angeles, Edgar to took over as president. He also married Inez Apperson from Vermont that year. She was eight years younger than him.

Severe financial problems beset the company in 1922. The following year Don P. McCord was elected as the new president and "Brothers" was dropped from the name. Edgar stepped down to second vice-president. A year later, Edgar decided to sell his share in the company and retire from the automotive business all together. He certainly left the struggling company at

Inez Apperson. (Courtesy of the Haynes Museum.)

the right time. A year later the Apperson Company went bankrupt and gave way to the Pioneer Automobile Company.

Edgar left for Wisconsin to live there and spend more time hunting and fishing with his second wife and foster son, Gilbert Alvord. In 1932, they moved to Arizona. He invested in farm lands in the Salt River Valley near Phoenix. He spent winters in Arizona and traveled to Wyoming or Wisconsin during the hot summer months. He was also an honorary member of the Horseless Carriage Club, Valley of the Sun region.

In 1942, his wife died. During World War II, Edgar once helped out a South Phoenix machine shop owner who was overwhelmed with work after his workers all left for the war effort. Edgar ran a lathe for three weeks just for the fun of it.

On May 31, 1946, Edgar was one of the first to be installed into the auto industry's Hall of Fame in Detroit. Also selected at the ceremony were W.C. Durant, J. Frank Duryea, Henry Ford, George Holley, Frank Kwilinski, Charles B. King, Charles W. Nash, Barney Oldfield, Ransom E. Olds, John Van Bensenoten, Alred P. Sloan Jr., Charles Synder and John Zaugg. He was also honored with the highly prized Charles Clifton Award for his pioneering work in the automotive field.

At 86, he returned to Kokomo for the ribbon cutting of a street named in his honor: Apperson Way.

Top: Edgar Apperson in his later years at his log cabin in Montana. (Courtesy of the Haynes Museum.) *Bottom:* Edgar Apperson cuts the ribbon to Apperson Way in Kokomo on Oct. 15, 1955. (Courtesy of Howard County Historical Society, Kokomo, Indiana.)

Ironically, Apperson Way begins across the street from the old Haynes plant.

Edgar Apperson chats with Mary Landon, who used to work for him, during the dedication of Apperson Way. (Courtesy of Howard County Historical Society, Kokomo, Indiana.)

Edgar Apperson (center) receives congratulations during the dedication of Apperson Way. (Courtesy of Howard County Historical Society, Kokomo, Indiana.)

On Oct. 22, 1955, the dedication ceremonies were held in front of American Legion Post 6. He told a reporter then: "The highway slaughter today makes me doubtful of my contribution. I cringe every time I pick up a newspaper and read about highway accidents. It will never be stopped until manufacturers govern autos so they can't move faster than 50 miles per hour."

A couple of years later a newspaper reporter in Phoenix interviewed him and asked him about the first car. "It was a far cry from the mechanical miracles of today, but it ran," he said. "It will run yet."

He died at age 89, on May 12, 1959, in a Phoenix rest home. He chose to be cremated. His only survivor was his foster son, Gilbert E. Alvord, a Salt River Valley rancher.

Appendix I

Haynes-Apperson Models

One-Cylinder

Trap, 4 passenger, 1,500 lbs, $1,000

Two-cylinder, 7/8 hp

Carriage, 2 passenger, $1,250
Carriage, 4 passenger, $1,500
Carriage, 6-8 passenger, $1,800

Two-cylinder, 7/8 hp

Business Wagon, 2 passenger, $1,000
Pleasure Carriage, 2 passenger, $1,250
Doctor's Carriage, $1,250
Carriage, 4 passenger, $1,500
Carriage, 6 passenger, $1,600
Carriage with trailer, 10-15 passenger, $1,800
Delivery Wagon, $1,800

Model A, Surrey, 9 hp, 4 passenger, $1,800

Model B, Phaeton, 9 hp, 2 passenger, 2,100 lbs, $1,500

Model C, Runabout, 6 hp, 2 passenger, 1,250 lbs, $1,200

Model F, Tonneau, 5 passenger, Four-cylinder, 93" wb, $2,450

Model G, Surrey, 9 hp, 4 passenger, 2,100 lbs, $1,800

Model H, Phaeton, 12 hp, 2 passenger, 1,900 lbs, $1,500

Model I, Runabout, 6 hp, 2 passenger, 1,300 lbs, $1,200

Model J, Light Touring Car, Two-cylinder, 2 passenger, 12 hp, 76" wb, $1,400

Appendix II

Apperson Models

Model A

Years produced: 1902-07
Engine: 2 and 4 cylinder
Horsepower: 16, 25, 40, 50/55
Wheelbase: 102", 114", 115", 116"
Body styles:
    Touring, 4 passenger, $2,500
    Touring, 6-passenger, $3,500
    Touring, 7-passenger, $4,150-5,000
    Special Touring, 7 passenger, $5,500
    Touring, 7 passenger, $4,000
    Chassis, 5 passenger, $3,500
    Chassis, 7 passenger, $4,250
    Chassis, 7 passenger, with full extension top, $4,700
    "Kimball" Limousine, $6,200
    Runabout, $4,500
    Jackrabbit Cup Racer, (60 hp., 100" wb), $5,000

Model B

Years produced: 1904-07
Engine: 2 and 4 cylinder
Horsepower: 24, 40/45
Wheelbase: 102", 112", 114"
Body Style:
    Touring, 4 passenger, $3,500
    Touring, 5 passenger, $3,500
    Touring, 7 passenger, $4,500
    Touring, 5 passenger, 3,800 lbs, $3,800
    Touring, 7 passenger, 4,200 lbs, $4,200
    "Kimball" Limousine, $5,600
    Runabout, light chassis, $3,800

Special Model

Years produced: 1905
Engine: 4 cylinder
Horsepower: 50
Wheelbase: 114"
Body Styles:
    Touring, 7 passenger, $5,150
    Limousine, 7 passenger, $6,500

Racing Model

Years produced: 1907
Engine: 4 cylinder
Horsepower: 96
Wheelbase: 110"
Body Style:
    Jackrabbit "Big Dick" racer, 2 passenger, $15,000

Model C

Years produced: 1906
Engine: 4 cylinder
Horsepower: 30/35
Wheelbase: 104"
Body Style:
    Special Touring, 7 passenger
Price: $5,500

Model I

Years produced: 1909
Engine: 4 cylinder
Horsepower: 35/40
Wheelbase: 128"
Body Styles:
    Touring, 5 passenger, $3,900
    Runabout, 3/4 passenger, $3,900

Model J-R

Years produced: 1908
Engine:
Horsepower: 50-55
Wheelbase:
Body Styles:
    Touring
Price:

Model K

Years produced: 1908
Engine: 4 cylinder
Horsepower: 50-55, 60
Wheelbase: 105", 114", 116"
Body Styles:
    Touring, 7 Passenger, $4,200
    Runabout, $4,000, $5,000
    Jackrabbit, $5,000
    Touring, 7 passenger (123" wb), $4,200
    Tonneau, $4,000
    Roadster, $4,250

Model M

Years produced: 1908-09
Engine: 4 cylinder
Horsepower: 30/35/40
Wheelbase: 106 1/2", 119"
Body Styles:
    Touring, 5 passenger, $3,350
    Roadster, 2/3 passenger, $3,000
    Roadster, 4 passenger, $2,750

Model O

Years produced: 1909-10
Engine: 4 cylinder
Horsepower: 30-35
Wheelbase: 119"
Body Styles:
    Touring, 5 passenger, $2,400
    Runabout, 3 passenger, $2,250
    Roadster, 4 passenger, $2,250
    Baby Tonneau, 5 passenger, $2,450

Model S

Years produced: 1909-10
Engine: 6 cylinder
Horsepower: 50/55
Wheelbase: 114"
Body Styles:
    Touring, 7 passenger, $5,000
    Runabout, 3 passenger, $5,000

Model 4-30

Years produced: 1910-11
Engine: 4 cylinder
Horsepower: 30, 32.4
Wheelbase: 114", 119"
Body Styles:
    Baby Tonneau, $2,100
    Jackrabbit Touring, 5 passenger, $2,000
    Jackrabbit Fore-Door Touring, $2,250

Model 4-40

Years produced: 1910-11, 15
Engine: 4 cylinder
Horsepower: 40

Bore & Stroke: 4 × 5
Wheelbase: 122"
Weight: 2,760 lbs
Serial Numbers: 8500-9000
Body Styles:
    5-passenger Touring
Price: $3,000 (1910), $4,200 (1911), $1,350 (1915)

Model 4-45 Light

Years produced: 1914-15
Engine: 4 cylinder
Horsepower: 32.40
Bore & Stroke: 4½ × 5
Serial Numbers: 5500-8000
Body Styles:
    Jackrabbit Touring, 5 passenger, 2,830 lbs, $1,600 (1914); 3,200 lbs, $1,685 (1915)
    Jackrabbit Roadster, 3,100 lbs, $1,750 (1915), $1,685 (1916)
    Jackrabbit Coupe, 4 passenger, 3,700 lbs, $2,100 (1915), $2,350 (1916)
    Jackrabbit Town Car, 4 passenger, $2,250
    Turtle-Back Roadster, 2 passenger, 3,510 lbs, $1,600
    Sedan Limousine, 5 passenger, 3,648 lbs, $2,500

Model 4-50

Years produced: 1910-11
Engine: 4 cylinder
Horsepower: 50
Wheelbase: 128"
Body Styles:
    Touring, 7 passenger
Price: $4,200

Model 4-55

Years produced: 1912-13
Engine: 4 cylinder
Horsepower: 55
Wheelbase: 118", 122"

Styles:
    Jackrabbit Touring, 5 passenger, $2,000
    Jackrabbit Special Touring, 7 passenger, $3,000
    Fourdore Touring

Model 4-65

Years produced: 1913
Engine: 4 cylinder
Horsepower: 65
Wheelbase: 128"
Styles:
    Jackrabbit "De Luxe" Touring, 7 passenger, $4,200

Model 6-40

Years produced: 1910
Engine: 6 cylinder
Horsepower: 40
Wheelbase: 128"
Body Styles:
    Touring, 7 passenger
Price: $4,200

Model 6R

Years produced: 1913
Engine: 6 cylinder
Horsepower: 60
Shipping weight: 2,000
Body Styles:
    Roadster
Price:

Model 6-45

Years produced: 1914-15
Engine: 6 cylinder
Bore & Stroke: 3¾ × 5
Horsepower: 29.40
Wheelbase: 128"
Serial Numbers: 6300 to 6400, 10000 to 12000
Body Styles:
    Touring, 5 passenger, 3,430 lbs, $2,200 (1914); 3,000 lbs, $1,485 (1915)

Touring, 7 passenger, 3,530 lbs, $2,300
Roadster, 2 passenger, 3,300 lbs, $2,200

Model 6-55

Years produced: 1914
Engine: 6 cylinder
Horsepower: 43
Wheelbase: 128"
    Touring, 5 passenger, $2,350
    Roadster, 2 passenger, $2,350

Model 6-60

Years produced: 1915
Engine: 6 cylinder
Bore & Stroke: 4¼ × 5
Horsepower: 32.40
Serial Numbers: 8000-8500
Styles:
    Roadster, 3,300 lbs, $2,200
    Touring, 5 passenger, 3,400 lbs, $2,200
    Touring, 7 passenger, 3,500 lbs, $2,350

Model 6-16

Years produced: 1916
Engine: 6 cylinder
Bore & Stroke: 3½ × 5
Horsepower: 29.40
Wheelbase: 128"
Serial Numbers: 15000 to 17000
Body Styles:
    Light Six Touring, 7 passenger, 3,150 lbs, $1,550
    Light Six Touring, 5 passenger, 3,100 lbs, $1,485
    Light Six Roadster, 4 passenger, 3,050 lbs, $1,550

Model 8-16

Years produced: 1916
Engine: 8 cylinder
Bore & Stroke: 3⅛ × 5
Horsepower: 31.25
Shipping Weight: See below
Serial Numbers: 12000 to 13000
Body Styles:
    Light Eight Touring, three or four door, 7 passenger, 3,200 lbs, $1,850
    Light Eight "Chummy" Roadster, 4 passenger, 3,200 lbs, $1,850
    "Speed Boy" Roadster, 4 passenger, 3,150 lbs, $2,000

Model 6-17-4

Years produced: 1917
Engine: 6 cylinder
Bore & Stroke: 3½ × 5
Horsepower: 29.40
Wheelbase: 130"
Shipping Weight: 3,100
Serial Numbers: 15000 to 17000
Body Style:
    Roadaplane Chummy Roadster, 4 passenger, 3,100 lbs, $1,750

Model 6-17-5

Years produced: 1917
Engine: 6 cylinder
Bore & Stroke: 3½ × 5
Horsepower: 29.40
Wheelbase: 130"
Shipping Weight: 3,200
Serial Numbers: 15000 to 17000
Body Styles:
    Beverly Light, 5 passenger, $1,690

Model 6-17-7

Years produced: 1917
Engine: 6 cylinder
Bore & Stroke: 3½ × 5
Horsepower: 29.40
Wheelbase: 130"
Shipping Weight: 3,250
Serial Numbers: 15000 to 17000
Body Styles:
    Roadaplane Touring, 7 passenger, 3,200 lbs, $1,750

Model 8-17-4

Years produced: 1917
Engine: 8 cylinder
Bore & Stroke: 3½ × 5
Horsepower: 29.40
Wheelbase: 130"
Shipping Weight: 3,140
Serial Numbers: 13000 to 15000
Body Styles:
    Roadaplane Chummy Roadster, 4 passenger, $2,000

Model 8-17-7

Years produced: 1917
Engine: 8 cylinder
Bore & Stroke: 3¼ × 5
Horsepower: 33.80
Wheelbase: 130"
Shipping Weight: 3,140
Serial Numbers: 13000 to 15000
Body Styles:
    Roadaplane Chummy Roadster, 4 passenger, $2,000

Model 8-17-8

Years produced: 1917
Engine: 8 cylinder
Bore & Stroke: 3¼ × 5
Horsepower: 33.80
Wheelbase: 130"
Shipping Weight: 3,290
Serial Numbers: 13000 to 15000
Body Styles:
    7-passenger Touring
Price: $2,000

Model 6-18-4

Years produced: 1918
Engine: 6 cylinder
Bore & Stroke: 3½ × 5
Horsepower: 29.40
Wheelbase: 130"
Serial Numbers: 15000 to 17000
Body Styles:
    Chummy Roadster, 4 passenger, 3,000 lbs, $1,990
    Touring, 7 passenger, 3,250 lbs, $1,990

Model 8-18

Years produced: 1918
Engine: 8 cylinder
Bore & Stroke: 3¼ × 5
Horsepower: 33.80
Wheelbase: 130"
Serial Numbers: 18000 to 19000
Body Styles:
    Chummy Roadster, 4 Passenger, 3,150 lbs, $2,550
    Touring, 7 passenger, 3,400 lbs, $2,550
    Silver Special Touring, 3,469 lbs, $3,500
    Sedan, 7 passenger, 3,600 lbs, $2,550

Model 8-19

Years produced: 1919
Engine: 8 cylinder
Bore & Stroke: 3¼ × 5
Horsepower: 33.80
Wheelbase: 130"
Serial Numbers: 19000 to 20000
Body Styles:
    Tourister, 4 passenger, 3,400 lbs, $4,000
    Anniversary Touring, 7 passenger, 3,460 lbs, $4,000
    Roadster, 4 passenger, 3,150 lbs
    Sedan, 7 passenger, 3,600 lbs, $2,550

Model 8-20

Years produced: 1920
Engine: 8 cylinder
Bore & Stroke: 3¼ × 5
Horsepower: 33.80
Wheelbase: 130"
Serial Numbers: 20000 to 21700
Body Styles:
    Touring, 7 passenger, 3,810 lbs, $2,950

Sportster, 4 passenger, 3,555 lbs, $2,950
Ace, 2 passenger, 3,290 lbs, $2,950
Sedan, 7 passenger, 4,020 lbs, $4,000
Sedanet, 4 passenger, 3,925 lbs, $4,000
Coupe, 4 passenger, 3,850 lbs, $4,000
Berlin, 7 passenger, 4,100 lbs, $4,000

Anniversary Model

Years produced: 1920-22
Engine: 8 cylinder
Bore & Stroke: 3¼ × 5
Horsepower: 33.80
Wheelbase: 130"
Shipping Weight: See below
Serial Numbers: 20000 to 21700
Body Styles:
    Touring, 7 passenger, 3,810 lbs, $4,000
    Tourister, 4 passenger, 3,750 lbs, $4,000
    Sedan, 7 passenger, 4,225 lbs, $5,500
    Cabriolet, 4 passenger, 3,880 lbs, $5,500
    Coupe, 4 passenger, 3,975 lbs, $5,500

Model 8-21

Years produced: 1921
Engine: 8 cylinder
Bore & Stroke: 3¼ × 5
Horsepower: 33.80
Wheelbase: 130"
Serial Numbers: 21700 and up
Body Styles:
    Open Sportster, 4 passenger, 3,550 lbs, $3,500
    Open Touring, 7 passenger, $3,500
    Anniversary Touring, 7 passenger, 3,810 lbs, $4,250
    Anniversary Tourister, 4 passenger, 3,750 lbs, $4,250
    Sedanet, 4 passenger, 3,925 lbs, $4,500
    Ace, 2 passenger, 3,290 lbs
    Sedan, 7 passenger, 4,020 lbs
    Coupe, 4 passenger, 3,850 lbs

Beverly Model

Years produced: 1922
Engine: 8 cylinder
Bore & Stroke: 3¼ × 5
Horsepower: 33.80
Wheelbase: 130"
Serial Numbers: 24000 and up
Body Styles:
    Sportster, 4 passenger, 3,550 lbs, $2,620
    Touring, 7 passenger, 3,600 lbs, $2,645
    Tourister, 4 passenger, 3,500 lbs, $2,995
    Sedanet, 4 passenger, 3,900 lbs, $3,895
    Sedan, 7 passenger, 4,000 lbs, $3,995
    Limousine Sedan, 7 passenger, 4,100 lbs, $4,195
    Sportster Tourequipt, 4 passenger, 3,600 lbs, $2,995
    Tourister Tourequipt, 4 passenger, 3,600 lbs, $3,245

Model 6-23

Years produced: 1923
Engine: 6 cylinder
Bore & Stroke: 3¼ × 5
Horsepower: 33.40
Wheelbase: 120"
Serial Numbers: 1000 and up
Body Styles:
    Tourister, 5 passenger, 2,885 lbs, $2,645
    Sedan, 5 passenger, 3,250 lbs

Model 8-23S

Years produced: 1923
Engine: 8 cylinder
Bore & Stroke: 3¼ × 5
Horsepower: 33.80
Wheelbase: 130"
Serial Numbers: 30000 and up
Body Styles:
    Phaeton, 5 passenger, 4,050 lbs, $2,485
    Phaeton, 7 passenger, 4,300 lbs, $2,485
    Touring Sedan, 7 passenger, 4,500 lbs, $3,625
    Sedan, 5 passenger, 4,380 lbs, $3,695

Model 6-24

Years produced: 1924
Engine: 6 cylinder

Wheelbase: 120"
Body Styles:
    Phaeton, 5 passenger, 4,050 lbs, $2,485
    Phaeton, 7 passenger, 4,300 lbs, $2,485
    Touring Sedan, 7 passenger, 4,500 lbs, $3,625
    Sedan, 5 passenger, 4,380 lbs, $3,695

Model 8-24

Years produced: 1924
Engine: V-8
Horsepower: 70 hp
Wheelbase: 130" wb
Body Styles:
    Phaeton, 5 passenger, $2,485
    Phaeton, 7 passenger, $2,485
    Sedan, 5 passenger, $3,385
    Sedan, 7 passenger, $3,585

Model 6-25

Years produced: 1925
Engine: 6 cylinder
Wheelbase: 120"
Body Styles:
    Sport Phaeton, 5 passenger, $1,650
    Coupe, 2 passenger, $2,050
    Sedan, 5 passenger, $2,095
    Sport Sedan, 5 passenger, $2,100

Model 8-25

Years produced: 1925
Engine: Straightaway Eight
Body Styles:
    Sport Phaeton, 5 passenger, $2,485
    Coupe, 2 passenger, $2,450
    Four-Door Brougham, $2,800
    Sedan, 5 passenger, $2,850
    Phaeton, 5 passenger, $2,485
    Sport Phaeton, 5 passenger, $2,800
    Phaeton, 7 passenger, $2,535
    Sport Phaeton, 7 passenger, $2,900
    Sedan, 5 passenger, $3,485
    Sport Sedan, 5 passenger, $3,750
    Sedan, 7 passenger, $3,585
    Sport Sedan, 7 passenger, $3,850

Model Six

Years produced: 1926
Engine: 6 cylinder
Horsepower: 46 hp
Wheelbase: 120"
Body Styles:
    Phaeton, 5 passenger, $1,575
    Sport Phaeton, 5 passenger, $1,650
    Coupe, 4 passenger, $2,050
    Brougham, 5 passenger, $2,050
    Sedan, 5 passenger, $2,100

Model Eight

Years produced: 1926
Engine: 8 cylinder
Horsepower: 65 hp
Wheelbase: 130"
Body Styles:
    Phaeton, 5 passenger, $1995
    Brougham, 5 passenger, $2,450
    Coupe, 5 passenger, $2,450
    Sedan, 5 passenger, $2,595

Appendix III

Haynes Models

Model K, 4 cyl., 35/40 hp, 108" wb
King of Belgium Touring, $3,000

Model L, 2 cyl., 16/18 hp, 82" wb
Stanhope, 2-passenger, $1,350

Model M, 2 cyl., 16/18 hp, 82" wb
Light Tonneau, 4-passenger, $1,500
Tonneau, 5-passenger, $1,800

Model O, 4 cyl., 30/35 hp, 97" wb
Touring, 5 passenger, $2,250
Runabout, 2 passenger, $2,250

Model R, 4 cyl., 45/50 hp, 108" wb
Touring, 5 passenger, 2,750 lbs, $3,500

Model S, 4 cyl., 30 hp, 103" wb
Runabout, 2 passenger, $2,400
Touring, 5 passenger, $2,500
Limousine, 5 passenger, $3,500

Model T, 4 cyl., 50 hp, 108" wb
Touring, 7 passenger, $3,500
Limousine, 7 passenger, $4,500

Model U, 4 cyl., 60 hp, 118" wb
Touring, 7 passenger, $3,750
Roadster, 2 passenger, $3,750
Limousine, $4,750

Model V, 4 cy., 50 hp, 106" wb
Vanderbilt Speedster, $3,500

Model W, 4 cyl., 45 hp, 108" wb
Touring, 5 passenger, 2,400 lbs, $3,000

Series X, 4 cyl., 36 hp, 112" wb
Touring, 5-7 passenger, $3,000
X1 Runabout, 3 passenger, $2,900
X2 Baby Tonneau, 4 passenger, $3,000
X3 Double-seated Roadster, 4 passenger, $3,000
X4 Hiker, 2 passenger, $2,900

Model Y, 4 cyl., 40 hp, 125" wb
Touring, 7 passenger, $3,000
Close-Coupled Touring, $3,000
Newport Limousine, $3,800
Berlin Limousine, $3,900

Model 19, 4 cyl., 36 hp, 110 1/2" wb
Touring, 5 passenger, $2,000
Runabout, 3 passenger, $2,000

Model 20, 4 cyl., 28 hp, 114" wb
Suburban, 4 passenger, $2,100
Touring, 5 passenger, $2,000
Fore-Door Touring, $2,100
Roadster, 2 passenger, $2,000

Speedster, $1,650
Open Touring, $1,650

Model 21, 4 cyl., 40 hp, 120" wb
Touring, $2,100
Close-Coupled Touring, $2,100
Coupe, $2,450
Limousine, $2,750

Model 22, 4 cyl., 40 hp, 120" wb
Touring, 4-5 passenger, $2,250
Roadster, $2,250
Coupe, $2,750
Limousine, 7 passenger, $3,400
Berlin Limousine, 7 passenger, $3,500

Model 23, 6 cyl., 50 hp, 130" wb
Touring, 5 passenger, $2,500

Model 24, 4 cyl., 35 hp, 118" wb
Touring, 5 passenger, $1,785

Model 26, 6 cyl., 50 hp, 130" hp
Touring, 4 passenger, $2,700
Roadster, 2 passenger, $2,700
Touring, 5 passenger, $2,700
Coupe, 4 passenger, $2,700

Model 27, 6 cyl., 50 hp, 136" wb
Touring, 6-7 passenger, $2,785
Limousine, 7 passenger, $3,850

Model 28, 4 cyl., 35 hp, 118" wb
Touring, 4-5 passenger, $1,985
Roadster, 2 passenger, $1,985
Coupe, 4 passenger, $2,700

Model 30, 6 cyl., 55 hp, 121" wb
Light Six Touring, 5 passenger, $1,485
Roadster, 2 passenger, $1,485
Touring, 7 passenger, $1,550
Cabriolet, 3 passenger, $1,750

Model 31, 6 cyl., 65 hp, 121" wb
Touring, $2,250
Coupe, $3,000

Model 32, 6 cyl., 48 hp, 121" wb
Touring, $1,660
Coupe, $2,500

Model 34, 6 cyl., 55 hp, 121" wb
Roadster, 3 passenger, $1,485
Light Six Touring, 5 passenger, $1,385

Model 35, 6 cyl., 55 hp, 127" wb
Kokomo Six Touring, $1,495

Model 36, Light Six, 6 cyl., 29.4 hp, 121" wb
Touring, 5 passenger, $1,485
Roadster, 4 passenger, $1,585
Touring, 7 passenger, $1,585
Sedan, 5 passenger, $2,150
Sedan, 7 passenger, $2,250

Model 37, Light Six, 6 cyl., 29.4 hp, 127" wb
Roadster, 4 passenger, $1,485
Touring, 7 passenger, $1,585
Sedan, 5 passenger, $2,150

Light Twelve (1917), 12 cyl., 36.3 hp, 127" wb
Touring, 7 passenger, $2,085
Touring, 5 passenger, $1,985
Roadster, 4 passenger, $2,085
Sedan, 5 passenger, $2,650
Sedan, 7 passenger, $2,750
Town Car, 5 passenger, $3,985
Fourdore Roadster, 4 passenger, $2,785
Coupe, 4 passenger, $3,335

Model 38, Light Six, 6 cyl., 29.4 hp, 121" wb
Touring, 5 passenger, $1,725
Touring, 7 passenger, $1,825
Sedan, 7 passenger, $2,585
Coupe, 4 passenger, $3,250
Fourdore Roadster, 4 passenger, $1,825

Model 39, Light Six, 6 cyl., 29.4 hp, 127" wb
Fourdore Roadster, 4 passenger, $1,825
Touring, 5 passenger, $1,725
Touring, 7 passenger, $1,825
Sedan, 7 passenger, $2,585
Coupe, 4 passenger, $2,535
Town Car, 5 passenger, $3,250

Model 40/41, 12 cyl., 60 hp, 127" wb
Roadster, $1,595
Touring, 5 passenger, $1,885
Touring, 7 passenger, $1,985

Model 45, Light Six, 51 hp, 127" wb
Touring, 7 passenger, $2,685
Roadster, 4 passenger, $2,685
Coupe, 4 passenger, $3,300
Sedan, 7 passenger, $3,550
Limousine, 7 passenger, $4,200

Model 46, Light Twelve, 62 hp, 172" wb
Touring, 7 passenger, $3,450
Roadster, 4 passenger, $3,450
Coupe, 4 passenger, $4,000
Sedan, 7 passenger, $4,200
Limousine, 7 passenger, $4,950

Model 47, Light Six, 50 hp, 132" wb
Touring, 7 passenger, $2,935
Tourister, 4 passenger, $2,935
Speedster, 2 passenger, $3,500
Brougham, 5 passenger, $3,950
Sedan, 7 passenger, $4,250
Suburban, 7 passenger, $4,250

Model 48, Light Twelve, 70 hp, 132" wb
Touring, 7 passenger, $3,635
Tourister, 4 passenger, $3,635
Speedster, 2 passenger, $4,200
Coupe, 4 passenger, $4,350
Brougham, 5 passenger, $4,650
Suburban, 7 passenger, $4,950
Sedan, 7 passenger, $4,950

Model 55, 6 cyl., 50 hp, 121" wb
Touring, 5 passenger, $1,785
Roadster, 2 passenger, $1,835
Sedan, 5 passenger, $2,835

Model 75, 6 cyl., 75 hp, 132" wb
Touring, 7 passenger, $2,485
Tourister, 4 passenger, $2,485
Speedster, 2 passenger, $2,685
Brougham, 5 passenger, $3,185
Sedan, 7 passenger, $3,485
Suburban, 7 passenger, $3,485

Model 57, 6 cyl., 55 hp, 121" wb
Touring, 5 passenger, $1,595
Sedan, 5 passenger, $2,595
Sport Touring, 5 passenger, $1,850
Sport Sedan, 5 passenger, $2,695
Sport Brougham, 5 passenger, $2,395

Model 60, 6 cyl., 50 hp, 121" wb
Brougham, 5 passenger, $2,200
Touring, 5 passenger, $1,295
Special Touring, 5 passenger, $1,395
Roadster, 2 passenger, $1,695
Sedan, 5 passenger, $1,895
Special Sedan, 5 passenger, $1,945

Model 77, 6 cyl., 70 hp, 132" wb
Touring, 7 passenger, $2,395
Brougham, 5 passenger, $3.095
Sedan, 7 passenger, $3,395
Sport Touring, 7 passenger. $2,550
Blue Ribbon Speedster, $3,250
Suburban, 7 passenger, $3,395

Appendix IV

Roster of Employees

Alphabetical list of known employees at Apperson and Haynes plants.

Mary Beymer Abney
John Aerne
Duck Alrie, drill press, Apperson Brothers Automobile Company
Clarence Arthur, truck driver, Apperson Brothers Automobile Company
Walter Arthur, metallurgist, Haynes Automobile Company
Joseph Baer
Daisy Bagwell
Ruth Bagwell.
Paul Barker
Earl B. Barnes
Orville Barnett, clerk in lathe department, Haynes Automobile Company
Russell Bassett, final testing, Haynes Automobile Company
H.A. Bauer
Court Beaman
W. Alf Beckingham
F. Kent Beecher
Jack A. Benell, assistant general manager, Haynes Automobile Company
Ernest Berry
Gusta Billheimer, foreman, drill press department, Haynes Automobile Company

Charles Bischoff
B.C. Bixton
Jess Bowers, general foreman of the machine shop, Haynes Automobile Company
Hazel Morgan Brady, billing clerk, Haynes Automobile Company, 1917–24
Lester Brammell
John J. Briney, pattern maker, Haynes Automobile Company, who died in the 1911 fire.
Clay Brown, Haynes Automobile Company
George Brown
R.A. Brown, screw machine department, Haynes Automobile Company
Melba Richards Burge, cost department, Haynes Automobile Company, 1916-1917
C.M. Burr, stores manager, Haynes Automobile Company
Paul T. Caldwell
C.C. Cartwright, board of directors, Haynes Automobile Company
Harry Chalfant
George W. Charles, Haynes Automobile Company

Roster of Employees

George Clark

Lela Butz Conner, trimmer, Haynes Automobile Company, 1900–1920

Otis Coppock

Floyd Cornwell, foreman, lathe department, Haynes Automobile Company

Otto Coy

James Cragun, shipping foreman, Haynes Automobile Company

Robert Crawford

Charles Crick, production manager, Haynes Automobile Company

Homer Crispen

Raymond V. Crull

Harry S. Crum, manager of service department, Haynes Automobile Company

Charles Currens, sheet metal crib, Haynes Automobile Company, 1921–22

Charles Daniels

George L. Davis

A.G. Dawson

Fred Dearinger

W.E. DeVinney, Apperson Brothers Automobile Company, 1919–920

E.W. Divens, assistant traffic manager, Haynes Automobile Company

B.F. Dixon

John Dixon

H.E. Doty

Joy Doyle, lathe department, Haynes Automobile Company

Arnold Eads, lathe operator and inspector, Haynes Automobile Company; lathe and screw machine operator, Apperson Brothers Automobile Company, 1918

Clarence Eads, floor boards department and parts department, Haynes Automobile Company, 1921–22

Howard Eads, drill press operator, Apperson Brothers Automobile Company, 1912–13

Oscar Clifton Eads, test block department, Apperson Brothers Automobile Company, 1920

Raymond Eads, screw machine set-up man, Haynes Automobile Company, 1915–23

James B. Eccleston

George Elliott, manager, Haynes Automobile Company

George Ellis, foreman, crank case machining, Haynes Automobile Company

J.W. Enders

Harry Eversole, foreman, sheet metal department, Haynes Automobile Company

Vern Faust, test driver, Haynes Automobile Company, 1916–24

George Fitzsimons

Charley Frakes, foreman, crank shaft department, Haynes Automobile Company

Chester Gilmore, Haynes Automobile Company, 1921–22; Apperson Automobile Company, 1925

Della May Goins, Haynes Automobile Company

Vance L. Gordon, foreman, Haynes Automobile Company

Al Gourley, foreman, Haynes Automobile Company

James A. Gragun, shipping foreman, Haynes Automobile Company

R.T. Gray

Darrell Griffey, timekeeper, Apperson Brothers Automobile Company, 1922–24

Verian J. Griffin

Ed Grist, Haynes Automobile Company

S. Grist, general foreman of the assembly departments, Haynes Automobile Company

Al Gunn, plating room, Apperson Brothers Automobile Company

Joe E. Habben, assembler, Haynes Automobile Company, 1918–19

D. Hamilton, foreman, Haynes Automobile Company

Harley E. Hamilton

June H. Hamilton

Harris Hanshue

Walter P. Hanson, advertising department, Haynes Automobile Company
Dorthy Creswell Hanswell
Roy E. Harper, electric gear shift department, Haynes Automobile Company, 1913–21
J. Frank Harris, experimental department, Haynes Automobile Company
Joseph Hartzell, tool room, Haynes Automobile Company
Floyd E. Hawley, Haynes Automobile Company; machinist, Apperson Brothers Automobile Company, 1915–16
Elwood Haynes, president. Haynes-Apperson Automobile Company and Haynes Automotive Company
Martha Beymer Haynes
Walter M. Haynes, director, Haynes Automotive Company
Zering Haynes, Apperson Brothers Automobile Company
F.C. Headington
Glen Heckman, foreman final assembly, Haynes Automobile Company
Maxine Elilas Henry, Haynes Automobile Company
Harvey Herrick
N. A. Hill, factory manager, Haynes Automobile Company
A.W. Hilman, Haynes Automobile Company
Clarence L. Hines
Bernie Hite, foreman, Haynes Automobile Company
Woodson Hobbs
Russell Hoover
Gloria Rhonemus Hostetler
Charles Hostetler
Fred Hostetler
S.M. How, sales manager, Haynes Automobile Company
Jim Ingels, Apperson Brothers Automobile Company
T.E. Jarrad
Webb Jay
D.E. Jenkins, assistant chief engineer, Haynes Automobile Company
J.W. Johnson
Harry S. Jones
Myrthy Jones
Alvie M. Kaufman, milling machine operator and foreman of the crankcase and transmission department, Haynes Automobile Company
Marion Kelly, body maker and inspector, Haynes Automobile Company
Russell Kelvic
W.G. Kibler, manager of purchasing department, Haynes Automobile Company
Ed Knare
Clarence LaMarr
Eva Lane
Bert A. Lee, maintenance electrician, Apperson Brothers Automobile Company
P.A. Lewis, filing and reaming department, Haynes Automobile Company
Clifford G. Lindsay, final assembly, Haynes Automobile Company
John Lucas
Jacob H. McCann
Everett S. McClain, Apperson Brothers Automobile Company, 1920; Haynes Automobile Company, 1924
Nelson McClain
E.J. McCarthy
F. Fay Hutchins McCarty
Don P. McCord
Leone Redman McLaughlin, secretary, service department, Haynes Automobile Company, 1917–1919
J.N. Mahan, drilling machines, Haynes Automobile Company, 1918–1920
C.M. Mallory, manager of traffic department, Haynes Automobile Company
Jonathan Maxwell, Haynes-Apperson Automobile Company, 1896–1898
Alleen Miller, stenographer, Haynes Automobile Company, 1922–23
Platt Hatt Miller, Apperson Brothers Automobile Company
William Ora Miller, plating and polishing departments, Apperson Brothers Automobile Company, 1915–19

Harry Moore

R.S. Moore, construction engineer, Haynes Automobile Company

Diehl Moran, Haynes Automobile Company, 1917–25

George A. Murray, tin shop, Haynes Automobile Company, 1917

Thomas F. Newby, assistant service manager, Haynes Automobile Company

Eugene M. Newlin

Georgia Newman, IBM operator, Haynes Automobile Company

Helen Newman, billing department, Haynes Automobile Company, 1922–24

J.H. Newmark

Frank N. Nutt, chief engineer, Haynes Automobile Company

Glen R. Osborn

Howard E. Osborn

Thomas Otis

Gladys Murray Parkhurst, sales department, Haynes Automobile Company, 1921–23

J.D. Peck, Haynes Automobile Company

Hazel Settle Pendergrass, timekeeper, Haynes Automobile Company, 1920

Nettie Perkins

C.E. Pierson, foreman of the forge shop, Haynes Automobile Company

William Politz, foreman, Haynes Automobile Company

Lora Poole, Haynes Automobile Company

G.U. Radoye, director of advertising and sales promotion, Haynes Automobile Company

C.R. Ray, foreman, Haynes Automobile Company

Pearl Reitz, drill press operator, Haynes Automobile Company

Andrew Richards

Edna McMillian Rioth, sewing machine, Apperson Brothers Automobile Company, 1920–26

Joseph G. Roberts

Harold Rose, Haynes Automobile Company, 1922–24

Plennie Rose

W.F. Rose, chief inspector, Haynes Automobile Company

Hank A. Rossiter, manager of cost department, Haynes Automobile Company

Raymond Ruddell

Dewey Runyon

N.H. Runyon, foreman, cam shaft department, Haynes Automobile Company

Frank E. Russel, sales department, Haynes Automobile Company

James A. Sampsel, foreman, connecting rod department, Haynes Automobile Company

Frank E. Saunders

Ray C. Saunders

A. G. Seiberling, vice president, Haynes Automobile Company; production manager, Apperson Brothers Company

Tom J. Sellers, Haynes Automobile Company, 1922; stockroom, Apperson Automobile Company, 1923

Donald Shenk, grinder operator, Haynes Automobile Company

George Shepard, final assembly department, Apperson Brothers Automobile Company, 1924

Noble Shepherd

Harold Shockley, sheet metal shop, Apperson Brothers Automobile Company, 1923

Nellie Shrock, Apperson Brothers Automobile Company

Edna McMillian Smith

Eva Smith, Haynes Automotive Company; Apperson Brothers Automobile Company

Orville E. Smith, machinist, Haynes Automobile Company

Theopolis Smith

Frank Sommers, foreman, milling department, Haynes Automobile Company

A.E. Starbuck, treasurer, Haynes Automobile Company

John C. Steiner, machine shop, Haynes Automobile Company, 1922

Alice Stinger
George H. Stout
Bruce Tabor, Haynes Automobile Company
Everett H. Tanner
A.L. Thalman
Meredith Thomas, assembly department, Haynes Automobile Company, 1907–09
George Thompson, motor department, Haynes Automobile Company, 1915
T.L. Tincher
Stephen Tudor
Earl Turner
Charles W. Tway
M.M. Uitts
C.W. Ulrich, factory superintendent, Haynes Automobile Company
N.H. Van Sicklen
L. R. Wagner
Clark Wallace, sales, Haynes Automobile Company
Orville Waltman, body assembly section, Haynes Automobile Company, 1919–23
D. L. Watson
Carroll E. Weideman
Audia Wise Werbe
Charles Westfall, final assembly line, Haynes Automobile Company, 1914; heat treatment section, Apperson Brothers Automobile Company
Mary Ruby Wiley
Ona Wiley
A.N. Wilhelm, plant engineer, Haynes Automobile Company
Owen Winegardner
Max H. Winters
Jessie Wise
Oliver Wolford, Haynes Automobile Company; Apperson Brothers Automobile Company
Bernice Fisher Woodward
Stephen V. Woodward
Frank M. Woolary, foreman, Haynes Automobile Company
J. Wright
Warren B. Wrightman
Florence Wrightsman

Appendix V

Biographical Sketches

Bernice Haynes The daughter of Elwood Haynes was born on Dec. 17, 1892, in Greentown. She graduated from Western College for Women in Oxford, Ohio. Then she went to work for her father as a secretary at the Haynes-Stellite Corp. In 1920, she married prominent Kokomo attorney Glen R. Hillis, who became the 1944 Republican candidate for governor. Glen passed away in 1965, while Bernice died on June 26, 1976. They had a daughter, Margaret, and three sons: Elwood, Robert and Joseph. She was a member of the First Presbyterian Church, Daughters of the American Revolution, Sisterhood of the P.E.O. and Morning Musicale. She also served on the board of the YWCA and Kokomo Junior College.

Jacob March Haynes The father of Elwood Haynes was the son of Henry and Achsah (March) Haynes. He was born in Monson, Massachusetts, on April 12, 1817. Jacob began working in his father's harness and carriage trimming shop in Southbridge, Massachusetts, as a teenager. In 1842, he began studying law in Worcester before moving to Muncie, Indiana, the following year. He taught school while studying law. He was admitted to the bar in 1844, the same year he moved to Portland, Indiana, a small town of about 25 homes. He opened a law practice in Portland. In 1845, he was elected as judge of the Court of Common Pleas for the Randolph and Jay counties. He served in that capacity until 1877. Jacob went back to practicing law until his death on February 5, 1903. He was married twice. His first wife was Hilinda Sophia Haines who bore eight children before her passing in May 1885. Two years later he married Sarah Watson.

March Haynes The son of Elwood Haynes was born in Kokomo on Jan. 3, 1896. After a public school education, he attended the Babson Institute of Boston for a year. He then was employed by the Haynes Stellite Company from 1912 to 1922. He returned to Babson, from which he graduated. He then served as secretary to his father until Elwood died in 1925. After that he became an investor and a director of the Peoples Bank of Portland. He also was a director for a tile manufacturing firm in Portland. He was married to Hazel Marie Carter on February 19, 1923. That marriage soon ended and he married Ester (Kennedy) Briggs on June 18, 1928. The couple named a son after his father. He lived until he was 72 and passed away in January 1968, in San Mateo, California. He was a member of the First Presbyterian Church of Kokomo and Elks Lodge.

Walter March Haynes The brother of Elwood Haynes was born in September 1853. He was president of Peoples Bank of Portland and a director of the Haynes Automobile Company. He died on Easter Sunday in 1929.

Elwood "Bud" Hillis The grandson of Elwood Haynes followed in the footsteps of his grandfather and became a Republican. He also ran for Congress like Elwood, but unlike his grandfather, he was elected in 1970. He served in Congress until 1986. He has moved from Indiana to Colorado in 2001 to be closer to his children. A Kokomo post office was renamed in his honor in December 2001.

Jonathan Dixon Maxwell Maxwell worked for the Riverside Machine Works when Elwood Haynes brought in his plans for the first car. He worked on that first car. Then when Haynes and the Apperson brothers formed their company, he was considered their first employee. In 1898 he left the company and headed to Detroit to work for R.E. Olds. Then, in 1903, he teamed up with the Briscoe brothers to produce the Maxwell-Briscoe automobile, a $500 two-cylinder runabout. The name of the auto was later changed to the Maxwell.

Alton G. Seiberling Seiberling worked for both Haynes and Apperson automotive companies for many years in high positions. Born in 1865, he was first hired by Haynes Automobile Company in 1905 as a superintendent. He worked two years for the company before he decided to sell his stock and leave for the rival Apperson Brothers Automobile Company as production manager in 1907. He was responsible for increasing production and the company soon incorporated as a result. However, in the fall of 1913, he resigned and became the factory manager back at Haynes. Two months later he was promoted to general manager. Later he was promoted to vice president. When the business declined in 1923, Seiberling was held responsible and was fired. When the plant failed, he lost his home and most of his wealth. He moved to Chicago and lived until 1952. He went by his initials: A.G.

Howdy Wilcox Wilcox, whom the Haynes Automotive Company used to promote its Model 75 Speedster, drove a Peugeot to victory in the 1919 Indianapolis 500, which led him to become the winner of the championship trail that year. He also drove in another ten Indy races during his racing career. Wilcox also won the Santa Monica 400 in 1916.

Appendix VI

Haynes-Apperson Specifications

THE HAYNES-APPERSON CO., KOKOMO, IND.

Price with top $1350

Model: **TWO - PASSENGER TOURING CAR.**

Body: Folding front seat.

Color: Olive green.

Seating capacity: Two and four persons

Total weight: 1500 pounds.

Wheel base: 81 inches.

Wheel tread: 56 inches.

Tire dimensions, front: 32 x 3½ inches.

Tire dimensions, rear: 32 x 3½ inches.

Steering: Irreversible wheel.

Brakes: Two on differential.

Gasoline capacity: 6 gallons.

Frame: Angle iron.

Horse-power: 16-18.

Number of cylinders: Two.

Cylinders arranged: Horizontal, opposed.

Cooling: Water.

Ignition: Jump spark.

Drive: Chain.

Transmission: Individual clutch.

Speeds: Three forward, one reverse.

Descriptive catalogue sent upon application to the above-named company.

THE HAYNES-APPERSON CO., KOKOMO, IND.

Price

without top

$1500

Model: **LIGHT TOURING CAR.**

Body: Four-passenger, divided front seat, side entrance.

Color: Dark green.

Seating capacity: Four persons.

Total weight: 1500 pounds.

Wheel base: 81 inches.

Wheel tread: 56 inches.

Tire dimensions, front: 32 x 3½ inches.

Tire dimensions, rear: 32 x 3½ inches.

Steering: Irreversible wheel.

Brakes: One on each rear hub

Gasoline capacity: 6 gallons.

Frame: Pressed steel.

Horse-power: 16-18.

Number of cylinders: Two.

Cylinders arranged: Horizontal, opposed.

Cooling: Water and fan

Ignition: Jump spark.

Drive: Shaft, with roller gear and sprockets

Transmission: Individual clutch direct on high gear.

Speeds: Three forward, one reverse.

Descriptive catalogue sent upon application to the above-named company.

THE HAYNES-APPERSON CO., KOKOMO, IND.

Price
with top
$3200
without top
$3000

Model: **FOUR-CYLINDER.**

Body: **Side entrance, folding top, divided seats.**

Color: **Dark green.**

Seating capacity: **Five persons.**

Total weight: **2800 pounds.**

Wheel base: **108 inches.**

Wheel tread: **56 inches.**

Tire dimensions, front: **34 x 4½ inches.**

Tire dimensions, rear: **34 x 4½ inches**

Steering: **Irreversible wheel.**

Brakes: **Rear hubs, also emergency on driving shaft.**

Gasoline capacity: **14 gallons.**

Frame: **Pressed steel.**

Horse-power: **35-40.**

Number of cylinders: **Four.**

Cylinders arranged: **Vertical, separate.**

Cooling: **Water and fan.**

Ignition: **Jump spark.**

Drive: **Shaft with roller gear and sprocket.**

Transmission: **Individual clutch direct on high gear.**

Speeds: **Three forward, one reverse.**

Descriptive catalogue sent upon application to the above-named company.

Appendix VII

Apperson Specifications

APPERSON BROTHERS AUTOMOBILE COMPANY, KOKOMO, IND.

Price
with top
$4150
without top
$4000

Model: TOURING CAR MODEL "A."

Body: Wood.

Color: Optional.

Seating capacity: Seven persons.

Total weight: 2600 pounds.

Wheel base: 108 inches.

Wheel tread: 56 inches.

Tire dimensions, front: 815 x 105 m/m.

Tire dimensions, rear: 875 x 120 m/m.

Steering: Worm and segmit, irreversible.

Brakes: Foot and hand emergency.

Gasoline capacity: 23 gallons.

Frame: Pressed steel.

Horse-power: 40.

Number of cylinders: Four.

Cylinders arranged: Separately.

Cooling: Water, radiator and fan.

Ignition: Jump spark.

Drive: Double chain.

Transmission: Sliding gear.

Speeds: Four forward and one reverse.

Style of top: Full cape top.

Descriptive catalogue sent upon application to the above-named company.

Apperson Specifications

APPERSON BROTHERS AUTOMOBILE COMPANY, KOKOMO, IND.

Price

with top
$3650
without top
$3500

Model: TOURING MODEL "B."

Body: Wood.

Color: Optional.

Seating capacity: Five persons.

Total weight: 2400 pounds.

Wheel base: 102 inches.

Wheel tread: 56 inches.

Tire dimensions, front: 815 x 105 m/m.

Tire dimensions, rear: 875 x 105 m/m.

Steering: Worm and segmit, irreversible.

Brakes: Foot and hand emergency.

Gasoline capacity: 23 gallons.

Frame: Pressed steel.

Horse-power: 24.

Number of cylinders: Four.

Cylinders arranged: Vertical separately.

Cooling: Water, radiator and fan.

Ignition: Jump spark.

Drive: Shaft or double chain.

Transmission: Sliding gear.

Speeds: Either three or four forward and one reverse.

Style of top: Full cape top.

Descriptive catalogue sent upon application to the above-named company.

APPERSON BROTHERS AUTOMOBILE COMPANY, KOKOMO, IND.

Price

with limousine body $6500

with standard wood body $5150

Model: APPERSON SPECIAL.

Body: Wood.

Color: Optional.

Seating capacity: Seven persons.

Total weight: 2800 pounds.

Wheel base: 114 inches.

Wheel tread: 56 inches.

Tire dimensions, front: 815 x 105 m/m.

Tire dimensions, rear: 875 x 120 m/m.

Steering: Worm and segmit, irreversible.

Brakes: Foot and hand emergency, double acting.

Gasoline capacity: 23 gallons.

Frame: Pressed steel.

Horse-power: 50.

Number of cylinders: Four.

Cylinders arranged: Vertical in front.

Cooling: Water, radiator, pump and fan.

Ignition: Jump spark.

Drive: Double chain.

Transmission: Sliding gear.

Speeds: Four forward and one reverse.

Style of top: Full collapsible or victoria on open car.

Descriptive catalogue sent upon application to the above-named company.

Appendix VIII

Haynes Specifications

SPECIFICATIONS

Engine:—"HAYNES" Two Cylinder, Double Opposed Balanced. Roller bearings, adjustable on crank shaft. *The first roller bearing gasoline motor ever built.*

Valves:—Mechanically operated. Bushings readily and inexpensively replaced when worn. Water cooled. Jackets cast integral. Cylinders 5" x 5". Horse-power 16-18. Engine almost absolutely silent.

Frame:—Angle iron.

Wheels:—32" Wood artillery. Twelve spokes. 3½" tires.

Wheel Base:—81", Tread 56", Clearance 10".

Springs:—Full elliptic.

Axles:—Front, rectangular steel 1⅛" x 1¼". Rear, one piece nickel steel combined with revolving sleeve.

Radiator:—Tubular, 17,000 sq. in cooling surface.

Water Capacity:—Six gallons.

Gasoline Capacity:—Six gallons.

Transmission:—"HAYNES" individual clutch, three speeds forward and one reverse, CONTROLLED BY ONE LEVER.

Drive:—Single chain from counter shaft to sprocket on rear axle.

Steering:—Wheel. "HAYNES" tilting post.

Bearings:—Rollers throughout, including wheels, shafts, etc.

Brake:—Powerful double band on rear axle. Operated by foot lever.

Lubrication:—Mechanical force feed pump.

Ignition:—Jump spark.

Throttle:—Governed by foot button.

Carburetor:—Automatic.

Muffler:—"HAYNES". Highly efficient.

Weight:—1500 pounds.

Passengers:—Two or four.

Equipment:—Folding top. Storm front and side curtains. One acetylene and two oil lamps. Horn.

Price:—$1350.00.

The HAYNES-Apperson Co.,
KOKOMO, IND., U. S. A.
BRANCHES

New York, 1715 Broadway.   Chicago, 1420 Michigan Ave.

Haynes Specifications

SPECIFICATIONS MODEL O

BODY. Aluminum and wood.
COLOR. Royal green, maroon or black.
SEATING CAPACITY. Five persons.
WEIGHT. 2250 lbs.
WHEEL BASE. 97 in.
WHEEL TREAD. 56 in.
TIRE DIMENSIONS. 32 in. x 4 in., front and rear.
STEERING. Wheel with irreversible worm gear.
BRAKES. Two external bands operated by hand lever, two internal bands operated by foot pedal; on 12 in. drums on rear wheels.
GASOLINE CAPACITY. 18 gallons.
FRAME. Pressed steel, reinforced with wood.
HORSE POWER. Rated 30. (Actually tests much higher).
NUMBER OF CYLINDERS. Four, arranged vertically in front.
COOLING. Water, by gear driven pump and cellular radiator.
IGNITION. Jump spark: one storage battery, one set dry cells.
DRIVE. Shaft.
TRANSMISSION. Sliding gears.
SPEEDS. Three forward, one reverse.
TOPS. Any style desired (extra).

SPECIFICATIONS MODEL R

BODY. Aluminum and wood.
COLOR. Royal green, maroon or black.
SEATING CAPACITY. Five persons—two extra seats can be added.
WEIGHT. 2750 lbs.
WHEEL BASE. 108 in.
WHEEL TREAD. 56 in.
TIRE DIMENSIONS. 34 in. x 4½ in. front and rear.
STEERING. Wheel with irreversible worm gear.
BRAKES. Two external bands operated by hand lever, two internal bands operated by foot pedal; on 12 in. drums on rear wheels.
GASOLINE CAPACITY. 20 gallons.
FRAME. Pressed steel, reinforced with wood.
HORSE POWER. 50.
NUMBER OF CYLINDERS. Four, arranged vertically in front.
COOLING. Water, by gear driven pump and cellular radiator.
IGNITION. Jump spark: one storage battery, one set dry cells.
DRIVE. Shaft.
TRANSMISSION. Sliding gears.
SPEEDS. Three forward, one reverse.
TOPS. Any style desired (extra).

The Haynes Automobile Company

Detailed Specifications
Model 34, America's Greatest "Light Six."   Model 35, The Kokomo "Six"

Body Styles—Model 34, five-passenger touring and three-passenger roadster. Model 35, seven-passenger touring. Aisleway between front seats on both touring models. Front seats adjustable forward and back. Roadster of "So-Sha-Belle" design, with three individual seats. Center seat set back between two front seats.

Unit Power Plant—3 point suspension, 6 cylinder, 3½x5 inch en bloc motor, light, high power, high speed type. Actually develops 55 horsepower.

Wheelbase—Model 34, 121 inches; Model 35, 127 inches, with turning radius slightly over 21 feet.

Left hand drive, center control with walking stick type gear shift lever. Enter front compartment from either side.

Weight—Model 34, 2950 pounds, giving more than one horse-power to each 55 pounds. Model 35, 3050 pounds.

Leece-Neville separate unit starting and lighting system. No gears to shift. Cranks through chain. No noise or fuss.

Generator-Storage battery system of ignition. Gives greater flexibility at ordinary driving speeds. System is dual.

Economical Rayfield carburetor, no intake manifold used.

Stewart vacuum gasoline system with supply tank at rear of chassis. Indicating gauge in tank.

Splash and force feed lubrication. Pump delivers one-half gallon of oil per minute.

Forced water circulation. Water space between all cylinders and around all valve seats. Large centrifugal pump. Haynes "Light Six" cars never overheat.

Clutch—Built in Haynes factory. Three plate dry disc type with facings of Raybestos. Requires very slight pressure on pedal to operate. Cannot grab. Holds under hardest pulls.

Steering Gear—Complete worm gear type. Nickel steel, heat treated. Built in Haynes factory. Steering wheel is notched.

Transmission—Selective sliding gear type, three speeds forward, one reverse. Heat treated, nickel steel gears.

Haynes full floating rear axle. Built in Haynes factory. Axle shafts, pinion gear and shaft nickel steel.

Helical or spiral bevel type drive gear used in rear axle.

Springs 38 inches in front, 54 inches long in rear. Self lubricating, flat type insures easy riding. Chrome vanadium steel. Bronze bushings used in eyes. Spring bolts hardened and ground.

Crowned fenders. Low center of gravity with low running boards. Road clearance 10½ inches. Long sweeping stream lines.

Tires—Goodyear and United States. Model 34, 34x4 inches. Model 35, 35x4½ inches. Goodyear, quick detachable, demountable rims. Non-skid tires on rear wheels. Extra rim.

Front and rear license brackets.

Motor Driven Tire Pump—Cannot pump oil. Hose and tire pressure gauge.

Stewart-Warner speedometer, driven from propeller shaft.

Improved one-man five bow top that can actually be operated by one man.

Collins curtains, top cover.

Windshield—Clear and rain vision ventilating.

Strapless, quick acting, single lock tire carrier at rear of chassis.

Running boards absolutely clear.

Entire interior of body lined with real hand-buffed leather.

Headlights with "No-Glare" Mazda bulbs and dimming device that saves two-thirds of the current. No extra bulbs. Outside focusing button.

Sparton electric horn under hood. Button in center of steering wheel.

Adjustable foot pedals. Foot and robe rails. Trouble lamp with cord. Boyce Moto-Meter. Waltham clock.

Automatic circuit breaker. Protects electric system. Eliminates fuses.

Auxiliary Seats—Two extra seats in Model 35. Drop down into floor when not in use. Entirely disappearing—may be removed if desired. Only two rings visible when seats are down.

Complete kit of high grade tools containing set of wrenches, hammer, punches, chisel, pliers, etc. Tire repair kit.

Color—Body Brewster Green, dark; black hood, fenders and chassis.

Enclosed detachable tops for winter driving, all models at slight additional cost.

Wire wheels (five) $100 extra.

Two Models—Three Body Styles

Model 34—5-passenger Touring Car . . . $1385
  In Canada, Duty Paid, $1825

Model 34—3-passenger "So-Sha-Belle Roadster".$1485
  In Canada, Duty Paid, $1955

Model 35—7-passenger Touring Car . . . $1495
  In Canada, Duty Paid, $1975

All prices f. o. b. Kokomo, Indiana

RESPONSIVE POWER WITH ECONOMY OF OPERATION

THE HAYNES LIGHT SIX IN BRIEF

MOTOR—Unit power plant, three point suspension, 50 horsepower, L-head type; cylinders 3½ x 5 inches, cast en bloc.

MODEL 45 TOURING—Double cowl type seven-passenger touring, with disappearing auxiliary seats. Convenient package receptacle in back of front seat.

MODEL 45 ROADSTER—A distinctively individual four-door, four-passenger roadster, exceptionally roomy.

MODEL 45 SEDAN—Seven-passenger, all-season SEDAN; windows drop into body, auxiliary seats fold into backs of front seats.

MODEL 45 COUPÉ—Four-passenger; disappearing windows make this car ideal for all seasons.

MODEL 45 LIMOUSINE—Seven-passenger; auxiliary seats fold away, windows drop into body.

COLORS—All open models: medium-shade Brewster green. All closed models: classic Haynes blue.

UPHOLSTERY—Ultra-fashionable French plaited style, over genuine curled hair and extra quality cushion springs. Open models come in high-grade dull-finish, hand-buffed, long-grain leather. Closed cars in serviceable and attractive mohair velvet. Back of front seat in model 45 roadster is upholstered in leather.

ELECTRICAL EQUIPMENT—Haynes Special two-unit Leece-Neville starting and lighting system. Bendix drive starter—starting button on toe-board. Willard battery.

LAMPS—Haynes special design lamps equipped with nitrogen bulbs. Small light is frosted. Lamps have extra heavy safety connectors.

CLUTCH—Single driven dry plate, Borg and Beck patent, with floating Raybestos friction rings; simple and easy to operate; holds under hardest strain.

TRANSMISSION—Selective sliding gear type; three speeds forward, one reverse. Heat-treated nickel steel gears. Gearshift and emergency brake levers curved back within easy reach.

SPRINGS—Semi-elliptic front and rear, of long-lived, special analysis, heat-treated steel. Exceptional length and width insure easy riding. Rear: 58 inches long, 2¼ inches wide. Front: 39 inches long, 2¼ inches wide.

WHEELBASE—All models 127 inches.

FRAME—Six-inch channel section side-rails of high-grade steel give great strength without excessive weight, prevent sagging, and hold body rigid over uneven roads. Stanch cross members prevent side sway.

COOLING—A large centrifugal pump forces cool water around the cylinders and valve seats. The fan is 15 inches in diameter. A copper honeycomb radiator is used, this being the most efficient type. Overheating is practically impossible with this motor when a proper amount of oil is carried.

LUBRICATION—Circulating splash system. Constant supply of oil assured by plunger type pump, with capacity of one-half gallon per minute at 1000 R. P. M. Oil passes through filter to pump. Oil lever gage on crankcase.

CARBURETOR—Mounted high, and attached directly to cylinder block; elimination of manifold makes better carburetion and consequently greater mileage.

AXLES—Front: I-beam, with wheel spindles and steering knuckles of drop-forged, heat-treated nickel steel. Rear: Haynes three-quarter floating. Pressed steel axle housing carries all weight—heat-treated nickel steel shafts drive car. Noiseless spiral bevel drive gears.

STEERING WHEEL—All closed styles have quick-adjustable sliding type. Rim is solid walnut, with aluminum spider.

TIRES—Open and closed models: Firestone and U. S. Fabric tires. Size, 34 x 4½ inches.

CURTAINS—Close fitting Haynes design; handy snap fasteners; curtains open with doors. Curtains and top made of durable and attractive Neverleek.

WHEELS—Wood, additional charge for wire wheels.

VENTILATOR—All models equipped with ventilator located in front cowl, easily regulated from driver's seat.

EQUIPMENT—Boyce Moto-Meter, Stewart vacuum gasoline system, speedometer, motor-driven electric horn, complete tool and tire repair kit, eight-day clock, engine-driven tire pump, cowl light, tonneau light, foot and robe rails, automatic circuit breaker, ammeter, single-lock tire carrier, and extra rim. Coupé has vanity case. Sedan has both vanity and smoking cases. Perfection heaters in all closed cars which are also equipped with Hartford shock absorbers. Sedan and Coupé styles have running-board rubber mats.

INFREQUENT SHIFTING INSURES RIDING EASE

SPECIFICATIONS HAYNES LIGHT TWELVE

MOTOR—Unit power plant, three point suspension, 70 horsepower, valve-in-head type; cylinders 2¾ x 5 inches, cast six en bloc.

BODIES—MODEL 46 TOURING: Double cowl type, seven-passenger touring, with disappearing auxiliary seats. Convenient package receptacle in back of front seat.

MODEL 46 ROADSTER—A distinctively individual four-door and roomy four-passenger roadster.

MODEL 46 COUPÉ—Four-passenger; disappearing windows make this car ideal for all seasons.

MODEL 46 SEDAN—Seven-passenger, all-season SEDAN; windows drop into body, auxiliary seats fold into backs of front seats.

COLORS—Open models: medium-shade Brewster green. Closed models: classic Haynes blue.

UPHOLSTERY—Open models: long-grain, bright-finish, hand-buffed leather, French plaited style, over genuine curled hair and extra quality cushion springs. Back of front seat in roadster upholstered in leather. Closed cars: serviceable and attractive mohair velvet.

ELECTRICAL EQUIPMENT—Haynes Special two-unit Leece-Neville starting and lighting system. Bendix drive starter—starting button on toe-board. Willard battery.

LAMPS—Haynes special design lamps equipped with nitrogen bulbs. Small light is frosted. Lamps have extra heavy safety connectors.

CLUTCH—Single driven dry plate, Borg and Beck patent, with floating Raybestos friction rings; simple and easy to operate; holds under hardest strain.

TRANSMISSION—Selective sliding gear type, three speeds forward, one reverse. Heat-treated nickel steel gears. Gearshift and emergency brake levers curved back within easy reach.

SPRINGS—Semi-elliptic front and rear, of long-lived, special analysis, heat-treated steel. Exceptional length and width insure easy riding. Rear: 58 inches long, 2¼ inches wide. Front: 39 inches long, 2¼ inches wide.

FRAME—Six-inch channel section side-rails of high-grade steel give great strength without excessive weight, prevent sagging, and hold body rigid over uneven roads. Stanch cross members prevent side sway.

WHEELBASE—All models 127 inches.

COOLING—A large centrifugal pump forces cool water around the cylinders and valve seats. The fan is 18 inches in diameter. A copper honeycomb radiator is used, this being the most efficient type. Thermostatic control assures an even temperature. Overheating is practically impossible with this motor when a proper amount of oil is carried.

LUBRICATION—Pressure feed system direct to camshaft drive chain, pump shaft bearing, and main bearings, thence to camshaft and to connecting rods through hollow crankshaft. Gear type pump, positive lubrication at all times. Pressure gage on instrument board.

CARBURETOR—Special single Rayfield, mounted in V between cylinder blocks; readily accessible for adjustments; manifold heated by hot water jackets, insuring perfect carburetion and maximum mileage.

AXLES—Front: I-beam, with wheel spindles and steering knuckles of drop-forged, heat-treated nickel steel. Rear: Haynes three-quarter floating. Pressed steel axle housing carries all weight—heat-treated nickel steel shafts drive car. Noiseless spiral bevel drive gears.

TIRES—Open and closed models: Firestone and U. S. Cord tires. Size, 34 x 4½ inches.

STEERING WHEEL—All open and closed styles have quick-adjustable sliding type. Rim is solid walnut with aluminum spider.

CURTAINS—Close fitting Haynes design; handy snap fasteners; curtains open with doors. Curtains and top made of durable and attractive Neverleek.

WHEELS—Five wire wheels standard equipment.

VENTILATOR—All models are equipped with ventilator, located in front cowl, easily regulated from driver's seat.

EQUIPMENT—Boyce Moto-Meter, Stewart vacuum gasoline system, speedometer, motor-driven electric horn, complete tool and tire repair kit, eight-day Waltham clock, engine-driven tire pump, cowl light, tonneau light, foot and robe rails, automatic circuit breaker, ammeter, Hartford shock absorbers, wire wheel carrier, and extra wire wheel. Perfection heater in closed cars. Sedan and Coupé styles have running-board rubber mats. Coupé has vanity case. Sedan has both vanity and smoking cases. Additional light in center cowl of seven-passenger open car.

Model 26 Specifications

Weight of motor: 1,000 lbs
Number of cylinders: 6
Firing order: 1-4-2-6-3-5
Bore: 4¼
Stroke: 5½
Horsepower rating: 43.35
Make of carburetor: Stromberg
Gas tank capacity: 21 gallons
Oil reserve capacity: 15 quarts
Oil system: splash and gravity feed to main bearings and idler gear
Radiator make: Fedders
Radiator type: Cellular
Cooling: centrifugal pump
Type of clutch: Contracting band
Type of transmission: Selective
Control: Vulcan Electric Gear Shift, hand shift optional
Speeds: 3 forward, 1 reverse
Type of steering gear: worm and worm
Type of frame: double drop
Wheels: artillery
Wheelbase: 130"
Size tires: 36 × 4½
Weight of car: 3,800 lbs
Type of front springs: semi-elliptic
5-passenger open body touring car price: $2,500
4-passenger closed body coupe price: $3,000
Electric gear shift: $200
Standard colors for open-body cars: Indiana-Blue and Pacific-Tour gram with black gear, hood and fenders.
Standard colors for enclosed-body cars: Black throughout and Brewster Green with black gear, hood and fenders.
Upholstery: hand buffed leather, long curled hair, deep cushions.
Starting and lighting: Leece-Neville electrical system.
Cowl Board equipment: electric lights, sight oil feed, automatic cutout for electric light, auxiliary air pressure pump with gauge, Warner 60-mile dial autometer, rim wind clock.
Standard equipment: Top, top cover, mechanical tire pump, rain-vision ventilating windshield, Vulcan electric gear shift, two large electric head lights, electric side lights, electric tail light, full cowl board equipment, Leece-Neville electric starter, generator, 60 ampere hour storage battery, coat and foot rails, electric horn, tire irons, full tool equipment, one extra demountable rim, shock absorber.

Model 27 Specifications

Weight of motor: 1,000 lbs
Number of cylinders: 6
Firing order: 1-4-2-6-3-5
Bore: 4¼
Stroke: 5½
Horsepower rating: 43.35
Make of carburetor: Stromberg
Gas tank capacity: 21 gallons
Oil reserve capacity: 15 quarts
Oil system: splash and gravity feed to main bearings and idler gear
Radiator make: Fedders
Radiator type: Cellular
Cooling: centrifugal pump
Type of clutch: Contracting band
Type of transmission: Selective
Control: Vulcan Electric Gear Shift, hand shift optional
Speeds: 3 forward, 1 reverse
Type of steering gear: worm and worm
Type of frame: double drop
Wheels: artillery
Wheelbase: 136"
Size tires: 36 × 4½
Weight of car: 3,800 lbs
Type of front springs: semi-elliptic
7-passenger open body touring car price: $2,500
7-passenger limousine: $3,650
Electric gear shift: $200
Standard colors for open-body cars: Indiana-Blue and Pacific-Tour gram with black gear, hood and fenders.
Standard colors for enclosed-body cars: Black throughout and Brewster Green with black gear, hood and fenders.
Upholstery: hand buffed leather, long curled hair, deep cushions.
Starting and lighting: Leece-Neville electrical system.
Cowl Board equipment: electric lights, sight oil feed, automatic cutout for electric light, auxiliary air pressure pump with gauge, Warner 60-mile dial autometer, rim wind clock.
Standard equipment: Top, top cover, mechanical tire pump, rain-vision ventilating windshield, Vulcan electric gear shift, two large electric head lights, electric side lights, electric tail light, full cowl board equipment, Leece-Neville electric starter, generator, 60 ampere hour storage battery, coat and foot rails, electric horn, tire irons, full tool equipment, one extra demountable rim, shock absorber.

Model 28 Specifications

Weight of motor: 875 lbs
Number of cylinders: 4
Firing order: 1-3-4-2
Bore: 4¼
Stroke: 5½
Horsepower rating: 28.9
Make of carburetor: Stromberg
Gas tank capacity: 21 gallons
Oil reserve capacity: 10 quarts
Oil system: splash and gravity feed to main bearings and idler gear
Radiator make: Fedders
Radiator type: Cellular
Cooling: centrifugal pump
Type of clutch: Contracting band
Type of transmission: Selective
Control: Vulcan Electric Gear Shift, hand shift optional
Speeds: 3 forward, 1 reverse
Type of steering gear: worm and worm
Type of frame: double drop
Wheels: artillery
Wheelbase: 118"
Size tires: 36 × 4½
Weight of car: 3,800 lbs
Type of front springs: semi-elliptic
2-passenger open body roadster price: $1,785
5-passenger touring body price: $1,785
4-passenger coupe body price: $1,785
Electric gear shift: $200
Standard colors for open-body cars: Indiana-Blue and Pacific-Tour gram with black gear, hood and fenders.
Standard colors for enclosed-body cars: Black throughout and Brewster Green with black gear, hood and fenders.
Upholstery: hand buffed leather, long curled hair, deep cushions.
Starting and lighting: Leece-Neville electrical system.
Cowl Board equipment: electric lights, sight oil feed, automatic cutout for electric light, auxiliary air pressure pump with gauge, Warner 60-mile dial autometer, rim wind clock.
Standard equipment: Top, top cover, mechanical tire pump, rain-vision ventilating windshield, Vulcan electric gear shift, two large electric head lights, electric side lights, electric tail light, full cowl board equipment, Leece-Neville electric starter, generator, 60 ampere hour storage battery, coat and foot rails, electric horn, tire irons, full tool equipment, one extra demountable rim, shock absorber.

Bibliography

America on Wheels (General Publishing Group, 1996), p. 17.
The American Automobile (Smithmark Publishers, 1992), p. 15, 19.
Arizona Republic, May 31, 1946.
Articles of Incorporation, Haynes-Apperson Company, Archives Division, Indiana State Library.
The Automobile, June 19, 1913; August 19, 1915.
Automobile Quarterly, Vol. VI, No. 2, pp.208–9; Vol. XIII, No. 1, p. 40; Vol. XII, No. 4, pp. 394–95, Vol. XIX, No. 4, p. 407.
Biographical Memoirs of Jay County, Indiana (Chicago: B.F. Bowen Company, 1901), pp. 291–292.
Bogue et al. v. *Bennett*, 156 Indiana 478–86.
Car & Parts, January 1984, pp. 42–43.
A Century of Automotive Style (Lamm-Morada Publishing, 1996), p. 17, 48.
Chamber of Commerce Annual, 1923.
Chicago Times-Herald, November 29, 1895; December 6, 1895.
Collector's History of the Automobile (Bonanza Books, 1978).
The Complete Encyclopedia of Motorcars, 1885–1968 (George Rainbird Ltd, 1968), p. 47.
The Complete Motorist, Haynes Automobile Company, 1913–1914.
Country Life, April 1920.
Cruise IN: A Guide to Indiana's Automotive Past and Present (Publishing Resources, 1997).

Detroit News, Feb. 1, 1925.
Economic Geography, XXXVII (1961), pp. 221–22.
Forbes Magazine, March 1, 1925, pp. 681–82.
Gray, Ralph D. *Alloys and Automobiles: The Life of Elwood Haynes* (Indiana Historical Society,1979).
The Haynes, 1905 models brochure.
Haynes, Sumner, Speech, October 9, 1932, Haynes Papers.
Haynes-Apperson Company Catalog, 1904, p. 6.
Haynes Pioneer, various issues.
Haynes Successful Selling, October 27, 1923.
History of Howard County, Indiana, I, pp. 248–49.
Horseless Age, July 1896, p. 10; November 1896; September 1898, p. 1; October 1898, p. 10; April 1899, p. 32; January 1900; February 6, 1901, p. 76; April 24, 1901, p. 81; December 3, 1902, p. v; December 31, 1902, p. ii.
The Horseless Carriage Gazette, January-February 1963.
Indianapolis Star, June 29, 1913; July 1, 1913; August 3, 1913; July 17, 1960.
Kokomo Daily Tribune, July 15, 1894; May 24, 1915; June 12, 1920; January 3, 1924; September 3, 1924; July 19, 1926; October 19, 1955; Nov. 3, 1963; Aug. 12, 1981.
Kokomo Dispatch, August 28, 1897; April 26, 1898; April 5, 1899; June 17, 1899; October 11, 1901; July 10, 1903; March 1, 1911; October 7, 1916; April 3, 1921.

Merrily We Roll Along: The Early Days of the Automobile (Shanachie Entertainment Corp., 1993).

MoTor, November 1925.

Motor Age, June 17, 1920.

Motor Trend, June 1964, p. 56.

Portland Sun, November 4, 1887; February 1, 1889.

Pusch, Charles F., Letter, Dec. 14, 1911, Haynes Papers.

Scientific American, March 1, 1902, p. 141; January 16, 1909, p. 40.

Sintz Gas Engine Company, Letter, July 18, 1894, Haynes Papers.

Standard Catalog of American Cars, 1805–1942 (Krause Publications, 1989), p. 53.

Stellite: A History of the Haynes Stellite Company, 1912–1972.

Story of Progress, 1893–1922 (Haynes Automobile Company).

Traces (Indiana Historical Society, Spring 1994), p. 17.

Treasury of Early American Automobiles, 1877–1925 (Bonanza Books, 1950), p. 3.

True Magazine, March 1952.

Twelfth Annual Catalog, Worcester County Free Institute of Industrial Science, pp. 32–33.

Vintagecars.about.com.

Index

Ace 69, 71, 191
Adams, Norb v
Alexandria, Indiana 135
Algonquin Hill Climb 84
Allen Enterprises 133
Allentown, Pennsylvania 2
Alloys and Automobiles: The Life of Elwood Haynes 221
Altadina, California 178
Alvord, Gilbert 180, 183
America on Wheels 221
The American Automobile 221
American Chemical Society 160
American Institute of Metals 160
American Society for Metals 145
American Stainless Steel Corporation 136, 160, 164
Anniversary Eight 64
Anniversary Model 69, 180
Anniversary Touring 64, 71, 190
Anniversary Tourister 71
Apperson, Edgar 4, 6, 20, 27, 31, 39, 39, 47, 51, 53, 63, 66, 67, 73, 78, 79, 157, 158, 172–183
Apperson, Elmer 6, 11, 17, 27, 29, 39, 41, 53, 62, 67, 78, 157, 172–174, 175
Apperson, Inez 180
Apperson, Dr. James 172
Apperson, Oscar W. 174
Apperson brothers ix, x, 1, 4, 10, 14, 17, 27, 29, 44, 148, 157
Apperson Brothers Automobile Company ix, 3, 4, 39–78, 94, 103, 129, 130, 131, 151, 169, 174, 180, 196–200, 202, 207–210

Apperson Brothers Models: **4-30** 50, 52, 187; **4-40** 50, 52, 60, 187; **4-45** 52, 54, 56, 57, 60, 188; **4-50** 50, 52, 188; **4-55** 52, 54, 188; **4-65** 52, 188; **6** 49; **6-16** 62, 63, 189; **6-17-4** 189; **6-17-5** 189; **6-17-7** 189; **6-18** 63, 64; **6-18-4** 190; **6-23** 75; **6-23S** 75; **6-24** 76; **6-40** 50, 188; **6-45** 60, 188; **6-55** 189; **6-48** 60; **6-60** 57, 60, 189; **8-16** 62, 189; **8-17** 63; **8-17-4** 190; **8-17-7** 190; **8-17-8** 190; **8-18** 63, 190; **8-19** 64, 190; **8-20** 190; **8-21** 66, 71; **8-24** 76, 192; **8-25** 192; **A** 39, 41, 42, 43, 47, 186, 208; **B** 41, 42, 43, 47, 186, 208; **C** 186; **I** 48, 49, 186; **J-R** 187; **K** 47, 49, 187; **M** 47, 48, 49, 187; **O** 48, 49, 187; **S** 47, 187; **Special** 186, 210; **Racing** 186; **Roadaplane** 62, 189; **V-8** 60
Apperson Way 134, 181–183
Arizona Republic 221
Ascot Park 49
Associated Advertising Clubs of the World 3
Atlanta 49
Auburn v, 158
Auburn Cord Duesenberg Museum v, 31, 72, 89, 90, 147–148, 157
The Automobile 221
Automobile Club of America tour 68
Automobile League 13
Automobile Quarterly 221
Automobile Trade Journal 77

Automotive Heritage Museum 24, 29, 75, 93, 126, 128, 138, 146–147

Babson Institute of Boston 201
baby tonneau 49, 92, 187, 193
Bailey, L. Scott 2
Ball, Harry 49
Barrett-Jackson Classic Collector Car Auction 139
Basile, Charles 71
Bates, J.F. 49
"Battle of Kokomo" 64
Bell, Alexander Graham 3, 162
Benz 10, 11, 12, 66
Benz, Karl 4
Berlin 69, 191
Berlin Limousine 98, 100, 193
Beverly 75
Beverly Hills Board Track 174
Beverly Hills Light 71
Beverly Light 63, 189
Beverly Model 73
Bill, Jon v
Blue Book 131
Blue Ribbon Speedster 126, 195
Boonstra, Henry 164
Boottail Wicker 139
Boston 35
Bradenton, Florida 103
Branston, C.A. 161
Brearley, Harry 164
Bretton Woods, New Hampshire 83
Briarcliff race 47
Briney, John J. 92
Brooklyn 20, 33, 37, 158

223

brougham 78, 122, 123, 126, 129, 192, 193, 194, 195
Buffalo, New York 21, 29, 31, 37
Buffum 60
Buick 49
Buick Model B 37
business wagon 185
Buyer, Steve 150

Cabot Corporation 136
cabriolet 69, 110, 191
Cadillac 37, 60
Car & Parts 221
carriage 185
Catskill, New York 15
Chamber of Commerce Annual 221
Chapin, Roy 26
Charles, G.W. 17
Charles River Track 83
Cheyenne, Wyoming 49
Chicago 5, 10, 11, 13, 14, 18, 27, 29, 37, 41, 49, 103, 202
Chicago Dealer's Race 114
Chicago Heights 137
Chicago Motor Club 83
Chicago Times-Herald 10, 221
Chicago World's Fair 6, 156
Chrysler Corporation ix, 131
Chummy Roadster 59, 61, 63, 68, 189
Civil War 152
Cleveland 24
Cloverleaf Roadster 137
clutch-drive automobile 3
Cobe Cup 48
The Collector's History of the Automobile 2, 221
colonial coupe 98, 99
Columbus, Ohio 15
The Complete Motorist 102, 221
Consolidated Motors Corporation 126
Cord 78
Corona road race 61
Country Life 221
coupe 57, 60, 69, 71, 76, 78, 100, 105, 106, 110, 117, 118, 122, 191
Crawford, Robert 102, 161
Crick, C.W. 126
Croker, Frank 47
Crosley Radio 131
Crown Point, Indiana 48
Crown Point Cemetery 174
Cruise IN: A Guide to Indiana's Automotive Past and Present 221
Czecho-Slovakia 117

Daimler, Gottlieb 4
Daytona Beach 47
De LaVergne Refrigeration Company 11
Delco Electronics 131

delivery wagon 185
Delphi Electronics 131
Denver 49
Detroit 26, 27, 33, 178
Detroit News 221
Diamond Tires 48
Dietz Regal oil lights 37
doctor's carriage 185
Dorris Company 126, 169
Duesenberg 78
Durant, W.C. 181
Duryea 12
Duryea, Charles 2, 10, 166, 167
Duryea, Frank 2, 10, 181
Duryea brothers 1, 2, 3, 10, 11, 13, 14
Duryea Motor Wagon Company 2, 3, 13, 14
Dyke, A.L. 59

Eames, Hayden 128, 129
Eccleston, Jesse 57
Edison, Thomas A. 3, 102
Edwards, Olive 174
Eisenhower, Dwight D. 103
Eisenhower, Mamie Doud 148
electric car 11, 23
electric engine 5
electric shifting 104, 105
Elks 47
England 15
Essen, Germany 44
Etherington, Dale v, 137, 151
Evanston, Illinois 11

Fairmount Park, Philadelphia 48, 49
Falls Engine 75
Ferris Trophy 48
Fiat 50
Fisher, Carl G. 48
Forbes Magazine 221
Ford 49
Ford, Henry 1, 3, 14, 181
Ford, Percy 114, 115
Ford Model A 35
Ford Model K 41
Ford Model T 3, 56
Ford Quadricycle 151
Fort Erie Track 31, 83
Founders Day 48
fourdore 116, 117
fourdore roadster 117
Fox, Alvin 137, 138
Franklin Mint 151
Frazer, Kay v, 142, 143
Fresno 103
Friedman auto 29
Frost, Jack 17, 141, 149
Frye, Jack 41
Fulton, Robert 162

Gamaliel 102
gasoline-powered engine 2, 21, 23

General Motors 64
Glidden, Charles J. 83
Glidden Tours 83, 139
Gollner 136–137
Good Roads Day 114
Goode, Frank 56
Graves, Vernon 131
Gray, Ralph D. 4, 221
Gray, R.T. 104
Greece 117
Griffey, David v, ix, 90, 137, 138
Grosse Pointe Track 33

Haines, Hilinda Sophia 152, 201
Haines, Russ 139
Hanly, J. Frank 162
Hanshue, Harris 48, 49, 52, 71
Harding, Hugh 49
Harding, Pres. Warren 166
Harlem Mile Track 41
Hartford, Connecticut 24
Hartford Suspension Company 46
Haynes, Bernice 137, 154, 156, 158, 159, 201
Haynes, Calvin 17, 158
Haynes, Charles 86
Haynes, Elwood ix, x, 1–11, 13, 14, 15, 17, 20, 23, 28, 29, 33, 64, 65, 66, 67, 79, 83, 102, 104, 109, 119, 134, 136, 140, 141, 142, 147, 148, 152–171, 172, 175, 176
Haynes, Henry 152
Haynes, Jacob 152, 153, 201
Haynes, John W. 83
Haynes, March 137, 158, 165, 201
Haynes, Sumner 140, 221
Haynes, Walter 17, 158, 202
Haynes-Apperson Automobile Company 3, 4, 13, 14–38, 41, 158, 160, 176, 196–200, 202, 221
Haynes-Apperson car 4, 11, 13, 15, 24, 29, 31, 33, 34, 35, 37, 39, 114, 139, 151, 157, 176, 203–206
Haynes-Apperson Festival 137, 148, 149
Haynes-Apperson Models: A 31, 32, 185; B 31, 185; C 31, 185; F 35, 185; G 31, 35, 185; H 31, 35, 185; I 31, 35, 185; J 37, 38, 185; R 38
Haynes Automobile Company ix, 3, 38, 44, 52, 69, 79–133, 144, 147, 151, 160–161, 202, 211–219
Haynes Aviation Field 164
Haynes Creed 118
Haynes-Duryea Company 167
Haynes Models: **19** 92, 95, 193; **20** 92, 93, 100, 193; **21** 98, 100, 194; **22** 100, 120, 194; **23** 100, 194; **24** 100, 194; **26** 105, 106, 194, 217; **27** 101, 105, 106, 194, 217; **28** 105, 106, 194, 217; **30** 110, 194; **31** 110, 194; **32** 110, 194; **34** 112,

114, 137, 194, 214; **35** 112, 114, 194, 214; **36** 115, 194; **37** 115, 139, 194; **38** 117, 194; **39** 117, 194; **40** 112, 114, 194; **41** 112, 114, 194; **45** 119, 148, 195; **46** 119, 195; **47** 121, 122, 137, 195; **48** 121, 122, 123, 195; **55** 123, 195; **57** 126; **60** 127, 128, 129, 195; **75** 122, 123, 125, 126, 127, 137, 138, 195, 202; **77** 122, 126, 195; **K** 81, 83, 98, 193; **L** 79, 80, 83, 193; **M** 79, 83, 193; **O** 84, 85, 193, 213; **R** 83, 84, 85, 193, 213; **S** 86, 88, 193; **T** 87, 88, 193; **V** 88, 193; **W** 89, 193; **X** 83, 88, 92, 193; **X1** 92, 193; **X2** 92; **X3** 92; **X4** 92; **Y** 92, 98, 99, 100
Haynes Monument 166–168
Haynes Museum v, 8, 18, 19, 28, 30, 41, 43, 47, 58, 60, 61, 73, 76, 80, 81, 82, 88, 94, 96, 97, 98, 99, 101, 124, 125, 141, 142–145, 155, 163, 166, 168
The Haynes Pioneer 3, 102
Haynes Stellite Factory ix, 134–136, 161, 164, 201
Heare, Eddie 50
Heberton Hill 110
Heilman Motor Car Company 110
Hiker 92
Hillis, Elwood "Bud" 201
Hillis, Glen R. 201
Holley, George 181
Hoosier State Automobile Association 166
Hoover, Herbert 140
The Horseless Age 14, 15, 160, 221
horseless carriage ix, 2, 15
Horseless Carriage Contest 10
Hot Wheels 151
Howard, Edward J. 114
Howard County Historical Society v, 16, 20, 21, 22, 23, 25, 27, 30, 32, 45, 48, 54, 70, 89, 127, 142, 149, 150, 18, 183
Howard Shipbuilding Company 114
Hubbard, Burtt J. 52, 60, 61
Hudson 78
Huffman, W.S. v
Hunt, J.F. 165
Hunt Porcelain, Inc. 165
Hutchings, F.W. 102
hydrocarbon engine 23

Indiana Board of Education 165
Indiana Fairgrounds 47, 114
Indiana Historical Society v, 44, 46, 53, 55, 58, 62, 68, 74, 77
Indiana Natural Gas & Oil Company 6, 29
Indiana State Library 165
Indiana University 1, 165
Indianapolis 102, 161

Indianapolis 500 50, 51, 122
Indianapolis Motor Speedway 48, 51
Indianapolis Star 221
Indo-China 117
International Congress of Applied Chemistry 160
Isgrigg, Paul 147, 148

Jack Rabbit 41, 53, 55, 56, 69, 75
Jackrabbit 42, 44, 45, 48, 50, 52, 54, 56, 137, 173, 187, 188
Jackrabbit "Big Dick" racer 46, 47, 49, 178, 186
Jackrabbit Coupe 54, 188
Jackrabbit Cup Racer 47
Jackrabbit "De Luxe" Touring 52, 188
Jackrabbit Fore-Door Touring 52, 187
Jackrabbit Roadster 52, 54, 188
Jackrabbit Special Touring 52, 54
Jackrabbit Touring 52, 54, 187
Jackrabbit Town Car 52, 54, 188
Jennings, M.W. 110
John Robinson Circus 15
John Scott Medal 165
Johns Hopkins University 155

Kenosha, Wisconsin 24
"Kimball" Limousine 47, 186
King, Charles 14, 181
King, J.C. 27
King of Belgium Touring 83, 193
Knight, Harry 50
Knox, C.B. 20
Kokomo, Indiana v, ix, x, 3, 6, 16, 17, 20, 21, 22, 23, 25, 27, 30, 32, 45, 48, 54, 70, 83, 89, 102, 110, 118, 126, 128, 131, 136, 139, 141, 142, 148, 164, 172, 179, 201
Kokomo Daily Tribune 7, 67, 221
Kokomo Dispatch 221
Kokomo Rubber Company 17
Kokomo Six Touring 114, 194
Korean War 135
Kraft, Harry 6, 156
Kreb carburetor 42
Krupp Gun Works 44, 47
Kwilinski, Frank 181

Ladies Home Journal 115
Lafayette, Indiana 18
Lambert, John W. 2, 14
Landon, Mary 173, 183
Lansing, Michigan 24
Lanterman, Bertha B. 156
Laundaulet 44
Lewis, P.C. 176
light eight touring 62
light six 107, 110, 112, 113, 115, 119, 215
light six cabriolet 110
light six roadster 62, 189

light six touring 62, 110, 114, 189
light tonneau 83
light touring car 36, 37, 38, 185, 205
light twelve 112, 113, 114, 115, 119, 216
Lilliput 151
limousine 42, 86, 88, 98, 100, 105, 106, 119, 193, 194, 195
limousine sedan 73
Locomobile 48
Long Island 27, 49
Long Island Endurance Contest 29, 31
Long Island Non-stop Contest 83
Los Angeles 41, 49, 103
Louisiana Purchase Exposition 21, 84
Louisville 83
Lycoming 76
Lytle, Herbert 47, 48, 49

Mack Sennett movie 65
Marion, Indiana 41
Mathewson, Christie 178
Maxwell, Johathan D. ix, 7, 67, 174, 202
Maxwell-Briscoe automobile 202
McClain, Nelson 35
McClure, Marshall 1
McCord, Don. P. 73, 180
McDonald & Campbell Trophy Run 49
McKinley, President 178
McReynolds, Thomas C., Sr. 39, 180
Mercedes 41
Milwaukee 2, 27
Minich, V.E. 83, 160
Monson, Massachusetts 201
Morse, Samuel 162
MoTor 222
Motor Age 44, 98, 222
Motor Age Cup Road Race 41
Motor Trend 222
Mueller, Oscar 10
Muncie, Indiana 201
Musey's magazine 81

Nadig, Henry 2
Nash 78
Nash, Charles W. 181
National Automobile Show 129
National Vigilance Committee 3
Natural Gas Company 65
Naughton, Willard 137
Nesta battery 41
New York Automobile Show 61, 112
New York-Boston-New York Reliability Contest 83
New York City 11, 26, 32, 35, 39, 41, 83, 103
New York Globe 67

New York-Pittsburgh Endurance Run 84
New York Reliability Contest 40
New York-Rochester Endurance Contest 83
New York-St. Louis Tour 84
New York to Buffalo Pan American Exposition race 173, 177
New York to Pittsburgh Run 84
Newark 103
Newbit, Wilbur D. 3
Newmark, J.H. 57
Newport Limousine 98, 99, 193
Niagara Falls 141
Northern Indiana Supply Company 133, 134
Nutt, Frank 83

Oakland 49, 103
Oakland Motor Company 57
Ohio City, Ohio 2
Ohio State Fair 15
Oldfield, Barney 178, 181
Olds, Ransom 1, 14, 26, 181, 202
Olds Motor Works 24
Oldsmobile 37, 38, 49
Oldsmobile Runabout 26
Omaha 49

Packard 41, 78
Packard, James Ward 20
Pan-Am Exposition 83
Pardington, A.R. 50
Paris 10, 44
Patten, James C. 161
Peerless 60
Pennville, Indiana 5
Pentecost, Laura 175
Peru, Indiana 17
Peugeot, Armand 4
phaeton 31, 33, 35, 37, 75, 76, 78, 185, 191, 192
Philadelphia 49
Phoenix 57, 183
Pioneer 7, 157, 160
Pioneer Automobile Company 78, 148, 180
Pittsburgh 110, 123
pleasure carriage 185
Pointe Gross Track 83
Pope Manufacturing 24
Portland, Indiana 5, 17, 65, 140, 152, 201, 202
Portland Natural Gas and Oil Company 155, 156
Portland Sun 222
Portola Cup 49
Price, Sam 56, 61
Prohibitionist Party 162, 164
Puerto Rico 18, 20
Pusch, Charles F. 222

Quadricycle 14
Quakertown, Pennsylvania 137

Race of the Century 10
Radoye, Gilbert U. 118, 128
Reliance Company 133
Riverhead Motor Carnival 49
Riverside Machine Shop 6, 7, 15, 39, 67, 133, 175
Roadaplane Chummy Roadster 63, 173, 190
roadster 48, 49, 57, 60, 64, 89, 92, 100, 105, 106, 110, 114, 115, 116, 119, 129, 187, 189, 190
Robertson, George 43, 48
Robertson, William 59
Ronen, France 10
Roosevelt, Pres. Theodore 92
Roosevelt Memorial Association 164
rotary gas valve engine 1
Rudolph, Wilma 148
runabout 22, 26, 29, 29, 30, 31, 33, 35, 37, 38, 47, 48, 49, 79, 85, 86, 88, 92, 93, 185, 187, 193

S.S. *Elwood Haynes* 141
Sacramento 103
St. Louis World's Fair 38
Salt Lake City 180
San Francisco 21, 37, 49, 102, 103, 161, 162, 172
San Francisco Hill Climb 49
Santa Barbara 102
Santa Cruz 103
Santa Monica 48, 202
Saratoga Springs, New York 176
Saturday Evening Post 111, 113, 116
Savannah, Georgia 47
Savannah Road Race 41
Scharchburg, Richard 3
Schloemer, Gottfried 2
Scientific American 19, 21, 31, 37, 92, 222
Scribner's Cosmopolitan 21, 46
sedan 63, 64, 69, 71, 73, 75, 76, 78, 115, 118, 119, 123, 126, 129, 190, 191, 192, 194, 195
sedan limousine 57, 188
sedanet 69, 71, 73
Seiberling, A.G. 3, 44, 104, 128, 202
Selden, George 1
Selden Patent 1
Shettler, Leon T. 49
Shite Mountain Road Test 84
Sieberling, A.G. 86, 103, 164
Silver, Conover T. 63
Silver-Apperson 63
Silver Special Touring 63
Sintz engine 2, 6, 8, 156
Sintz Gas Engine Company 222
Sloan, Alred P., Jr. 181
Smithsonian Institution 3, 65
"So-Sha-Belle" Roadster 112
Souder, Edward M. 67
Special Apperson 42

Special Sedan 129
Special Speedster 121, 124
Special Touring 129, 186, 187
Speed Boy Roadster 63
speedster 100, 194
sport phaeton 76, 78, 192
sport sedan 76, 78, 192
sport touring 126
sportster 66, 69, 73
Springfield, Massachusetts 2, 10, 14
Springfield Morning Union 2
Stanhope 83, 193
Star Machine Works 7, 172
stellite ix, 1, 222
Stout, George 49, 102
Stromberg Service Stations 105
Sturges Electric Moor Wagon 13
suburban 92, 98, 122, 123, 126, 193, 194, 195
Supreme Court 26
surrey 29, 30, 31, 33, 35, 37, 79, 185
Svedino's Automobile and Aviation Museum 148
Sweany, Dr. 15
Synder, Charles 181

Tampa, Florida 103
Tasmania 117
Taylor University 164
Tencher, T.L. 102
thermostat 1
Thomas 41
Thomas B. Jeffrey Company 24
Toepfer, Frank 2
Tonneau 35, 36, 37, 49, 60, 83, 185, 193
touring 41, 42, 43, 45, 47, 49, 52, 57, 60, 63, 69, 73, 85, 88, 89, 90, 92, 98, 100, 105, 106, 110, 114, 115, 117, 118, 119, 122, 123, 129, 186, 187, 188, 189, 190, 191, 193, 194, 195, 208, 209
touring sedan 75
tourister 122, 123, 190, 195
tourster 64, 69, 72, 73, 75
town car 117, 194
Traces 222
Trap 10, 16, 185
Treasury of Early American Automobiles 222
True Magazine 222
Tudor, Robert L. 129
Turtle-Back Roadster 57

Union Carbide Corporation 141, 164
Uniontown Mountain 123
U.S. Postal Service 150, 202

Valparaiso 172
Van Bensenoten, John 181
Vanderbilt, Cornelius 176

Index

Vanderbilt Cup 35, 43, 47, 49, 56, 83, 84, 86
Vanderbilt Speedster 86, 88
Vanderbilt racer 45
Van Kley, Bonnie J. v
Veterans of Foreign Wars 133
Victory Theater 119
Vietnam War 136
Vulcan Electric Gear Shifter 104

W. H. Smith Memorial Library v
Wagner, L.R. 83, 102
Wallace Spencer Huffman Collection 44, 46, 53, 55, 58, 62, 68, 74, 77
Warren, C.B. 104
Warren Auto Parts and Salvage Company 131, 132
Watson, Sarah 201
Webber, Dr. Ashley A. 158, 176, 177
Western College for Women 164
Wilcox, Howdy 122, 202
Wildcat Creek 54
Wilhelm, A.N. 104
Williamson & Spencer Funeral Home 140
Wilson, William Robert 167
Wilson, Woodrow 79
Winton, Alexander 14
Winton Motor Carriage Company 20, 21, 126, 169
Worcester, Massachusetts 177
Worcester Polytechnic Institute 153, 164
World War I 114, 117
World War II 141, 180
Wrightman, Warren B. 7, 157

Young Men's Christian Association 164, 201

Zaugg, John 181
Zintz 2